THE CULTURAL USES OF THE CAESARS
ON THE ENGLISH RENAISSANCE STAGE

General Editor's Preface

Helen Ostovich, McMaster University

Performance assumes a string of creative, analytical, and collaborative acts that, in defiance of theatrical ephemerality, live on through records, manuscripts, and printed books. The monographs and essay collections in this series offer original research which addresses theatre histories and performance histories in the context of the sixteenth and seventeenth century life. Of especial interest are studies in which women's activities are a central feature of discussion as financial or technical supporters (patrons, musicians, dancers, seamstresses, wig-makers, or 'gatherers'), if not authors or performers per se. Welcome too are critiques of early modern drama that not only take into account the production values of the plays, but also speculate on how intellectual advances or popular culture affect the theatre.

The series logo, selected by my colleague Mary V. Silcox, derives from Thomas Combe's duodecimo volume, The Theater of Fine Devices (London, 1592), Emblem VI, sig. B. The emblem of four masks has a verse which makes claims for the increasing complexity of early modern experience, a complexity that makes interpretation difficult. Hence the corresponding perhaps uneasy rise in sophistication:

> Masks will be more hereafter in request,
> And grow more deare than they did heretofore.

No longer simply signs of performance 'in play and iest', the mask has become the 'double face' worn 'in earnest' even by 'the best' of people, in order to manipulate or profit from the world around them. The books stamped with this design attempt to understand the complications of performance produced on stage and interpreted by the audience, whose experiences outside the theatre may reflect the emblem's argument:

> Most men do vse some colour'd shift
> For to conceal their craftie drift.

Centuries after their first presentations, the possible performance choices and meanings they engender still stir the imaginations of actors, audiences, and readers of early plays. The products of scholarly creativity in this series, I hope, will also stir imaginations to new ways of thinking about performance.

The Cultural Uses of the Caesars on the English Renaissance Stage

LISA HOPKINS
Sheffield Hallam University, UK

Routledge
Taylor & Francis Group

LONDON AND NEW YORK

First published 2008 by Ashgate Publishing

Published 2016 by Routledge
2 Park Square, Milton Park, Abingdon, Oxon OX14 4RN
711 Third Avenue, New York, NY 10017, USA

Routledge is an imprint of the Taylor & Francis Group, an informa business

British Library Cataloguing in Publication Data
Hopkins, Lisa, 1962–
The cultural uses of the Caesars on the English Renaissance stage. – (Studies in performance and early modern drama)
    1. English drama – Roman influences 2. English drama – Early modern and Elizabethan, 1500–1600 – History and criticism 3. English drama – 17th century – History and criticism 4. Kings and rulers in literature 5. Allusions in literature 6. Power (Social sciences) in literature 7. Politics and literature – Great Britain – History – 16th century 8. Politics and literature – Great Britain – History – 17th century 9. Rome – In literature
    I. Title
    822'.009352621

Library of Congress Cataloging-in-Publication Data
Hopkins, Lisa, 1962
  The cultural uses of the Caesars on the English Renaissance stage / by Lisa Hopkins.
    p. cm. — (Studies in performance and early modern drama)
  Includes bibliographical references.
  ISBN 978-0-7546-6263-1 (alk. paper)
  1. English drama—Roman influences. 2. English drama—Early modern and Elizabethan, 1500–1600—History and criticism. 3. English drama—17th century—History and criticism. 4. Kings and rulers in literature. 5. Rome—In literature. 6. Allusions in literature. 7. Power (Social sciences) in literature. 8. Politics and literature—Great Britain—History—16th century. 9. Politics and literature—Great Britain—History—17th century. I. Title.

PR127.H65 2008
822.0514—dc22

                                      2007039750
ISBN 9780754662631 (hbk)

Contents

Acknowledgements

I am grateful to Professor Prashant Sinha, Professor Rajiv Verma, and above all Professor Rupin Desai, who kindly enabled me to deliver a first draft of chapter two to a meeting of the Shakespeare Society of India, and to Bob White and Dorothea Kehler for much collegial conversation there; to David Mayall for help with gypsies, and to Matthew Woodcock for help with Olaus Magnus; and to the British Academy, who awarded me a conference grant to enable me to deliver a first draft of chapter seven as a paper at the Renaissance Society of America Annual Meeting 2004. An early draft of chapter three was prepared for a Shakespeare Association of America seminar on Marlowe; I am grateful to all the other members of the seminar and most particularly to Alan Dessen. My students Lyndsey Clarke, Samantha Gibbs, Sharon McDonnell, and Tracey Siddle helped enormously by all choosing Renaissance Roman plays to edit for the module of Editing a Renaissance Play as part of the MA English Studies (Renaissance Literature) at Sheffield Hallam University. Ian Baker, Matt Steggle, and my husband, Chris Hopkins, all painstakingly and uncomplainingly read draft chapters, and indeed in Matt's case the whole book; as always, I am grateful to work in such a collegial department. Annaliese Connolly unearthed a very helpful reference at a crucial time, and the anonymous reader for Ashgate offered some extremely acute advice and guidance. Thanks also to Erika Gaffney for her patience and support.

An earlier version of chapter four appeared in *Shakespeare* 1.2 (December 2005): 121–35, an earlier version of chapter five in *Antony and Cleopatra: New Critical Essays*, edited by Sara Deats (London: Routledge, 2004), 231–42, a small part of chapter one as part of 'Paris is Worth a Mass: *All's Well That Ends Well* and the Wars of Religion', in *Shakespeare and the Culture of Christianity in Early Modern England*, edited by Dennis Taylor (Fordham University Press, 2003), 369–81, and an earlier version of part of chapter seven as 'We were the Trojans: British national identities in 1633', *Renaissance Studies* 16.1 (March 2002), 36–51.

Introduction

'King nor Keisar'

The cultural impact of Rome in Renaissance England was all-pervasive. Although early modern England did not use the term 'Renaissance', it was acutely aware of itself as embodying a rebirth of classical culture and learning. The image of the Caesars was particularly prevalent: in Robert Greene's *The Comicall Historie of Alphonsus, King of Aragon*, for instance, the formulaic phrase 'King nor Keisar' recurs on a number of occasions, suggesting that the idea of being a Caesar is almost synonymous with rule.[1] Ideas about, or derived from, Rome, were liable to surface anywhere and everywhere. They even conditioned the material culture of the period, not only in the shape of the universal passion for and desire to imitate the architecture of Vitruvius but also in the fact that the most influential collector of his day, Sir Robert Cotton, organised his manuscripts under busts of the Roman emperors and labelled them accordingly. Other physical manifestations of the Roman emperors were to be found in great houses such as Theobalds, where, the traveller Paul Hentzner noted, in the summer-house in the garden 'are the twelve Roman emperors in white marble'; Hampton Court, where Hentzner noted plaster effigies of the Emperors,[2] and where a tapestry showed the murder of Julius Caesar;[3] Nonsuch Palace, whose exterior was covered in Roman scenes; Woodstock Palace, allegedly built by Julius Caesar; Raglan Castle in the Welsh Marches; the palace of Whitehall; the two residences of William Cavendish, Earl of Newcastle, Bolsover Castle, Derbyshire, and Welbeck Abbey in Nottinghamshire;[4] and Naworth Castle in Cumberland, where Lord William Howard amassed a collection of antiquities from the Roman fort at Birdoswald.[5] In 1588 London was even treated to a reconstruction of a Roman triumph when, to celebrate the defeat of the Spanish Armada, Elizabeth I had herself drawn through the streets on a 'chariot-throne' in imitation of a Roman conqueror.[6]

---

1   On the prevalence and history of the phrase, see Charles A. Pennel, 'Robert Greene and "King or Kaisar"', *Notes and Queries* n.s. 3 (1965), pp. 124–6. As an instance of its use, see for example Lodowick Lloyd, *The Pilgrimage of Princes* (1573), p.161, 'Of Luste': 'it hath vanquished Kynges and Kesars'.

2   Paul Hentzner, *Travels in England during the reign of Queen Elizabeth*. Online: http://etext.library.adelaide.edu.au/h/hentzner-travels/ Accessed 28.4.04.

3   James Shapiro, *1599: A Year in the Life of William Shakespeare* (London: Faber and Faber, 2005), p. 181.

4   See Lucy Worsley, 'The "artisan mannerist" style in British sculpture: a bawdy fountain at Bolsover Castle', *Renaissance Studies* 19.1 (2005), pp. 83–109.

5   Tony Wilmott, *Birdoswald Roman Fort: 1800 Years on Hadrian's Wall* (Stroud: Tempus, 2001), pp. 19–20.

6   Shapiro, *1599*, p. 179.

There was even a living embodiment of this reverence for Rome in the shape of the resonantly-named Sir Julius Caesar, master of the Court of Requests, and at least two Renaissance Englishwomen were the subject of iconography comparing them to women associated with the Caesars: Francis Meres in *Palladis Tamia* compares Mary Sidney to Octavia, daughter of the Emperor Claudius,[7] and a portrait said to be of Elizabeth Throckmorton, Lady Ralegh, though the attribution is very doubtful, shows her 'as Cleopatra, complete with brandished snake and bared breasts. In the corner of the portrait is a scroll with a quotation from a popular play of the time, Samuel Daniel's *Cleopatra*. The quotation contains the inflammatory lines "and now proud tyrant Caesar, do thy worst"'.[8] Whether or not the sitter was actually Lady Ralegh, its meaning is clear: it encodes defiance to the rule of a Renaissance monarch, and it represents that monarch as a Caesar.

In this book, I aim to trace the ways in which English Renaissance drama from the 1580s to the 1630s appropriated the cultural centrality of Rome and her Emperors for its own, often political, purposes. Much work has already been done in this field; however, my project is different in a number of respects. In the first place, it ranges widely across Renaissance drama, including two of the less popular Shakespeare plays (*Titus Andronicus* and *Cymbeline*) alongside two of the best-known, *Hamlet* and *Antony and Cleopatra*, and touching too on several non-Shakespearean plays that have been little considered in contemporary criticism. Secondly, whereas the Renaissance is generally conceived as a rebirth of classical values, I look at some areas in which the classical had, in some sense, never gone away, and consider the rival claims of Turkey and Russia to be centres of Caesarian power. Most centrally, though, I look at the widely various and highly charged uses which the drama of this period made of the idea of the Caesars, the group of men who for the Renaissance mind emblematised and incarnated so much of what Rome stood for. When Cleopatra in Shakespeare's *Antony and Cleopatra* says ''Tis paltry to be Caesar',[9] she is not just dismissing one individual; she is effectively rejecting earthly power itself, in the shape of one of its most conspicuous symbols, for Caesarian authority had become so closely identified with supreme power that its attributes were, as we shall see, appropriated by a wide variety of competing rulers in the Renaissance. At the same time, though, there is a widespread sense that if to be Caesarian means to be a great ruler, it also in some sense means to be a flawed or even a failed man; this is perhaps seen in sharpest focus in Shakespeare's *Julius Caesar*, where Caesar after his death acquires a monumental stature and psychological power he had failed to achieve in his life, just as, throughout the play, the memory and relics of the dead Pompey prove more insidiously threatening to Caesar and his cause than Pompey living had been. Perhaps most notably, the collective history of the Caesars encapsulated all the worst potential problems of a hereditary monarchy, since so many of them – most

---

7   Roy Kendall, *Christopher Marlowe and Richard Baines: Journeys through the Elizabethan Underground* (London: Associated University Presses, 2003), p. 159.

8   Anna Beer, *Bess: The Life of Lady Ralegh, Wife to Sir Walter* (London: Constable & Robinson, 2004), pp. 133–4.

9   William Shakespeare, *Antony and Cleopatra*, edited by Emrys Jones (Harmondsworth: Penguin, 1977), V.ii.2.

spectacularly Nero and Caligula – either were or became palpably unfit to rule. Bringing together the canonical and the non-canonical, historicising without being bound by a schema, this book offers a new view of the cultural uses of the Caesars on the English Renaissance stage.

The book is divided into three sections, which address the three central cultural uses of Rome on the English Renaissance stage. By the time of the Renaissance, the monolithic power that had been Rome was only a memory, and what remained of its power, authority and physical presence had travelled in three principal directions. In the first place, and most uncannily, the city of Rome itself was now the seat not of Emperors, but of Popes, and it is this new layer of Roman identity that is the subject of my first section. Secondly, and also, to Renaissance eyes, unnervingly, much of the power and even the title of the Caesars had gravitated eastward, first to Turkey, where the Ottoman Emperors claimed to be the inheritors of Caesarian power, and ultimately to Russia, where the former Grand Duke of Muscovy was now the Csar, and an increasingly important trade partner for England. My second section examines a number of plays which try to come to terms with this new and unfamiliar axis of power. Finally, England itself laid increasingly embattled claim to be the only true inheritor of the cultural authority of Rome via the Brutus myth and the idea of the *translatio imperii*. In my final section, I look at a number of plays in which this idea is used to offer a subtle but far-reaching indictment of the legitimacy and efficacy of the early Stuart kings.

The first section is called 'The Whore of Babylon', and addresses possibly the most vexed question of what Rome had come to mean for the English Renaissance, its role as bastion of Catholicism. As the period progressed, what Rome itself had become since the days of its greatness grew increasingly pertinent to the early modern English stage, since Romanness could easily be elided with Roman Catholicism. John E. Curran has observed that Caesar was often used as a type of the papacy,[10] while John Kerrigan argues that

> the British martyrs persecuted under Diocletian...could be used to demonstrate the existence of an ancient, British Christianity pre-existing the influence of the papacy, and...their persecution for refusing to worship the pagan idols of Rome could be seen as prefiguring the martyrdom of Marian Protestants who refused to worship the idols of the Roman church.[11]

Certainly in William Alexander's *Jvlivs Caesar* we find the startling statement that 'there in *Caesar* many Marians were';[12] this actually refers to supporters of Marius, but its resonances for an early modern audience would be very different, evoking the name of the Virgin Mary, while James I described the Catholic conspirator

---

10   John E. Curran, Jr, *Roman Invasions: The British History, Protestant Anti-Romanism, and the Historical Imagination in England, 1530–1660* (Newark: University of Delaware Press, 2002), p. 153.

11   John Kerrigan, 'The Romans in Britain, 1603–1614', in *The Accession of James I: Historical and Cultural Consequences*, edited by Glenn Burgess, Rowland Wymer and Jason Lawrence (Basingstoke: Palgrave, 2006), pp. 113–39, p. 114.

12   William Alexander, Earl of Stirling, *Jvlivs Caesar* (1637), II.ii.90.

Guy Fawkes 'as seeming to put on "a Roman resolution"'.[13] The equation was also reversible: as Clifford Ronan remarks, 'In *King John*...the papal invasion replicates an Ancient pagan Roman conquest'.[14] Indeed to some extent, the very physical fabric of Roman remains in England fed the idea of an underlying continuity between Romanness and Roman Catholicism: the Appleby schoolmaster Reginald Bainbrigg visited Birdoswald in 1599 and told Camden that 'The inhabitants did showe me the plaice where the churche stode', on which Tony Wilmott comments that

> Surviving remains of the exercise basilica with its great piers...would have closely resembled the remains of dissolved abbeys which were a prominent feature of the late sixteenth-century landscape of England. The Roman buildings would certainly have been in a state of decay, but in an area with a relatively small population and not many buildings for which cut stone had yet been needed, ancient structures might have remained as standing ruins for centuries as they still do in parts of North Africa and the Middle East.[15]

To Bainbrigg, then, it might well have seemed that Romans and Roman Catholics had left virtually identical ruins in England's landscape.

It is unsurprising, therefore, that Rome and Roman Catholicism are eerily conflated in *Titus Andronicus*,[16] while in Thomas Dekker's *The Whore of Babylon*, the Empress (of whom it says in the dramatis personae 'vnder whom is figured *Rome*', in the sense of the seat of the papacy), declares that

> Our Image, which (like *Romane Caesars*) stamp'd
> In gold, through the whole earth did currant passe;
> Is now blanch'd copper, or but guilded brasse.[17]

In John Fletcher's *Bonduca*, too, the association between Rome and Roman Catholicism is anachronistically invoked by the British characters as a means to demonise their Roman opponents. Bonduca herself says, 'Mercy and love are sins in Rome and hell',[18] and adds,

> If Rome be earthly, why should any knee
> With bending adoration worship her?
> She's vicious; and, your partial selves confess,
> Aspires the height of all impiety.   (IV.iv. p. 183)

---

13   Antonia Fraser, *The Gunpowder Plot: Terror and Faith in 1605* (London: Arrow, 1999), p. 174.

14   Clifford Ronan, *'Antike Roman': Power Symbology and the Roman Play in Early Modern England, 1585–1635'* (Athens: The University of Georgia Press, 1995), p. 119.

15   Wilmott, *Birdoswald Roman Fort*, pp. 144 and 146.

16   See Nabil Matar and Rudolph Stoekel, 'Europe's Mediterranean Frontier: The Moor', in *Shakespeare and Renaissance Europe*, edited by Andrew Hadfield and Paul Hammond (London: Thomson Learning, 2005), pp. 220–52, p. 229.

17   Thomas Dekker, *The Whore of Babylon* (London: 1606), ll. 39–41. Subsequent references will be given in the text.

18   John Fletcher, *Bonduca*, in *Beaumont and Fletcher*, vol. II, edited by J. St Loe Strachey (London: Ernest Benn, 1950), IV.iv.p. 183. All further quotations from the play will be taken from this edition and reference will be given in the text.

Bonduca's elder daughter, on the point of committing suicide, attacks one of the greatest of Roman myths in specifically Catholic language when she declares that

> your great saint Lucrece
> Died not for honour; Tarquin topped her well;
> And, mad she could not hold him, bled. (IV.iv. p. 188)[19]

And Petillius is so struck by the daughter's valour that he loves her even when she is dead, with the same kind of necrophilic devotion as is associated with Catholicism in *The Second Maiden's Tragedy* (anonymous, but probably by Thomas Middleton), while in Jasper Fisher's *Fuimus Troes*, where part of the point is that all the characters are Roman to some degree, Lantonus refers to

> That ceremonious fear, which bends the heart
> Of mortal creatures and displays itself
> In outward signs of true obedience,
> As prayer, kneeling, sacrifice and hymns. (II.vi.1–4)

In fact the analogy between Rome and Roman Catholicism was virtually invited by the fondness of successive popes for choosing classicising names such as Pius and Julius, especially since Pope Julius II, the 'second Caesar', chose his title 'as a conscious reference to Julius Caesar'[20] and

> grew his beard in imitation of his imperial namesake...who had stopped shaving as a pledge of vengeance on the Gauls. His compatriots spoke of his "Caesar-like soul" and the imperial destiny of this incumbent of Rome was promulgated through art and ideology.[21]

This association between Romans and Roman Catholics gained added force in the reign of Charles I, whose wife Henrietta Maria was a Catholic. I further argue that this association is often considered in tandem with Rome's status as source of many of the most privileged aesthetics of literary and cultural representation, not least because the Counter-Reformation had taken it upon itself to develop an aesthetic as well as a religious agenda, since it vigorously propounded its own 'Counter-Reformation stylistics'.[22]

This section has two chapters. The first, 'Reformation and Deformation: *Titus Andronicus*', focuses on one of the most troubled and puzzling of Shakespeare's plays to argue that this paradigmatic story of the fall of Rome to the Goths operates

---

19 For comment on the implications of considering Lucrece as a saint, see Anna Swärdh, *Rape and Religion in English Renaissance Literature: A Topical Study of Four Texts by Shakespeare, Drayton, and Middleton* (Uppsala: Acta Universitatis Upsaliensis, Studia Anglistica Upsaliensia 124, 2003), p. 135.

20 Nicholas Temple, 'Julius II as Second Caesar', in *Julius Caesar in Western Culture*, edited by Maria Wyke (Oxford: Blackwell, 2006), pp. 110–27, pp. 110 and 113.

21 Philip Crispin, 'Louis XII, Julius II and Pierre de Gringore's *Sottie du Jeu du Prince des Sots* (1512)', in *Mighty Europe 1400–1700. The Writing of an Early Modern Continent*, edited by Andrew Hiscock (Burlington: Ashgate, forthcoming).

22 Swärdh, *Rape and Religion in English Renaissance Literature*, p. 225.

in profoundly symbolic ways which both itemise and interrogate what Rome had come to mean to Renaissance England. The play never loses sight of the irony that while Rome was now at the centre of the hated Catholic rather than the revered classical world, the descendants of the Goths who had destroyed the city had since reinvented themselves as its heirs. This had been neatly illustrated by the tomb which the Holy Roman Emperor Maximilian had proposed to build for himself early in the sixteenth century:

> Maximilian's extravagant tomb project was designed as a virtual archaeological museum. If it had ever been assembled according to Maximilian's plans, the tomb would have included over forty life-size bronze statues of princely forbears – some, like Arthur and Theodoric, not strictly part of the lineage – thirty-four busts of Roman emperors, and 100 small statues of the "Hapsburg Saints."[23]

For Maximilian, Goths and Romans could sit easily alongside one another; moreover Maximilian himself, as a German, was the descendant of the historical Goths, and yet his title was Holy *Roman* Emperor.

Since Maximilian's time the situation had been further inflected by the wildfire spread of Lutheranism in Germany, the country with which the Goths were most closely associated. In *Titus Andronicus*, Romans and Goths thus come to represent not only military opponents in classical terms but religious ones in Christian terms, but the polarities in both cases are shifting and unstable. Moreover, the events of this play are not related to any specific, individual Caesar; rather it lies at the heart of *Titus Andronicus*'s project not to anchor itself to any particular historical moment or event, but rather to gesture suggestively at a whole sequence of events. References to the expulsion of the Tarquins sit, with wanton disregard of chronology, directly alongside references to the Aeneas story, while the march of the Goths on Rome takes us to yet a third historical period, and the name of Bassianus, as we shall see, alludes to the Roman occupation of Britain, and also activates audience memory of a debate about the nature and history of the 'historical' Bassianus which had recently flared up in Shakespeare's own Britain. This promiscuity of reference is not merely accidental, though; rather it enables Shakespeare to offer in effect a conspectus of *all* Rome's history rather than focusing on merely part of it. And in so doing, it further allows Shakespeare's flexible story of the past to reach out into his own present, to suggest that just as the identities and allegiances of his long-dead Goths and Romans are blurred and confused, so the debates and conflicts between still-living Protestants and Catholics might be less clear-cut than might have been supposed.

In the second chapter, 'Hamlet Among the Romans', I turn to *Hamlet*. Later in the book I shall be suggesting that one of the principal reasons the early modern English stage found the Caesars so useful was that they could so readily be used to figure contemporary English rulers. Although it could be used in relation to queens, this paradigm does not acquire its full potential until the accession of James VI

---

23 Christopher S. Wood, 'Maximilian I as Archeologist', *Renaissance Quarterly* 58.4 (winter 2005), pp. 1128–74, p. 1155.

and I, who had 'placed a Roman stamp on his reign'.[24] Fletcher's *Valentinian*, for instance, is not only a play about monarchy in general, but also one which reflected directly on James VI and I; Gordon McMullan observes that 'Fletcher's metaphoric geography is characteristically Protean: in *Valentinian*, a solo tragedy written around the same time as *Bonduca*, he presents a Rome whose instabilities can all too easily be equated with those of Jacobean England'.[25] It is my contention that *Hamlet* marks the moment of cultural transition at which the pattern begins to acquire its full valency. Although written and first acted in the reign of Elizabeth, the play, as I will explore in my discussion of it, gestures unmistakably towards James, and, while evoking a number of individual members of the Julio-Claudian family, is able to make particular use of the figure of Caligula, because while James was still an unknown quantity, there was a corresponding ambiguity about Caligula – he is effectively the hero in the anonymous *Claudius Tiberius Nero*, but he is notably less savoury in Jonson's *Sejanus*, and as we shall see he is closely related to Hamlet. In the final part of the chapter, I discuss how *Hamlet* draws on its many allusions to late Elizabethan Roman plays (including *Julius Caesar*) to stage a contest between modes of representation – violent and non-violent, classical and modern, and visual and aural – which activates an analogous debate about whether drama should have a political function, and, in so doing, alerts us to another important area of cultural concern into which plays about the Emperors tapped: in the first place, political debate, especially debate about the best system of rule, and in the second, and in parallel with this, a corresponding metatheatrical debate about the extent to which drama should engage with such issues.

Playwrights knew that they were playing a potentially dangerous game in using Roman history to make political points, and this is reflected not only in the fact that many of the plays about the Caesars tackle contentious political issues head-on, but also in a sustained concern in Roman plays with ways of narrating and of staging events. In Shakespeare's *Julius Caesar*, Brutus says to the other conspirators,

> Good gentlemen, look fresh and merrily;
> Let not our looks put on our purposes,
> But bear it as our Roman actors do,
> With untired spirits and formal constancy.[26]

And Cassius says,

> How many ages hence
> Shall this our lofty scene be acted over,
> In states unborn, and accents yet unknown! (III.i.111–113)

---

24   Jonathan Goldberg, *James I and the Politics of Literature: Jonson, Shakespeare, Donne, and Their Contemporaries* (Baltimore: The Johns Hopkins University Press, 1983), p. 165.

25   McMullan, *The Politics of Unease*, pp. 95–6.

26   William Shakespeare, *Julius Caesar*, edited by Norman Sanders (Harmondsworth: Penguin, 1967), II.i.224–7. All subsequent quotations will be taken from this edition and reference will be given in the text.

In both these cases, our attention is drawn not only to the inflammatory nature of what we have been shown but also, and even more urgently, to the way in which we have been shown it. As Jonathan Goldberg remarks, 'The Roman plays that came to claim the stage in the Jacobean period reflect the style of the monarch and James's sense of himself as royal actor. They bear, as *romanitas* does in the Renaissance, a strong notion of public life, the continuities of history, the recreation of Rome as England's imperial ideal'.[27] They are also, though, fundamentally conditioned by a sustained theatrical self-consciousness, most neatly illustrated in the title of Massinger's *The Roman Actor*.

As a related concern, English Renaissance playwrights also often make the point that being a poet could be a dangerous avocation in imperial Rome. Lucan and Seneca had been forced to commit suicide, and Ovid had been banished. On the English Renaissance stage, Cinna the poet is murdered onstage in Shakespeare's *Julius Caesar*, and in the anonymous *Claudius Tiberius Nero*, Caligula reports of Tiberius that

> He slew a poet for this little cause,
> Because that in a doleful tragedy,
> He railed on Agamemnon's cruelty. (V.x.47–9)

Nevertheless, despite the peril associated with them, Roman modes of literary representation remained prestigious, influential, and much reflected on. Literature, and particularly verse, was believed to have had special properties in ancient Rome. Quite apart from the literary magic of works like the *Aeneid*, whose prestige cut across all factional allegiances – Luther on his deathbed wrote 'Do not lay hands on the divine *Aeneid*, but bow down and honour its tracks'[28] – there was an acute consciousness of the supposedly literal magic of the Sibylline verses. Thus Casca in the anonymous *Caesar's Revenge* says

> Well did the Cibills vnrespected verse.
> Bid thee beware of Crocadilish Nile.[29]

Agrippina, The Roman Actor, and above all *Sejanus* – in which Shakespeare himself acted – are all openly interested in historiography. Ultimately, I conclude that *Hamlet* aligns itself with other early modern plays about the Caesars as part of a wider project of using the stage to critique contemporary rule, in this case that of the incoming James of Scotland. It may do so in an oblique rather than a direct way, but it also insists that things must be fully brought to light and acted out, not merely narrated or alluded to – and in doing so it not only declares solidarity with the collective cultural enterprise and aesthetic of early modern drama as a whole but lays bare a crucial aspect of its workings.

---

27 Goldberg, *James I and the Politics of Literature*, p. 165.

28 W.A. Sessions, *Henry Howard, The Poet Earl of Surrey: A Life* (Oxford: Oxford University Press, 1999), p. 262.

29 *The tragedie of Caesar and Pompey or Caesars reuenge* (London, 1607), II.iv.49–50. Subsequent references will be given in the text.

The second section is entitled 'Caesar and the Czar', and turns its attention to some of the ways in which images of the Caesars impacted on England's growing push towards overseas exploration and colonisation. It consists of two chapters. The first, 'Tamburlaine and Julius Caesar', explores the intersection of references to Tamburlaine and references to Julius Caesar in a number of early modern plays. Julius Caesar was the paradigmatic Roman, and so closely associated with the concept of Caesarism that he was often referred to simply as 'Caesar'. He paradoxically expressed both the height of Roman achievement and the depths of its vulnerability to female temptation,[30] in the shape of Cleopatra, a figure who regularly casts a shadow over the image of Rome as home of heroism and manliness. Julius Caesar's achievement was widely considered to have been phenomenal, and he was understood as 'the prime example of a *fortunatus*, a man signally favored by Fortune'.[31] In the first place, he was considered invincible on the battlefield, and military might endured in the public consciousness as the essence of ancient Roman identity; indeed Anthony Miller sees this as central to the early modern interest in Rome.[32] Julius Caesar was also an author of considerable note. As well as being a historian whose work remained central in Renaissance educational practices,[33] he was reported by Suetonius to have written at least one play and other works too:

> It is said that in his boyhood and early youth he also wrote pieces called *In Praise of Hercules* and *The Tragedy of Oedipus* and *Collected Sayings*; but nearly a century later the Emperor Augustus sent Pompeius Macer, his Surveyor of Libraries, a brief, frank letter forbidding him to circulate these minor works.[34]

Julius Caesar had shaped both the spatial and temporal dimensions of the Renaissance world, laying down the Julian Calendar, to which England still adhered even after the introduction of the Gregorian one on the continent, and giving his name to various cities. He was also credited with having built the Tower of London, as *Richard III* reminds us when the young Edward V in *Richard III*, contemplating the Tower, asks of his uncle 'Did Julius Caesar build that place, my lord?'.[35] Most notably, his career

---

30 On the extremes and paradoxes which characterised Caesar's reputation, see for instance Suzanne F. Kistler, 'The Significance of the Missing Hero in Chapman's *Caesar and Pompey*', *Modern Language Quarterly* 40 (1979), pp. 339–57, p. 341: 'The gap is... wide between the popular mythology of the time about Caesar, glorified as one of the Nine Worthies, and the educated view of writers like Elyot, Muret, Garnier, Jonson, and Montaigne, who consistently reflected a divided, ambivalent repsonse to him'.

31 Rolf Soellner, 'Chapman's *Caesar and Pompey* and the Fortunes of Prince Henry', *Medieval and Renaissance Drama in England* 2 (1985), pp. 135–51, p. 144.

32 Anthony Miller, *Roman Triumphs and Early Modern English Culture* (Basingstoke: Palgrave, 2001), p. 4.

33 On the use of Caesar in education, see Curran, *Roman Invasions*, p. 150. For the importance of the Caesar story in relation to Stoicism, see Geoffrey Miles, *Shakespeare and the Constant Romans* (Oxford: Clarendon Press, 1996).

34 Suetonius, *The Twelve Caesars*, translated by Robert Graves (Harmondsworth: Penguin, 1957), p. 35.

35 William Shakespeare, *Richard III*, edited by E. A. J. Honigmann (Harmondsworth: Penguin, 1968), III.i.69. All further quotations from the play will be taken from this edition and reference will be given in the text.

crystallised the issue of the proper mode of rule. Although he did not directly seek the crown, he is repeatedly represented by Renaissance writers as having done so indirectly, and the Republic certainly did not long survive him. The conjunction of two such iconic figures of power as Julius Caesar and Tamburlaine is, therefore, a peculiarly energising and revealing one in a number of plays, and I argue that the coupling of the two allows dramatists to plot the changing contours of the political and economic world and the receding of the legacy of classical culture, as power gravitated increasingly in the threatening direction of the Ottoman Turks.

The second chapter of this section argues that despite the apparent problems of dating, Shakespeare's play *The Winter's Tale* can profitably be read in the light of the story of the Algonquian princess Pocahontas. As many scholars have observed, the classical past and the New World were rarely far apart in early modern thought. The chapter argues that there is not merely an incidental but a structural parallel, with deep roots in early modern thought systems, between the events of *The Winter's Tale* and those surrounding the visit of Pocahontas to London some four or five years after the play was first performed, so that the later of the two events can indeed help us to read the earlier. It suggests that excessive attention to Pocahontas' relationships with first John Smith and then John Rolfe have prevented us from noticing a much less visible but culturally no less interesting one with Henry, Prince of Wales, and above all with the mode of relationship between England and America which Prince Henry encouraged and with which he ultimately came virtually to be identified, which was one mediated through the classical past. Throughout Prince Henry's life in England there was a strong association between him and the figure of Marcellus, nephew and heir apparent of the Emperor Augustus, who died young and whose loss was lamented in the *Aeneid*. Pocahontas too was a figure to whom strong Virgilian resonances accrued. In *The Winter's Tale*, the princess from a new land replaces the lost prince who had died in the old, and the discourse of the classical mingles powerfully with that of the trade and exploration which drove the quest for the New World. To read *The Winter's Tale* in the light of the Pocahontas story allows us a lens through which to read the culturally crucial intersection of the Virgilian with the Virginian, and of the New World with the Old.

The third section, 'The Romans in Britain', focuses directly on the use of the Caesars to figure the Stuart kings. It opens with a chapter on 'Cleopatra and the Myth of Scota', which argues that *Antony and Cleopatra* plays off the English and Welsh myth of origin from Rome and ultimately Troy against the alternative Scottish version of descent from Scota, daughter of Pharaoh. This, I suggest, allows Shakespeare to activate a wide range of disreputable and undesirable associations for James I and other Scots, not least because Scotland had been deliberately excluded from the Roman empire by Hadrian's Wall. In Shakespeare's *Antony and Cleopatra* the use of the Augustus persona may initially seem flattering to James but, as I shall show, closer examination reveals that Shakespeare has activated some unexpectedly explosive associations which can be detonated by reading James as Augustus. This is followed by '*Cymbeline*: The Romans in Wales', which turns its attention more directly to the rôle of the *translatio imperii* in British history. *Cymbeline*, like *Titus Andronicus*, gestures at a number of different historical periods: its Romans feel more like Italians, and Ros King points out that 'the names given by Belarius to

Guiderius and Arviragus – Polydore and Cadwal respectively – encompass the complete world or span not just of the Britain myth but also of Saxon English history', in that Polydore was a younger son of Priam, whose ghost is seen by Brutus before he leaves for Britain, and Cadwallader was 'the last Celtic King of Britain'.[36] However, at the heart of the play is once again the figure of Augustus, and James's desire to be seen in relation to him, and in this the play goes right to the heart of what *Romanitas* meant to early modern Britain. This play too, I argue, incriminates James I by suggesting that his emphasis on the unity of England and Scotland is undermined if it is viewed in the context of Wales. Finally, 'He, Claudius: Charles I and the Claudius story' looks at the ways in which the figure of the Emperor Claudius could be mapped onto that of Charles I and the kinds of political capital that could be made from this.

The use of the Caesars to discuss contemporary issues was not confined to the early seventeenth century. It continued well after the Restoration: for instance, Nathaniel Lee's *Lucius Junius Brutus*, dedicated to 'the Right Honourable CHARLES, Earl of *DORSET* and *MIDDLESEX*, One of the Gentlemen of his MAJESTIES BED-CHAMBER, &c.', is obviously a lament for the Duke of Monmouth. It is, however, suggestive that Lee's play makes its point by referring back to the earlier period when the use of the correspondence between English kings and Caesars had first come into its own, since *Lucius Junius Brutus* retroactively rewrites *Hamlet* by building strongly on the echoes of the Brutus story there. Brutus directly echoes the words of Old Hamlet to Young Hamlet when he says to his son Titus (later to become clearly identified as a type of Monmouth), 'Remember me; look on thy Father's suff'rings…If thou hast nature, worth, or honour in thee';[37] later, Titus will muse Hamlet-like on death. Equally, Brutus' other son Tiberius swears his co-conspirators to silence, like Hamlet after his meeting with the Ghost, and hopes, Hal-like, 'to redeem the time' (III.i.80). *Antony and Cleopatra* is also echoed when Titus conjures Teraminta, 'Leap to my heart, and ride upon the pants' (III.iii.61), while the Priest's 'Now drink the Blood, / To make the Conjuration good' echoes both the rhythms and the mood of *Macbeth* (IV.113–114), as is underlined by Tiberius' comment on ambition immediately afterwards, and Sempronia's remark on the eloquence of a child's silent pleading recalls that of Volumnia in similar circumstances. All these references to Shakespeare strengthen the sense of this ostensibly Roman play as something actually profoundly related to England and its traditions, which not only sharpens the perception of the parallel with Monmouth, but also ironically underlines the extent to which this is a strategy with a proven track record with regard to his ancestors. This, the last elegiac appearance of a Caesar figure in conjunction with a Stuart one, serves merely to underline the closeness of the fit which, for perhaps the greatest half-century in the history of the English stage, made allusion to the Caesars so culturally rich and resonant.

---

36   Ros King, *Cymbeline: Constructions of Britain* (Aldershot: Ashgate, 2005), pp. 73–4.

37   Nathaniel Lee, *Lucius Junius Brutus*, edited by John Loftis (London: Edward Arnold, 1967), II. 366–8. All further quotations from the play will be taken from this edition and reference will be given in the text.

Chapter One

Reformation and Deformation:
Titus Andronicus

Mention of Rome inevitably evoked the question of proper modes of governance. This is particularly clear in Fletcher's *Valentinian*, a play in which, as Gordon McMullan observes, 'The central and by now familiar problem of *Valentinian* is the level of loyalty owed by virtuous courtiers to a corrupt king and court'.[1] This is a debate with which Fletcher had experimented in many other settings, but which he clearly found worked particularly well in Rome, where it could be centred on one of the Caesars. It is because of this emphasis on rule that in terms of the Renaissance understanding of Roman history, the expulsion of the Tarquins is the central event, referred to in a wide variety of texts. For instance, in the anonymous *Caesar's Revenge* (also known as *Caesar and Pompey*), Brutus unequivocally declares that

> An other Tarquin is to bee expeld,
> An other Brutus liues to act the deede.[2]

Perhaps the most remarkable thing here is the ease with which the long-ago story of the Tarquins can be mapped onto a much later episode in Rome's history, and this is a pattern which will be repeated elsewhere in Renaissance plays about Rome. It is as though, for the early modern playwrights who write about Rome, the expulsion of the Tarquins was not a single event, but one which was insistently replayed throughout the long course of Rome's history – and one which was to become particularly resonant after the demise of the Republic, when there was always a lurking potential parallel waiting to be activated between Tarquin, last monarch before the Republic, and the Caesars who restored monarchical rule after the Republic.

Not only the Caesar of *Caesar's Revenge* but any character in almost any Roman play who is perceived as vicious is liable to find himself identified with Tarquin, particularly if that character is a Caesar. Thus in *Claudius Tiberius Nero* (another anonymous play, published in 1607), Caligula refers to Tiberius as 'this proud Tarquinius',[3] and in *The Roman Actor* Aretinus claims that Palphurius Sura, Junius Rusticus and Lamia

---

1   Gordon McMullan, *The Politics of Unease in the Plays of John Fletcher* (Amherst: University of Massachusetts Press, 1994), p. 96.

2   *The tragedie of Caesar and Pompey or Caesars reuenge* (London, 1607), III.v.29–30. Subsequent references will be given in the text.

3   *Claudius Tiberius Nero*, V.iii.25. I quote from the version of the play edited by my student Sharon McDonnell as part of the MA English Studies (Renaissance Literature) at Sheffield Hallam University and available online at http://extra.shu.ac.uk/emls/iemls/resources.html

conclude there was
A Lucrece once, a Collatine, and a Brutus;
But nothing Roman left in you but
The lust of Tarquin.[4]

In William Alexander's *Jvlivs Caesar*, Anthony recalls how 'chast *Lucretia* (by proud *Tarquin* stain'd) / Wash'd with her bloud the violated bed',[5] and in Fletcher's *Valentinian* Lucina says to Valentinian 'The sins of Tarquin be remembered in thee'.[6]

The continuing importance and resonance of the Tarquins' story is shown perhaps most clearly by the recurrent, almost casually allusive references to it in the earliest of Shakespeare's Roman plays, *Titus Andronicus*. This is hardly surprising, because *Titus Andronicus* is a play which has the question of appropriate modes of governance at the heart of its concerns: Andrew Hadfield argues that *Titus Andronicus* 'make[s] a conspicuous effort to show that extremes of government are less desirable than a balanced and mixed constitution, which makes all the estates within society co-operate', since 'the fictional classical Rome created by the play cannot be ruled without the support of its citizens'.[7] I think, however, that the play is less programmatic than that. *Titus Andronicus* pits ideas and models together and registers the extent to which they jar, but it does not ultimately have a solution to offer, any more than it can offer clear contemporary equivalences for the blurred and shifting religious and national identities it charts.

Part of this juxtaposing process is the way in which the play deliberately brings together emblems of specific but different moments in Rome's past. Peter Culhane points out that although Shakespeare paid several imaginative visits to Rome, spread right across his career – 'In his writing career Shakespeare turned to Rome as a setting in six works: *Lucrece* and *Titus Andronicus* at the start, the three "Plutarchian" plays in the middle, and *Cymbeline* towards the end' – *Titus* offers a unique experience amongst these in that it 'contains more Latin than any other work by Shakespeare, and there are more occurrences of the word "Rome" and its cognates than in any other Shakespeare play'.[8] Moreover, as Robert S. Miola notes, 'The city is named frequently, occurring more times in this play than in *Julius Caesar* and *Antony and Cleopatra* combined'.[9] And yet the Rome of this play is more loosely defined than

---

4   Philip Massinger, *The Roman Actor*, in *Five Stuart Tragedies*, edited by A.K. McIlwraith (London: Oxford University Press, 1953), II.i.132–5. All further quotations from the play will be taken from this edition and reference will be given in the text.

5   William Alexander, Earl of Stirling, *Jvlivs Caesar* (1637), II.i.257–8.

6   John Fletcher, *Valentinian*, edited by Martin Wiggins (Oxford: Oxford University Press, 1998), III.i.91. Subsequent references will be given in the text.

7   Andrew Hadfield, 'Shakespeare and republicanism: history and cultural materialism', *Textual Practice* 17.3 (2003), pp. 461–83, pp. 474 and 473.

8   Peter Culhane, 'Livy and Titus Andronicus', *English* 55 (spring 2006), pp. 1–13, pp. 1 and 3.

9   Robert S. Miola, *Shakespeare's Rome* (Cambridge: Cambridge University Press), p. 43.

that of any other of Shakespeare's plays or poems, because in it elements of sharply different periods of the city's history are startlingly juxtaposed.

Throughout *Titus Andronicus*, characters are prodigal with references to key moments of Rome's past, though Peter Culhane, suggesting that 'Shakespeare's schooling in the culture of ancient Rome left him with an ambivalent or even hostile attitude towards the severe ideals of virtue that Roman writers espoused', argues that these are used principally to ironic effect:

> The play is laden with deliberate use of classical precedents by the characters; however, these Roman precedents are responsible for the play's descent into violence...this use of Roman examples points to a double critique. First, it suggests that the Roman ethics were alien from those of sixteenth century England. Second, it suggests that classical Latin was not a simple source of moral lessons for Renaissance England, as some humanist uses seemed to imply.[10]

The expulsion of the Tarquins is only one of the moments to which the play refers, though it is certainly an important one. Aaron carelessly remarks, 'Lucrece was not more chaste / Than this Lavinia, Bassianus' love',[11] and Lucius threatens that

> If Lucius live, he will requite your wrongs
> And make proud Saturnine and his empress
> Beg at the gates like Tarquin and his queen. (3.i.297–9)

Titus tells his daughter,

> Give signs, sweet girl – for here are none but friends –
> What Roman lord it was durst do the deed.
> Or slunk not Saturnine, as Tarquin erst,
> That left the camp to sin in Lucrece' bed? (4.i.61– 4)

And Marcus exhorts,

> My lord, kneel down with me; Lavinia, kneel;
> And kneel, sweet boy, the Roman Hector's hope,
> And swear with me – as, with the woeful fere
> And father of that chaste dishonoured dame,
> Lord Junius Brutus swore for Lucrece' rape –
> That we will prosecute by good advice
> Mortal revenge upon these traitorous Goths,
> And see their blood, or die with this reproach. (4.i.87–94)

In all these instances, Tarquin clearly serves to provide both an easily accessible type of tyranny and a foreshadowing of Saturninus' own doom. I want to argue, however, that the use of the figure is also achieving rather more than that.

---

10   Culhane, 'Livy and Titus Andronicus', pp. 1 and 6–7.

11   William Shakespeare, *Titus Andronicus*, edited by Jonathan Bate (London: Routledge, 1995), 2.i.109–10. All further quotations from the play will be taken from this edition and reference will be given in the text.

Titus Andronicus, uniquely among all the Shakespearean Roman plays which followed it, is not founded on any known classical events; instead the play looks like the story that, since it wasn't true – as Ronald Broude points out, 'the events represented in *Titus Andronicus* have no basis in historical fact' –[12] had to be invented, so economically do its events recapitulate both the fall of classical Rome and what Rome had come to mean to the Renaissance. The idea of recapitulation – of fast-forwarded and miniaturised selective reproduction of crucial episodes in a long-term sequence of events – is indeed key to the ways in which this play works. As Lukas Erne points out,

> *Titus Andronicus*, contrary to Shakespeare's other Roman tragedies *Julius Caesar, Antony and Cleopatra* and *Coriolanus*, does not deal with a specific, well-defined portion of Roman history. Rather, it unfolds in what seems an amalgamation of historical moments, early and late, Rome at the moment of military expansion and Rome at the moment of near collapse. When Titus first enters with pomp and circumstance as he returns from another successful battle, the times seem to be those of military conquest and prowess, yet the Goths standing in Rome as the play closes suggest Roman decline if not fall.[13]

A key element in the play's ability to collapse chronology in this way is its evocation not only of Junius Brutus but also of elements associated with the story of a much earlier Brutus, Aeneas' great-grandson, supposed founder of Britain.

Alongside the allusions to the Tarquins' story, *Titus Andronicus* also shows a marked debt to Virgil, weaving together a series of allusions to and quotations from him in which Troy fuses with Rome in a way inevitably suggestive of the *translatio imperii*, so that the whole history of Rome from inception to fall is emblematically conjured up for us, not least because the name of Lavinia inevitably recalls that of Aeneas' bride.[14] The effect is thus that of a seamless mixing of allusions to two markedly different periods of Rome's history, in which one seems constantly to blur into the other. As Jonathan Bate remarks in his edition of the play,

> Like Tarquin, Saturninus abuses the electoral process; like Lucretia, Lavinia is raped; as a consequence, Lucius, following in the footsteps of Lucius Junius Brutus, brings political change. Like Aeneas, Titus is "surnamed Pius", and, as in the *Aeneid*, the main threat to him is an exotic woman from a rival empire. But in a deliberate debasement of the famous encounter between Aeneas and Dido in a cave during a hunt, Tamora's sexual involvement is with the Moor, not with a Roman, and Virgil's celebrated image of the impassioned woman as a stricken deer (*Aen.* 4.68–73) is displaced on to the rape of Lavinia.[15]

---

12   Ronald Broude, 'Roman and Goth in *Titus Andronicus*', *Shakespeare Studies* 6 (1970), pp. 27–34, p. 30.

13   Lukas Erne, '"Popish Tricks" and "a Ruinous Monastery": *Titus Andronicus* and the Question of Shakespeare's Catholicism', in *The Limits of Textuality*, edited by Lukas Erne and Guillemette Bolens (Tübingen: Narr, 2000), pp. 135–55, p. 144.

14   On the play's interest in the *translatio imperii*, see also Liz Oakley-Brown, '*Titus Andronicus* and the cultural politics of translation in early modern England', *Renaissance Studies* 19.3 (June 2005), pp. 325–47, p. 326.

15   *Titus Andronicus*, ed. Bate, introduction, p. 18.

This is not, however, a mere hodge-podge. By avoiding specificity, *Titus Andronicus* gains in applicability: its loosely anchored material, which cannot be mapped onto any known set of historical events, conjures up not just a part of Rome's long story, but all of it. For instance, Titus and Aaron are both names with Jewish resonances, and Aaron strongly recalls Marlowe's Barabas, so that we remember among many other episodes of Rome's history the Emperor Titus's campaign against Jerusalem.

The presence of the Aeneas material also means, however, that Rome's is not the only past to which *Titus Andronicus* alludes, for the descendants of Aeneas famously came to Britain, and *Titus Andronicus* can be seen as alluding to Britain almost as much as to Rome. Indeed Anna Swärdh argues that the play also reproduces in miniature the history of the Reformation in England, with the events of the first half recalling those of the reign of Mary and the earlier part of that of Elizabeth and then moving through to bring the audience up to what was, at the time of the play's earliest performances, the present moment. As one particular instance of the many correspondences she sees, Swärdh links Titus' surname Pius not only to Aeneas, as Bate does, but also to Pope Pius V, who excommunicated Elizabeth,[16] and so too do Lukas Erne[17] and John Klause, who points out that 'Like Titus, [Pope] Pius was at his election offered (but, unlike Titus, did not reject) the white *pallium* (Shakespeare's "palliament" [i.i.182]), which popes had come to wear in imitation of the Roman emperors'.[18]

As part of these systematic allusions to both the Roman and the English pasts, this paradigmatic story of the fall of Rome to the Goths operates in profoundly symbolic ways. At its heart, it offers us a series of striking visual emblems of what the idea of Romanness had most urgently and centrally meant to each of the two pasts, classical and Christian, on which it reflects. Firstly, as Anthony Brian Taylor remarks, 'As he confronts the symbolic figure of Lavinia, her Virgilian name recalling the city's rise, her plight, raped and devastated by "barbarous Goths," foretelling its fall, it is Rome itself that stands bleeding before Marcus',[19] and Anthony Young adds that 'numerous commentators have pointed out how Lavinia's loss of tongue and hands resemble the loss of speech and writing, the elements of civilization, to the forces of darkness and barbarism',[20] thus summing up the logic of classical Rome's self-appointed mission to 'civilise' as much of the rest of the world as it could reach, and its ultimate failure to do so. Secondly, Lukas Erne relates the numerous instances of mutilation in the play to the Pauline theory of the Church as the body of Christ, and hence to what Rome meant to Shakespeare's contemporaries: 'the Reformation

---

16   Anna Swärdh, *Rape and Religion in English Renaissance Literature: A Topical Study of Four Texts by Shakespeare, Drayton, and Middleton* (Uppsala: Acta Universitatis Upsaliensis, Studia Anglistica Upsaliensia 124, 2003), pp. 118–19 and 82–3.

17   Erne, '"Popish Tricks" and "a Ruinous Monastery"', p. 148.

18   John Klause, 'Politics, Heresy, and Martyrdom in Shakespeare's Sonnet 124 and *Titus Andronicus*', in *Shakespeare's Sonnets: Critical Essays*, edited by James Schiffer (London: Garland, 1999), pp. 219–40, p. 234.

19   Anthony Brian Taylor, 'Lucius, the Severely Flawed Redeemer of *Titus Andronicus*', *Connotations* 6.2 (1996–97), pp. 138–57, p. 149.

20   Anthony Young, '"Ripen Justice in this Commonweal": Political Decay and Regeneration in *Titus Andronicus*', *Renaissance Papers* (1998), pp. 39–51, p. 47.

resulted in what Roman Catholics considered a mutilation of the Pauline body as several members cut themselves off from communion with the one Church'.[21] It is perhaps symbolic of this that both the banquets in the play are blighted ones, where the flesh of sons is consumed in a ghastly parody rather than an echo of the body and the blood of Christ.

Both these sets of emblematic representations focus not on the triumphs or grandeur of Rome but on loss, mutilation and conflict. This is a play which, whichever period it is homing in on, is interested in Rome's downfall and decline rather than its greatness. Hence, it is no surprise that during the course of the play as a whole, Shakespeare does not merely echo Virgil: he also subverts him. One of the ways in which he does this is by introducing an alternative, or conflicting voice. Heather James observes that 'Ovid dominates the central acts of the play at a direct cost to Vergil as a source for cultural decorum for Titus, Rome, and the play itself',[22] even if it is, as Michael Pincombe has argued, an Ovid mediated through Seneca.[23] 'Gracious Lavinia, Rome's rich ornament' (I.i.55) is not wooed in any heroic contest, as her namesake was by Aeneas, but raped, in an echo of the recurrent threat of *Metamorphoses*. At other points, Virgil is evoked only to be denied. Bassianus' quasi-abduction of Lavinia from Saturninus echoes Aeneas' rivalry with Turnus, but Bassianus is no Aeneas, founder of a dynasty: rather he is unceremoniously murdered, without even the dignity of a heroic fight, before he has sired a child – nothing but a dynastic red herring in the long, genealogically-driven story of Rome. Another ironic Virgilian echo is found in the words of the First Goth to Lucius:

> We'll follow where thou lead'st,
> Like stinging bees in hottest summer's day
> Led by their master to the flowered fields. (5.i.13–15)

Here what Reuben Brower astutely identifies as 'The Virgilian simile of warrior bees'[24] becomes an emblem not of Roman unity but of Roman vulnerability to external attack.

Other strategies for subverting and belittling the sense of Rome's greatness can also be seen at work. Titus himself, initially seen as like the successful Greeks when his brother Marcus says of him that 'Ten years are spent since first he undertook / This cause of Rome' (I.i.31–2), is soon aligned with the defeated Trojan king Priam, except that he is, it seems, only half the man that Priam was:

---

21 Erne, '"Popish Tricks" and "a Ruinous Monastery"', p. 149.

22 Heather James, *Shakespeare's Troy: Drama, politics, and the translation of empire* (Cambridge: Cambridge University Press, 1997), p. 43. Peter Culhane argues that Livy is also 'a highly significant source of *Titus Andronicus*...the use of Livy in this play reveals much about Shakespeare's scepticism of humanist adoption of Roman literature' (Culhane, 'Livy and Titus Andronicus', p. 1).

23 Michael Pincombe, 'Classical and Contemporary Sources of the "Gloomy Woods" of *Titus Andronicus*: Ovid, Seneca, Spenser', in *Shakespearean Continuities: Essays in Honour of E. A. J. Honigmann*, edited by John Batchelor, Tom Cain and Claire Lamont (Basingstoke: Macmillan, 1997), pp. 40–55.

24 Reuben Brower, *Hero and Saint: Shakespeare and the Graeco-Roman Historical Tradition* (Oxford: The Clarendon Press, 1971), p. 190.

Romans, of five-and-twenty valiant sons,
Half of the number that King Priam had,
Behold the poor remains, alive and dead. (I.i.82–4)

This seems quite deliberately suggestive of a diminution and a falling-off of the Trojan heritage of which Rome was so proud, especially since, as Richard Harvey's *Philadelphvs* contends, a member of Brutus' line in England also produced fifty children: '*Ebranke* a very goodly person among thousands and strong, begat *Brute* the second, and nineteene sonnes and thirtie daughters: these fiftie children were borne unto him of twentie women'.[25] The Roman equivalent, however, can equal neither the heroic original nor his British counterpart.

The Priam story, Rome's foundational moment, continues to figure prominently in *Titus*. As P. Jeffrey Ford observes, 'The historical moment is kept in the foreground throughout the play by repeated allusions to the fall of Troy, so that in this concluding phase of Roman civilization we are reminded of the fall of the civilization from which Rome was born'.[26] After this initial reference to Priam, Titus and his family are repeatedly associated with the suffering Trojans. Titus when he sees Lavinia asks,

What fool hath added water to the sea?
Or brought a faggot to bright-burning Troy? (3.i.69–70)

Later, he asks his brother,

Ah, wherefore dost thou urge the name of hands
To bid Aeneas tell the tale twice o'er
How Troy was burnt and he made miserable? (3.ii.26–8)

And the Boy, thinking of Lavinia, declares, 'I have read that Hecuba of Troy / Ran mad for sorrow' (4.i.20–21).

The comparison is, however, not without its attendant ironies. In the first place this *ur*-story of colonisation proves to be one that can itself be colonised by Titus's enemies, as when Demetrius says to Tamora,

Then, madam, stand resolved, but hope withal
The self-same gods that armed the queen of Troy
With opportunity of sharp revenge
Upon the Thracian tyrant in his tent
May favour Tamora, the queen of Goths
(When Goths were Goths and Tamora was queen),
To quit the bloody wrongs upon her foes. (I.i.138–44)

Secondly, the fall of Troy was also a story that, at least in the hands of Lydgate, could disturbingly prove to be about treachery and about the untrustworthiness of identity

---

25 Richard Harvey, *Philadelphvs, or A Defence of Brutes, and the Brutans History* (London: John Wolfe, 1593), p. 16.

26 P. Jeffrey Ford, 'Bloody Spectacle in Shakespeare's Roman Plays: The Politics and Aesthetics of Violence', *Iowa State Journal of Research* 54.4 (May 1980), pp. 481–9, p. 485.

rather than its stability, and this is echoed in *Titus Andronicus* when an unnamed Roman lord exhorts Marcus,

> Speak, Rome's dear friend, as erst our ancestor
> When with his solemn tongue he did discourse
> To lovesick Dido's sad-attending ear
> The story of that baleful burning night
> When subtle Greeks surprised King Priam's Troy.
> Tell us what Sinon hath bewitched our ears,
> Or who hath brought the fatal engine in
> That gives our Troy, our Rome, the civil wound.   (5.iii.79–86)

Despite the play's attempts to demonise and externalise its enemies, it is only too clear that Rome's only Sinons are internal ones: Brecken Rose Hancock, for instance, suggests a parallel between Lucius and the Goths,[27] while Anthony Brian Taylor compares Titus bringing the Goths to Rome to the Trojans admitting the horse.[28] To evoke the idea of Rome's Trojan ancestry, then, proves to trouble the sense of *Romanitas* as much as to confirm it.

Another motif from the story of Rome's foundation to figure prominently in the play (and again one with strong Virgilian overtones) is the tale of Aeneas' affair with Dido.[29] This is, as Jonathan Bate observes, clearly evoked when Tamora says,

> after conflict such as was supposed
> The wandering prince and Dido once enjoyed,
> When with a happy storm they were surprised
> And curtained with a counsel-keeping cave,
> We may, each wreathed in the other's arms,
> Our pastimes done, possess a golden slumber.   (2.ii.21–6)

Again, though, the story is ironically handled, because there is a sharp glance here towards the quasi-comic treatment of the story in Marlowe's *Dido, Queen of Carthage*.[30] Marlowe has already been evoked elsewhere in the play when Tamora declares 'I'll find a day to massacre them all' (I.i.455) and when Aaron, Barabas-like, says 'I must talk of murders, rapes and massacres' (5.i.63);[31] according to *OED*, the word 'massacre' entered the English language in 1578 in the aftermath of the St Bartholomew's Day Massacre, with which it remained closely associated, and on

---

27   Brecken Rose Hancock, 'Roman or Revenger: The Definition and Distortion of Masculine Identity in *Titus Andronicus*', *Early Modern Literary Studies* 10.1 (May 2004). Online: http://extra.shu.ac.uk/emls/10-1/hancroma.htm

28   Taylor, 'Lucius, the Severely Flawed Redeemer of *Titus Andronicus*', p. 151.

29   Heather James asks 'What does it mean that Aeneas's tale to Dido might serve as an analogue to the myth of republican Rome...*Titus Andronicus*'s odd allusion tends to revolutionize what we think "lovesick Dido" hears with her "sad-attending ear"' ('Dido's Ear: Tragedy and the Politics of Response', *Shakespeare Quarterly* 52.3 [Fall, 2001], pp. 360–82, p. 367).

30   Brower notes that *Titus* 'is in many ways reminiscent of Marlowe's *Dido Queen of Carthage*' (*Hero and Saint*, p. 174).

31   On Marlovian language in the play, see Bate, *Titus Andronicus*, introduction, p. 87.

which Marlowe's play *The Massacre at Paris* centres, and indeed the extent to which *Titus Andronicus* might be seen as directly reminiscent of the St Bartholomew's Day Massacre is indicated by the moment in the anonymous, smartly self-conscious university play *Pathomachia: Or: The Battell of Affections* (not published until 1630 though written earlier, maybe c. 1616) when Malice compares Hatred to '*Tamira* Queene of the *Gothes*, or *Katherine de Medices*'.[32]

The presence of *Dido, Queen of Carthage* in *Titus Andronicus* is seen most clearly when Marcus tells Titus,

> O noble father, you lament in vain:
> The tribunes hear you not, no man is by,
> And you recount your sorrows to a stone.   (3.i.27–9)

This closely echoes the scene in *Dido, Queen of Carthage* in which Aeneas mistakes a stone for Priam:

> O, yet this stone doth make Aeneas weep!
> And would my prayers, as Pygmalion's did,
> Could give it life, that under his conduct
> We might sail back to Troy, and be revenged
> On these hard-hearted Grecians which rejoice
> That nothing now is left of Priamus!
> O, Priamus is left, and this is he!
> Come, come aboard, pursue the hateful Greeks![33]

One might in addition notice a macabre parallel in the severing of one of Titus' hands and both of Lavinia's in *Titus Andronicus*, and both those of Marlowe's Priam, who, 'Forgetting both his want of strength and hands' (II.i.252), grotesquely continues to try to use them, in the speech which Shakespeare seems also to be remembering in the Player King's speech in *Hamlet*. It might also be worth remembering that in *The Massacre at Paris*, Admiral Coligny had his hands cut off (Scene Five, 42). And another play of Marlowe's may also be being remembered: Anthony Miller argues that 'The triumphs of *Titus Andronicus* derive part of their energy from the sense of peril and of nationhood generated in the Armada years. The play is akin to *Tamburlaine* not only in date and bloody horror but also in its use of triumph to redraw the boundaries of civility'.[34] Marlowe in general, then, seems to be a pervasive background presence, and *Dido, Queen of Carthage* is particularly so.

As Heather James convincingly argues, the cumulative effect of the allusions to Dido (and *Dido*) in *Titus Andronicus* is that 'Meticulously citing Rome's own authorities, Shakespeare suggests that the founding acts of empire contain the seeds

---

32   Henry More (?), *Pathomachia: or, The battell of affections* (London, 1630), I.i. Further references will be given in the text.

33   Christopher Marlowe, *Dido, Queen of Carthage*, in *Christopher Marlowe: The Complete Plays*, edited by Mark Thornton Burnett (London: Everyman, 1999), II.i.15–22.

34   Anthony Miller, *Roman Triumphs and Early Modern English Culture* (Basingstoke: Palgrave, 2001), p. 128.

of its ruin'.[35] More specifically, they also work, as *Dido, Queen of Carthage* itself can be seen to do, to bridge the gap between the two historical periods remembered by the play by incriminating Elizabeth I, since the two queens, Elizabeth and Dido, were often compared, not least because Dido's other name was Elissa. As Donald Stump points out, the epilogue to William Gager's Latin play on *Dido* openly draws the comparison between Dido and Elizabeth, and in particular, Stump directly relates Marlowe's *Dido* to Elizabeth's proposed marriage to Alençon.[36]

A comparison with Dido was by no means necessarily flattering to Elizabeth, but then to some extent all allusion to or iconographical representation of the queen, other than those which she sanctioned herself, was potentially perilous.[37] Indeed Shakespeare would have been on such dangerous ground here that Anthony Brian Taylor, challenging Frances Yates's influential view that there is a clear reference to Elizabeth as Astraea in *Titus Andronicus*, argues that an allusion to the queen cannot have been intended in the play because it would have been too risky:

> Close examination of the beginning of the *Book of Martyrs*...makes it extremely doubtful that Shakespeare would have wished an audience to identify his characer with the legendary King Lucius and then, by implication, with Elizabeth. In the small space devoted to king Lucius, there are two salient facts: the first is that he introduced Christianity into Britain; the second is that he died childless with disastrous consequences for his country. *Titus Andronicus* was written when the Queen was well past child-bearing age; as a young playwright at the beginning of his career, Shakespeare would have had to have displayed a good deal less sense than we normally credit him with, to have invited his audience to link Elizabeth, even by remote implication, with a ruler who was the epitome of the Elizabethan nightmare.[38]

However Andrew Hadfield argues that 'obliquely, but not beyond the bounds of possibility, Tamora, as the wicked queen of the Goths, may be a representation of Elizabeth',[39] and certainly when Taylor describes how 'The play opens...with the quarrel of two brothers over who should rule Rome, which is being violated and torn apart. And when the scene shifts from the city to the forest, the second, darker movement also gets underway with a quarrel between two brothers',[40] what he thus makes it sound like is *Gorboduc*, a play with clear reference to Elizabeth and the succession question. More generally, Anthony Young observes that '[t]he Saturninus-Bassianus conflict at the beginning of the play illustrates some of the points about

---

35   James, *Shakespeare's Troy*, p. 44.

36   Donald Stump, 'Marlowe's Travesty of Virgil: Dido and Elizabethan Dreams of Empire', *Comparative Drama* 34 (2000), pp. 79–107, p. 79.

37   See for instance Susan Frye, *Elizabeth I and the Competition for Representation* (New York: Oxford University Press, 1993).

38   Taylor, 'Lucius, the Severely Flawed Redeemer of *Titus Andronicus*', p. 139.

39   Andrew Hadfield, 'Tarquin's Everlasting Banishment: Republicanism and Constitutionalism in *The Rape of Lucrece* and *Titus Andronicus*', *Parergon* 19.1 (2002), pp. 77–104, p. 101.

40   Taylor, 'Lucius, the Severely Flawed Redeemer of *Titus Andronicus*', p. 142.

monarchial rule that would have been of great interest to a nation with no certain successor for the throne'.[41]

I think the idea of Elizabeth is present here. I have argued elsewhere that incrimination of Elizabeth is a favourite tactic of Marlowe's,[42] and Shakespeare is clearly remembering Marlowe in this play. It is, therefore, unsurprising that Heather James declares that in *Titus Andronicus* Shakespeare's 'critique of Elizabethan political iconography begins with the figure of Lavinia and ends with Tamora, who parodies the guises that Queen Elizabeth appropriated from Vergil – Dido, Astraea, and the *Venus armata* [armed Venus]'.[43] Most particularly, James argues that in the shooting scene 'Shot in the lap, Astraea, virgin goddess of justice and forerunner among Elizabeth I's celebratory guises, is anatomically exposed as the whoring queen of Goths'.[44] Reuben Brower is, I think, too cautious when he says that 'It is just possible that the bookish part of the audience for this bookish play would have detected in Titus' words from Ovid, "*Terras Astraeaea reliquit*" [Astraea flies from the earth]…an allusion to Elizabeth-Astraea';[45] her presence seems to me quite unmistakable, and clearly advertised. As Andrew Hadfield argues, 'For Shakespeare and Peele…the comparison between transitional Rome, caught between empire and republic, and dying Elizabethan England, about to be ruled by a new, unknown dynasty, is there for the audience and readers of the published play-text to make'.[46]

The most suggestive link between Titus' Rome and Elizabeth's England comes in the fact that, as Clifford Chalmers Huffman points out,

> just a year before *Titus* appeared in print for the first time the name of Emperor Bassianus was the subject of a notable reformulation which brings it close to Shakespeare's character: this treatment occurs in R. H[arvey]'s *Philadelphus, or A Defence of Brutes, and the Brutans History*.[47]

In many Renaissance accounts both before and after Harvey's, the Emperor Bassianus is responsible for the deaths of both his father, Alexander Severus, and his half-brother, Geta, and marries his stepmother (something which might lie behind Saturninus' sudden passion for the older Tamora);[48] but Harvey tells a very different story. His

---

41 Young, '"Ripen Justice in this Commonweal"', p. 40.

42 Lisa Hopkins, *Christopher Marlowe: A Literary Life* (Basingstoke: Palgrave, 2000), pp. 107–16.

43 James, *Shakespeare's Troy*, p. 48.

44 James, *Shakespeare's Troy*, p. 72.

45 Brower, *Hero and Saint*, p. 194.

46 Hadfield, 'Shakespeare and republicanism', p. 474.

47 Clifford Chalmers Huffman, 'Bassianus and the British History in *Titus Andronicus*', *English Language Notes* 11 (March 1974), pp. 175–81, p. 176.

48 See for instance John Clapham, *The historie of Great Britannie* (London, 1606), Part One, book III, chapter nine; John Speed, *The history of Great Britaine* (London, 1611), and Pedro Mexia, *The imperiall historie*, translated by Edward Grimeston (London, 1623). For another, considerably later play featuring Bassianus, see Hilton Kelliher, 'A Hitherto Unrecognized Cavalier Dramatist: James Compton, Third Earl of Northampton', *British Library Journal* 6 (1980), pp. 158–87, p. 177. Kelliher also notes a neo-Latin play from 1618, *Antoninus Bassianus Caracalla*. For discussion of Compton's work, which reverts to

Bassianus is an icon of Britishness (he is chosen as emperor over his brother because his mother was British). His brother's death is merely noted, with no cause specified; then we are told that '*Bassian* and the *Brutans* slew Geta, and the *Romanes* by night', making this sound more like an act of patriotism than of power-seeking, as it is in most authors.[49] Nor is there any mention of the alleged marriage to his stepmother, Julia. Huffman observes that Harvey's book 'would have gained a fair notoriety, for the book figures in the Harvey-Nashe quarrel, and carries within it an address, dated 14 June 1592, to the author's brother Gabriel',[50] and indeed *Philadelphus* openly advertises the Nashe-Harvey feud, since the commendation to Gabriel Harvey refers to Nashe's alias of 'Pierce Pennilesse': 'the schollers head without moderation is like the merchantes purse pennilesse without all credite'.[51] Shakespeare could have been expected to take an interest in this, since Nashe dedicated to his own patron Southampton,[52] and he himself seems to have used Nashe's *Christs Teares Over Ierusalem* as a source for *Titus Andronicus*;[53] moreover, Nashe was a friend of Marlowe and was named on the title-page of *Dido, Queen of Carthage* as co-author of the play, though it is unclear what the extent of his involvement actually was. Certainly Huffman points out that Harvey's book 'must have been well known since Nashe refers, in *Have With You to Saffron-Walden* (1596), to "*Dick* the true *Brute* or noble *Troian*"'.[54] Harvey's work also carries a dedication to Essex which refers to his generosity to Harvey, and Essex seems to have been a figure of considerable interest to Shakespeare elsewhere, since, as I shall discuss in chapter three, the final chorus of *Henry V* appears to allude to him directly. Finally, the Shakespeare of the sonnets might well have been expected to take notice of the coyness of Harvey's declaration that '*Memprise* solde himselfe to adultery, he gaue his body to buggery and beastly loue, which was loue, sauing your reuerence',[55] while the Shakespeare who wrote the strangers scene in *Sir Thomas More* seems unlikely to have been sympathetic to the xenophobia of such statements as 'Straungers cannot be true friendes, if they and we haue at any time been at ods'.[56] Harvey's would, then, have been a text in which Shakespeare could have been expected to take an interest, though not necessarily to agree with it.

Harvey's Bassianus is an important figure in the history of Britain. He is the son of the Emperor Severus, and John Peacock notes that many sixteenth-century writers, including Sir Thomas Elyot, praised Severus because he was felt to be peculiarly British, since he was thought to be buried in York, and he was also understood as

---

the traditional view of Bassianus as wicked, see Dale B.J. Randall, *Winter Fruit: English Drama 1642–1660* (Lexington: The University Press of Kentucky, 1995), p. 263.

49   Harvey, *Philadelphvs*, pp. 72 and 78.

50   Huffman, 'Bassianus and the British History in *Titus Andronicus*', p. 179.

51   Harvey, *Philadelphvs*, p. 14.

52   Hadfield, 'Tarquin's Everlasting Banishment', p. 79.

53   See Adrian Streete, 'Nashe, Shakespeare and the Bishops' Bible', *Notes and Queries* 47.1 (March 2000), pp. 56–8.

54   Huffman, 'Bassianus and the British History in *Titus Andronicus*', p. 180.

55   Harvey, *Philadelphvs*, p. 20.

56   Harvey, *Philadelphvs*, p. 86.

'a Christian emperor *avant la lettre*'.[57] Most notably, Severus was then believed to have built Hadrian's Wall. Spenser's name for the Wall is 'Gaulseuer', i.e. 'the wall of Severus', and the information that it had been built by the Emperor Severus is repeated in John Speed's 1610 map, where it is described as 'The Picts Wall'; in Leland, where it is 'the Pictish Wall';[58] in Drayton's *Poly-Olbion*;[59] and in Camden's *Britannia*, where we read that Severus 'reformed many things throwout the Island, and was the first that built a wall between the barbarous Britans and the Romans fourescore miles in length'.[60] Speed says that the Wall was started by Hadrian but completed by Severus, and it is Severus alone who is shown in the accompanying illustration.[61] Harvey's Bassianus is thus associated, via his father, with the physical structure that defined where Romanness ended and barbarism began. Moreover, although he was better known as Bassianus Caracalla, his alternative full name of 'Antoninus Bassianus' associates him with the Antonine Wall between the Firth of Forth and the Firth of Clyde, a second lasting legacy in the material fabric of Britain that had been originally intended to demarcate civility from savagery.

Shakespeare might also have remembered the Bassianus of Geoffrey of Monmouth, a pivotal figure in the religious history of England. In Geoffrey, Bassianus's story comes just after Geoffrey's account of how the Pope sent missionaries to King Lucius because he heard of his piety and 'Once the holy missionaries had put an end to paganism throughout almost the whole island, they dedicated to the One God and His Blessed Saints the temples which had been founded in honour of a multiplicity of

---

57   John Peacock, 'The Image of Charles I as a Roman emperor', in *The 1630s: Interdisciplinary essays on culture and politics in the Caroline era*, edited by Ian Atherton and Julie Sanders (Manchester: Manchester University Press, 2006), pp. 50–73, pp. 62 and 64.

58   John Chandler, *John Leland's Itinerary: Travels in Tudor England* (Stroud: Sutton, 1993), p. 341.

59   Michael Drayton, *Poly-Olbion*, in *The Complete Works of Michael Drayton*, edited by J. W. Hebel, 5 vols (Oxford: Basil Blackwell, 1933), Vol. 4, XXX.296.

60   William Camden, 'The Romans in Britaine', in *Britannia*, translated by Philemon Holland (1607). Online: http://e3.uci.edu/%7Epapyri/cambrit/romanseng.html

61   Michael Neill notes in *Putting History to the Question: Power, Politics, and Society in English Renaissance Drama* (New York: Columbia University Press, 2000) that in Speed's maps 'The "plots" of Cumberland and Northumberland...give particular attention to "The Picts Wall," describing its erection under Hadrian as a barrier against the barbarians of the north and enlarging its historical presence with marginal illustrations of surviving "monuments and Altars, [erected by Roman soldiers] with inscriptions to their idol Gods, for the prosperity of their Emperors and selves"' (p. 382), while Warner's *Albions England* notes, 'To passe by in silence *Iulius Agricola*, *Adrian*, *Lollius Vrbicus*, *Seuerus*, and others their seuerall workes and walles, erected heere in the Northern Regions for the same purpose: of which, besides *Seuerus* his forced vallie, with other strong and huge labors and fabrications, were reared at seuerall times two walles, the one of Turffe, and the other of Pyles and Timber strongly and artificially interposed, extending from Sea to Sea ouerthwarts the Countrey, estimated in length fowerscore, or, as haue some, about fiuescoore myles, incredible may it seeme that out of autenticke Authors is extant, were it not euen vnto this day to bee seene in the Ruines of the wall yet called the *Pictes* wall, raised of firme stone, containing in length as is aforesaid, in bredth throughout eight foote, and in height twelue' (William Warner, *Albions England* [1612] (Hildesheim: Georg Olms Verlag, 1971), p. 356 [2nd of the two so numbered]).

gods, assigning to them various categories of men in orders'. However, Christianity is abruptly expelled from the island after the betrayal of Bassianus by the Picts, after which came the persecution of Diocletian during which churches were destroyed and true believers martyred, events which Geoffrey describes in terms which would for a Renaissance audience have been irresistibly suggestive of the Reformation: 'all the churches were knocked down...The priests who had been elected and the faithful who were committed to their care were butchered side by side'.[62]

The prominence given to the Goths in *Titus Andronicus* certainly bears on the history of Britain, but in ways which are confusing and remind us of the complexity and instability of national and religious alignments and affiliations rather than offering a simple, clear-cut picture. As Harvey reminds us in the closing paragraph of *Philadelphvs*, 'It is a dangerous position to refuse the offpsring of *Brute*';[63] indeed it meant treading on a potential minefield, in ways which impinge directly on the later of the play's two time-frames, for the story of the *translatio imperii* to Britain via Aeneas's great-grandson Brutus and his descendants was not the only version of events extant. As Ronald Broude points out,

> ideas and emotions generated by the "racial," religious and political conflicts were most satisfyingly compressed in the *translatio imperii ad Teutonicos*, a tradition by which Roman dominion was understood to have passed to the Germans with the crowning of Charlemagne as Emperor of the Holy Roman Empire.[64]

This story had taken on new life in the wake of the Reformation, when it 'was re-interpreted in the Renaissance by German reformers, who began to see the Gothic overthrow of the Roman Empire as prefiguring the Protestant break-away from the Roman Catholic Church'.[65] The Goths, then, are figures with a surprising number of valencies. The editor of the Swedish-born, Rome-based writer Olaus Magnus, author of the influential *Description of the Northern Peoples*, sums up Magnus's attitude to Lutherans as being 'if only the Gothic heroes of old were alive today, they would deal fittingly with these filthy heretics!';[66] here Goths are *ur*-Germans to be deployed against degenerate modern Germans, and for Olaus Magnus' elder brother Johannes,

> the descent of the Goths was traced through the Scythians from Magog, son of Japhet and grandson of Noah, who found his way to present-day Finland and then sailed across to Sweden. Thus, the people he led, the Goths (or Getae), were an older and more religious race than the Romans. Unfortunately, like other tribes, they became idolaters (hence the building of the temple at Old Uppsala), though they were still able to pass on some of their antique virtue, valour, and wisdom to their progeny.[67]

---

62   Geoffrey of Monmouth, *The History of the Kings of Britain*, translated by Lewis Thorpe (Harmondsworth: Penguin, 1966), pp. 125 and 130.

63   Harvey, *Philadelphvs*, p. 107.

64   Broude, 'Roman and Goth in *Titus Andronicus*', p. 29.

65   Broude, 'Roman and Goth in *Titus Andronicus*', p. 30.

66   Olaus Magnus, *Description of the Northern Peoples* [1555], translated by Peter Fisher and Humphrey Higgens (London: The Hakluyt Society, 1996), 3 vols, vol. 1, introduction, p. ix.

67   Magnus, *Description of the Northern Peoples*, vol. 1, introduction, p. lxi.

Shakespeare very probably read at least some of Olaus Magnus,[68] and might in any case have encountered these ideas in other places too, so he would almost certainly be well aware that Goths could stand with ease for a wide variety of religious and national identities.

Titus Andronicus is centrally interested in how contemporary Roman identities, in the shape of Catholicism, relate to classical ones; indeed Lukas Erne argues that 'The fuzzy historical setting is further contorted when Imperial Rome and Reformation England seem to merge at the beginning of the last act'.[69] Above all, it uses the depiction of the old, classical Rome as a lens through which to examine what effects the break from the new, Catholic Rome has had for contemporary England. Jonathan Bate points to the many Reformation echoes in the play,[70] and J.Y. Michel relates the 're-edified' tomb in *Titus Andronicus* to what he sees as a collective Elizabethan interest in and defence of tombs in the wake of the Reformation and the dissolution of the monasteries. Michel argues that

> The blind violence which plagues *Titus Andronicus* may be seen as the symptom of a split between two opposed views which mirrored a theological divide. The Elizabethans who held on to Catholicism still thought that monuments showcased holy relics and symbolized an allegorical vision of death.

For Michel, *Titus* dramatises the way in which

> The Catholic viewpoint relied upon a sanctified death whose magical icons were supposed to be displayed to worshippers, triggering spontaneous belief and obedience. The Protestant viewpoint implied a barbaric death that had to be emprisoned [sic] and controlled before the civic body could correctly function.[71]

As Lukas Erne observes, 'It may be difficult to imagine today the urgency with which the question of the threatened unity of "Rome" posed itself to Catholics in the sixteenth century'.[72] This is a question which *Titus Andronicus* centrally addresses, but just as its principal trope is the ambiguous and shifting figure of the Goth, so it can find no easy answer to the questions it poses.

The theme of religious tension is declared even earlier in the play than the Virgilian one. Saturninus bases his claim to the throne on the fact that

> I am his first-born son that was the last
> That wore the imperial diadem of Rome. (I.i.5–6)

---

68   See Julie Maxwell, 'Counter-Reformation Versions of Saxo: A New Source for *Hamlet*?', *Renaissance Quarterly* 57.2 (summer 2004), pp. 518–60.

69   Erne, '"Popish Tricks" and "a Ruinous Monastery"', p. 144.

70   *Titus Andronicus*, ed. Bate, introduction, pp. 19–20.

71   J.Y. Michel, 'Monuments in Late Elizabethan Literature: A Conservatory of Vanishing Traditions', *Early Modern Literary Studies* 9.2 (September, 2003). Online: http://extra.shu.ac.uk/emls/09-2/michmonu.html

72   Erne, '"Popish Tricks" and "a Ruinous Monastery"', p. 147.

This has strong parallels to the idea of the apostolic succession. Saturninus's brother Bassianus, however, puts forward a very different and in some ways directly opposing rationale:

> But let desert in pure election shine,
> And, Romans, fight for freedom in your choice. (I.i.16–17)

The unmistakably Calvinist language of 'election' is provocatively juxtaposed with the idea of a revolutionary change in 'Roman' practice which clearly evokes the idea of Roman Catholicism. However, although two sharply contrasting positions may be delineated here, the factions associated with each position are much less securely identified. Despite Anna Swärdh's assertion that 'Throughout the play and with allegorical consistency, a number of factors contribute to establishing Titus' group of followers as "Catholic" and by exclusion the opposed group of Saturninus and the Goths as "anti-Catholic" or "Protestant"',[73] the play's allocation of religious identities is, I think, less schematic and clear-cut than this, in fitting reflection of the confusion and ambiguity in Shakespeare's own society – and indeed it is of course noticeable that the Goths are not united within themselves, but have, by the end of the play, split into two sharply polarised camps. Far from being the perquisite of an easily identifiable group, language associated with religion tends rather to float free, making allegiances as difficult to pin down as a specific historical period for the play is. Catholic language abounds in the play. Titus apostrophises his family tomb as

> O sacred receptacle of my joys,
> Sweet cell of virtue and nobility,
> How many sons hast thou of mine in store
> That thou wilt never render to me more! (I.i.95–8)

The idea of the 'cell' – the habitation of the Catholic Friar Laurence in *Romeo and Juliet*, a play close in date to this – is followed by even more open allusion when Saturninus decides to marry Tamora instantly,

> Sith priest and holy water are so near,
> And tapers burn so bright, and everything
> In readiness for Hymenaeus stand. (I.i.328–30).

It is also not only Catholic ritual and practice in general but rather more specific and urgent contemporary religious faultlines and schisms that are evoked when Lavinia is mutilated and the play becomes saturated with the language of martyrdom, so much so that John Klause terms it 'a "martyrial" drama'.[74] Lucius says, 'Speak, gentle sister: who hath martyred thee?' (3.i.82); Titus declares,

---

73   Swärdh, *Rape and Religion in English Renaissance Literature*, p. 81.

74   Klause, 'Politics, Heresy, and Martyrdom in Shakespeare's Sonnet 124 and *Titus Andronicus*', p. 224.

Thou hast no hands to wipe away thy tears,
Nor tongue to tell me who hath martyred thee. (3.i.107–8)

Later Titus says of Lavinia that 'I can interpret all her martyred signs' (3.ii.36), threatens Tamora's sons 'Hark, wretches, how I mean to martyr you' (5.ii.180), and tells Lavinia,

In thy dumb action I will be as perfect
As begging hermits in their holy prayers. (3.ii.40–41)

The rituals of Renaissance martyrdom are also evoked when Aaron says of the baby,

This maugre all the world I will keep safe,
Or some of you shall smoke for it in Rome. (4.ii.112–13)

Even more provocatively, this language of schism is in dangerous proximity to a term which opens up an actual and recent flashpoint of religious tension, when the Nurse says,

Here is the babe, as loathsome as a toad
Amongst the fair-faced breeders of our clime. (4.ii.69–70)

As Doris Adler has shown, references to toads in this period could all too clearly have been understood as referring to Elizabeth I's proposed marriage to the Duke of Alençon, whom she called her 'frog',[75] which had ultimately foundered on the religious differences between the couple. Again, then, criticism of the queen seems to be strongly implied, this time in a much more clearly focused way, with specific reference to religion.

Titus Andronicus's own attitude to the religious divide and to what Rome now means is as unclear as its characters' and indeed as its author's. On the one hand it is notable that the play's most openly Catholic character is a clown, who declares 'Nay, truly, sir, I could never say grace in all my life' (4.iii.99–100), salutes someone with 'God and Saint Stephen give you good e'en' (4.iv.42), and exclaims 'Hanged, by'Lady?' (4.iv.47). However there is also poignancy in the Goth's remark that

Renowned Lucius, from our troops I strayed
To gaze upon a ruinous monastery,
And as I earnestly did fix mine eye
Upon the wasted building, suddenly
I heard a child cry underneath a wall. (5.i.20–24)

And Aaron explicitly associates Lucius, the saviour-figure, with Catholicism when he says to him,

---

75 Doris Adler, 'Imaginary Toads in Real Gardens', *English Literary Renaissance* 11.3 (1981), pp. 235–60, pp. 238–9.

Yet for I know thou art religious
And hast a thing within thee called conscience,
With twenty popish tricks and ceremonies
Which I have seen thee careful to observe...   (5.i.74–7)

Perhaps the best indication of the play's overall position is to be found in Marcus's demonisation of Aaron as a 'misbelieving Moor' (5.iii.142) and his exhortation

O let me teach you how to knit again
This scattered corn into one mutual sheaf,
These broken limbs again into one body.   (5.iii.69–71)

What is important here is the unity of belief rather than its internal divisions. As Anna Swärdh suggests, 'the ending of the play can...tentatively be read as formulating a message of reconciliation and tolerance as the only way out of the situation of oppositional violence';[76] and it is certainly easier to downplay the differences between Protestantism and Catholicism if they are placed in the context of an entirely different belief system such as Aaron's.

This is perhaps best illustrated by the way in which this process operates in another play, *All's Well That Ends Well*. *All's Well*, too, uses the idea of the past to interrogate the present, and minimises the differences between the two Christian confessions by setting them against a belief system which is altogether other. Despite its contemporary setting, *All's Well* repeatedly reminds us of the far-distant past. The classical pull of the names of Diana and Helena is made explicit in the Clown's song:

Was this fair face the cause, quoth she,
        Why the Grecians sackèd Troy?
Fone done, done fond,
Was this King Priam's joy?[77]

In this play too, Marlowe is certainly evoked in the phrase 'Bajazeth's mule' at IV.1.41), and *Dido, Queen of Carthage* may well be remembered in the stone imagery of Lafew's remark that

                    I have seen a medicine
That's able to breathe life into a stone,
Quicken a rock, and make you dance canary
With sprightly fire and motion; whose simple touch
Is powerful to araise King Pippen, nay,
To give great Charlemain a pen in's hand
And write to her a love-line.   (II.i.72–8)

Mention of Charlemagne and Pepin, however, introduces a quite different motif, that of the play's Frenchness, and in particular its connections with French royalty: like

    76 Swärdh, *Rape and Religion in English Renaissance Literature*, p. 121.
    77 William Shakespeare, *All's Well That Ends Well*, edited by Barbara Everett (Harmondsworth: Penguin, 1970), I.iii.68–72. All further quotations from the play will be taken from this edition and reference will be given in the text.

Marlowe's, this is a play much interested in the massacre at Paris. This blending of past and present in a French context suggests that the ideological heart of *All's Well* is in a recent past whose troubles it thinks it can transcend by reference to a past still further back, in ways that will allow hope for the future. Thus the king's greeting to Bertram, 'Welcome to Paris' (I.ii.22), not only inaugurates a complex series of allusions in which Bertram will actually *be* Paris, choosing between the resonantly-named Diana and Helena, but also announces a geographical location. Moreover, though a classical model may be so strongly invoked, we are never allowed to forget the Frenchness of the setting either, since the motif of a doctor's daughter and a sexually wounded king so closely recalls the marriage between Catherine de' Medici (whose name meant literally 'of the doctors') and Henri II, unable to produce offspring for the first ten years of their marriage, while the sly link between the king's fistula and 'The fundamental reason of this war', which 'hath much blood let forth' (III.i.2–3), pokes fun at the French wars of religion and their complex interrelationships with questions of marriage and procreation. In this play, the 'virgin birth' of Helena's child can be brought about and offer hope for the future because it is pitted against the idea of the pre-Christian past. In this context, differences of confession rather than differences of belief system are minimised. There may indeed have been trouble between the two sides in the past, as seen most recently and devastatingly in the French Wars of Religion, but it is not too late to hope for better in the future, because, after all, all's well that ends well.

In *Titus Andronicus*, however, all definitely does not end well. In fact, the play is less interested in endings than in transitions. Brecken Rose Hancock suggests that

> It is not a coincidence that the son Titus executes is named 'Mutius.' Not only does Shakespeare recall Mutius Scaevola, who demonstrated the bravery of young men in Rome by unflinchingly burning off his own hand in the face of his enemy, but he alludes to a string of associated words that are intricately linked with the matter of the play; Mutius's death prefigures the 'muteness' and 'mutilation' that will plague the Andronici. Ironically, considering that Mutius's namesake is known for dramatically proving his loyalty to Rome, the name also implies 'mutiny,' the crime of which Titus accuses his son. It might also seem to Titus that his son is 'mutable,' or 'Inconstant in mind, will, or disposition' (*OED*) to wound so traitorously the 'honour' (1.1.370) of his father. Lastly, but I believe not least importantly, 'Mutius' holds the Latin root of all these words, that is, 'mutare,' 'to change' (*OED*).[78]

Change is, indeed, an idea strongly signalled in the play, which opens with a change of régime. Lukas Erne suggests that change is perhaps what *Titus Andronicus* is advocating most strongly, pointing out that this would have been an idea to which many in the audience might have been expected to be receptive: 'Shakespeare shows a Rome in need of reform', and many English Catholics thought this too,[79] so that the play may well be calling for change and action on both sides before any forward movement is possible for schism-torn England.

---

78 Hancock, 'Roman or Revenger'.
79 Erne, '"Popish Tricks" and "a Ruinous Monastery"', p. 148.

However many of the characters find change, or the prospect of change, profoundly painful – perhaps indeed impossible. Andrew Hadfield argues that Titus in particular 'is shown making a series of key mistakes which reveal that he does not possess the ability or the imagination to break free of traditional, constricting conventions and ideas', and provocatively suggests that we do not even know what happens at the end of the play, since the speech prefix of the acclamation of Lucius is disputed:

> Editors routinely alter it to 'All Romans', indicating that Lucius is a popular choice of emperor and that a proper order has been restored to Rome. However, it is equally possible that Lucius is staging an Andronici coup, having his brother [i.e. Marcus, actually his uncle] proclaim support for him, which would suggest that the ending shows a corrupted Rome which has failed to learn from its history and the same political errors will be repeated by the Andronici, who will inevitably degenerate into tyrants, propped up by the Goth army.[80]

Ultimately, then, this is a play that can only look nervously ahead to what an uncertain future may bring.

In *Titus Andronicus*, Caesarism and the *translatio imperii* do not offer sound foundations on which the future can build; instead they stand as terrible precedents threatening an unbreakable, self-repeating cycle of destruction and violence which was, as Shakespeare's audience would be only too well aware, still currently with them. As John Klause puts it, *Titus Andronicus* 'must have spoken with a special force to a certain part of his audience, moderate lay Catholics who might have seen the play even in its initial productions by the acting company of Lord Strange, a suspect Protestant whose ambience was Catholic',[81] especially if Klause is right to argue that Shakespeare modelled the message Titus sends to the Emperor via the clown on the petition which the Catholic layman Richard Shelley put into the hand of the queen in 1585. This episode was recorded by the Jesuit Robert Southwell, who was related to Shelley, in his 1591 pamphlet 'An Humble Supplication to Her Majestie',[82] and Southwell may well have been an associate and even a kinsman of Shakespeare.

Titus Andronicus, then, does not propose a solution; it laments, and ponders. Bassianus is a legitimate and auspicious heir with a resonant name, but he fails, and leaves no legacy. For ultimately, if the play does not take sides, it does register facts: the Goths are marching on, and the Romans are in retreat. Moreover, even if they were not, they are far from representing an ideal: they kill their own children and cling to outmoded ways, while though the first wave of Goths may have been destructive savages (as the first wave of Protestants were iconoclasts), the second wave proves amenable to a working alliance with Roman Lucius, and the Goth who finds Aaron did so because he wanted to go and look at the monastery. Perhaps in the

---

80   Hadfield, 'Shakespeare and republicanism', pp. 471 and 476.

81   Klause, 'Politics, Heresy, and Martyrdom in Shakespeare's Sonnet 124 and *Titus Andronicus*', p. 235.

82   Klause, 'Politics, Heresy, and Martyrdom in Shakespeare's Sonnet 124 and *Titus Andronicus*', p. 225.

end this tentative reconciliation is the best that can be hoped for in politically and religiously troubled *fin-de-siècle* England, and that curious, sightseeing Goth may yet stumble forward into a better future.

Titus Andronicus certainly does take us forward in one sense, since it leads directly on to the next play to which I turn. John Klause in his analysis of *Titus* observes that 'Not all...who suffer for "truth" or "justice" will become martyrs; some will become only psychological and political casualties, and perhaps executioners themselves. Shakespeare knew this very well, and would understand the problem even more deeply in writing *Hamlet*'.[83] Heather James finds another correspondence between the two plays when she points out that '*Titus Andronicus* and *Hamlet* provide concrete allusions to Dido as the original listener to Aeneas's tale',[84] and *Hamlet* too mixes Ovid and Virgil, as Caroline Hunt observes: 'the fall of Troy narrated by the Player is, as Harry Levin pointed out more than half a century ago, drawn not simply from the *Aeneid*, but also from the *Metamorphoses*'.[85] In the next chapter, I shall argue that *Hamlet* also follows on from *Titus Andronicus* in addressing the same cultural crisis of the proper mode of aesthetic representation, and the political and religious implications of what Rome, and above all the Caesarian tradition, had come to mean.

---

83 Klause, 'Politics, Heresy, and Martyrdom in Shakespeare's Sonnet 124 and *Titus Andronicus*', p. 237.

84 James, 'Dido's Ear', p. 382.

85 Caroline Hunt, 'Hamlet, Tiberius, and the Elephants' Graveyard', *Shakespeare Bulletin* 23.3 (Fall 2005), pp. 43–51, p. 48.

Chapter Two

Hamlet among the Romans

Shakespeare's *Hamlet* contains a number of significant references to Rome. Very early in the play, Horatio declares,

> In the most high and palmy state of Rome,
> A little ere the mightiest Julius fell,
> The graves stood tenantless and the sheeted dead
> Did squeak and gibber in the Roman streets;
> As stars with trains of fire and dews of blood,
> Disasters in the sun; and the moist star,
> Upon whose influence Neptune's empire stands,
> Was sick almost to doomsday with eclipse.[1]

This sets the scene for a number of other references to Rome, to individual Romans, and to contemporary plays set in Rome, not least – but not only – Shakespeare's own *Julius Caesar*. These are, I shall argue, constitutive for the meaning of *Hamlet* at every level, from the events it depicts to the way in which it chooses to represent them, and also condition its wider political meanings. Its sustained allusions both to Roman representational practices and to contemporary protocols for representing Rome allow *Hamlet* to focus its audience's attention on the principal difference between the classical stage and the early modern one, the diametrically opposed views on whether violence should be shown or described. This in turn offers an analogy for exploring whether the public display of violence (which Foucault would have it was a constitutive element of the early modern experience) has a legitimate rôle in the state, and, by extension, whether stage plays have a duty to bring issues to light to the fullest extent that they can, even if, as in 'The Mousetrap', this must perforce be done obliquely.

'I am more an antique Roman than a Dane' (V.ii.346) says Horatio at the close of *Hamlet*, and Clifford Ronan, taking this as the title of his important study on the Roman presence in Renaissance drama, argues that '*Hamlet*...is a Romanized play', not least because 'Several Roman plays press, as *Hamlet* does, questions about the double problem of *acting*',[2] while in Matt Haig's *Dead Fathers Club*, a modern riff on *Hamlet*, Philip, the Hamlet-figure, is obsessed with the Romans and points out the

---

1   William Shakespeare, *Hamlet*, edited by Harold Jenkins (London: Methuen, 1982), I.i.116–23. All further quotations from the play will be taken from this edition and reference will be given in the text.

2   Clifford Ronan, *'Antike Roman': Power Symbology and the Roman Play in Early Modern England, 1585–1635* (Athens: The University of Georgia Press, 1995), pp. 162 and 163.

parallel between the Romulus / Remus and Claudius / Old Hamlet pairings.[3] For all its setting in Elsinore, *Hamlet* as a whole could indeed be said to be as much if not more interested in antique Romans than in Danes, and particularly in the Julio-Claudians. This was the term used for those descendants of Julius Caesar who, starting with his great-nephew Octavius Caesar, who became the Emperor Augustus, provided a dynasty of Roman Emperors. Their history is a complicated one, understanding of which is not helped by numerous name changes, duplication of names, and (as in *Hamlet*) instances of incest and of marriage between close kin, but the version of it which Shakespeare would have known from his reading of Suetonius, Tacitus and Plutarch runs roughly as follows. After his defeat first of Brutus and Cassius and then of Mark Antony, Octavius Caesar succeeded to sole power as the Emperor Augustus. He married Livia, an ambitious divorcee who schemed for her elder son Tiberius to succeed him, and who was credited by some authors, such as Dio Cassius and Velleius Paterculus, with arranging the poisoning of several other possible heirs to ensure that this should be so. Tiberius did indeed become the next emperor, but his son Drusus predeceased him, and after the abortive attempt of Tiberius' chief minister Sejanus to snatch power by marrying Drusus' widow Livia the younger, the succession passed to the family of Tiberius' nephew Germanicus. After Germanicus' death, his widow Agrippina, his two elder sons Nero and Drusus, and his daughter Livia the younger (the same Livia who had married Tiberius' son Drusus) all died or were murdered, but Germanicus' youngest son Caligula remained alive and acceded to the throne. He proved so unbalanced and tyrannical that he too was soon murdered, and the succession passed to Germanicus' younger brother Claudius, who is famously supposed to have pretended all his life to be weak-minded so as to avoid being murdered. Claudius married as the last of his four wives his widowed niece Agrippina Minor, younger daughter of Germanicus, who is said to have poisoned him so that her own son Nero could succeed rather than Claudius' son Britannicus. Nero repaid his mother's schemes by murdering her, before himself coming to a bad end.

The relationship between *Hamlet* and the Julio-Claudians is signalled most clearly by the name of Hamlet's uncle Claudius, but there are other areas of strong correspondence. Both the historical and the dramatic families are much given to marriage within the family and to difficulties about who should be designated as the heir; both produce notable instances of poisoning, with Hamlet's father and, according to some authors, numerous members of the Julio-Claudian family all meeting their deaths in this way, invariably at the hands of another member of the family. Both feature matricide or the fear of it, and in both Julius Caesar functions as an authorising or authority figure. Both also feature family members who pretend to idiocy in order to avoid political complication.

The most celebrated of the Julio-Claudians was of course Julius Caesar himself, and he receives particular attention in *Hamlet*, perhaps not least because Shakespeare's own *Julius Caesar* had almost certainly been *Hamlet*'s immediate predecessor at

---

3   Matt Haig, *Dead Fathers Club* (London: Jonathan Cape, 2006), p. 180.

the Globe.[4] (It might also have been suggestive, in view of *Hamlet*'s concerns with parent-child relationships, that Suetonius records that Julius Caesar himself wrote a tragedy on the story of *Oedipus*.) When he speaks of a time 'A little ere the mightiest Julius fell' (I.i.117) Horatio, who doesn't know what's going on in contemporary Denmark, speaks almost as if he *remembered* this much more remote event, and in one way so of course he does, if he had acted in Shakespeare's play about it. Later, Polonius recalls how 'I did enact Julius Caesar. I was killed i'th'Capitol' (III.ii.102), almost certainly an extradiegetic reference to the fact that the same actor had indeed played both rôles, and Hamlet muses on how 'Imperious Caesar, dead and turn'd to clay, / Might stop a hole to keep the wind away' (V.i.206–7). Finally, Julius Caesar, like Hamlet, had a significant encounter with pirates, the fame of which is indicated by the fact that in his 1607 play *Jvlivs Caesar*, William Alexander has Caesar say

> I us'd those Pyrats who had me deceiv'd,
> Still as my servants (thundering threatnings forth)
> And gave them money more then they had crav'd,
> Whose ignorance too meanely priz'd my worth.[5]

That Alexander might have been aware of a parallel with *Hamlet* here is not impossible, since later in the play he clearly recalls *Hamlet* when the Chorus at the end of Act IV speaks of how '*like Camelions changing hue, / They onely feed on empty ayre*' (IV.i.435–6).

Other members of the Julio-Claudian family are also mentioned in *Hamlet*. Barnardo refers to 'Horatio and Marcellus, / The rivals of my watch' (I.i.13–14); Marcellus was the nephew and son-in-law of Augustus, whom the Emperor wished to make his heir before his premature death. When the Marcellus of the play arrives, he soon starts discussing the birth of Christ, which occurred during the reign of Augustus:

> Some say that ever 'gainst that season comes
> Wherein our Saviour's birth is celebrated,
> The bird of dawning singeth all night long.   (I.i.162–4)

This, Steve Sohmer has argued, is because the name of Marcellus recalls Marcellus the Centurion,[6] but an allusion to the family of Augustus is equally pertinent. Similarly, Hamlet prays, 'Let not ever / The soul of Nero enter this firm bosom' (III.ii.384–5). As well as being the stepson of the Emperor Claudius by the latter's marriage to Agrippina Minor, Nero was also Claudius's great-nephew, since Agrippina Minor was Claudius's niece as well as his wife. Both Nero and Hamlet thus have an incestuously-married uncle / father Claudius, to whom they may stand as heir if he can be disposed of, so the parallel is particularly pointed. Caroline Hunt also argues

---

4   See Steve Sohmer, 'Certain Speculations on *Hamlet*, the Calendar, and Martin Luther', *Early Modern Literary Studies* 2.1 (April, 1996), http://extra.shu.ac.uk/emls/02-1/sohmshak.html

5   William Alexander, Earl of Stirling, *Jvlivs Caesar* (1637), IV.i.317–20. Subsequent references will be given in the text.

6   Sohmer, 'Certain Speculations on *Hamlet*, the Calendar, and Martin Luther'.

for an allusion, if an oblique one, to Tiberius in *Hamlet* in the shape of the question 'What's Hecuba to him, or he to her?' (II.ii.553), since 'Hecuba was the subject of one of three famous questions with which the emperor Tiberius, according to Suetonius, tormented his grammarians...The first of these three rhetorical questions, "Who was Hecuba's mother?" ties in with Hamlet's difficulties about his own family loyalties, particularly his relationship to his mother'.[7]

As always in Renaissance drama, allusion to Rome in *Hamlet* carries in its wake a number of ideas and potential *topoi*: of cultural authority; of contestation over proper modes of governance; of a rigid behavioural code; of approved and prestigious modes of literary and dramatic representation; of religious belief, not least because Marlowe's Doctor Faustus, with whom Hamlet shares his education at Martin Luther's Wittenberg, had indulged in a provocative and blatantly anti-papal excursus to Rome; and of the *translatio imperii*. In *Hamlet* this last is directly raised by the Prince's wish to re-hear Aeneas' tale to Dido, which speaks precisely of how the seat of cultural authority came to be moved from Troy to Rome and thence, ultimately, to Britain, as in *Titus Andronicus*, and it brings with it an added layer of referentiality, making the play speak not only of ancient Rome but also of contemporary Britain. *Hamlet*'s odd glance at England, where all the men are as mad as he, may serve to alert us to the fact the the play is seriously interested in the ideas of succession and of legitimacy of government not only in Rome but in this current repository of the imperial authority of Troy and Rome. This is confirmed by the play's frequent intersections with the history of James VI of Scotland, probable heir to the English throne, and its setting in the homeland of his wife Anna of Denmark.

Denmark had indeed proved to be a prison for James Hepburn, Earl of Bothwell, James VI's stepfather, who had died insane as a prisoner in Denmark in 1578. The story of Bothwell seems to shadow that of *Hamlet* in that both pivot on the remarriage of a queen who may or may not have been responsible for her previous husband's death.[8] After the murder of her second husband Henry, Lord Darnley at Kirk o'Fields, Mary, Queen of Scots took Bothwell as her third husband despite his undoubted implication in the death of Darnley, thus leading to speculation that she herself had been involved; similarly, Gertrude is suspected by Hamlet of complicity with Claudius, once the play-within-the-play has convinced the prince of Claudius's own guilt in the matter of Old Hamlet's death. Andrew Hadfield, arguing that 'the plot of *Hamlet* seems saturated with suppressed and disguised references to Scottish history, all designed to express the anxiety felt by English subjects at the prospect of a Scotsman inheriting their throne', points to the striking similarities between the two stories:

> The murder of old Hamlet takes place in an orchard, as did the murder of Mary Stuart's second husband. His body broke out in boils...as did the dead body of Darnley, according

---

7   Caroline Hunt, 'Hamlet, Tiberius, and the Elephants' Graveyard', *Shakespeare Bulletin* 23.3 (Fall 2005), pp. 43–51, p. 44.

8   For discussion of this parallel, see Eric S. Mallin's *Inscribing the Time: Shakespeare and the End of Elizabethan England* (Berkeley: University of California Press, 1995), and Roland Mushat Frye, *The Renaissance Hamlet: Issues and Responses in 1600* (Princeton: Princeton University Press, 1984), pp. 27–37 and 102–10.

to Buchanan. It was commonly argued in anti-Marian propaganda that Mary's partner in crime and next husband, James, earl of Bothwell committed adultery with her before the death of Darnley, as old Hamlet argues was the case with Gertrude and Claudius; that the period of mourning was far too short, as Hamlet claimed was the case with his father; and that Bothwell was markedly inferior in appearance to Darnley, a judgement Hamlet claims anyone who saw Claudius beside his father would also make.[9]

Moreover, each queen had an only son who was severely traumatised by their discovery of these events. Hamlet, obviously, is deeply distressed by the Ghost's revelations to him and by the results of his own subsequent observations and investigations, and James VI and I suffered throughout his life from persistent gossip that he was the son not of Henry Darnley, his mother's husband, but of her alleged lover, the Italian musician David Rizzio, whom Darnley had murdered in Mary's chamber in a way not unlike Hamlet's killing of Polonius.[10]

Perhaps partly as a result of his traumatic early separation from his mother, James when he grew up evinced distinct difficulty in forming relationships with women, while *Hamlet* sees the collapse of the budding romance between Hamlet and Ophelia – whose description as a 'mermaid' by Gertrude at IV.vii.175 might even be reminiscent of the lewd caricatures depicting Mary, Queen of Scots in the shape of a mermaid, a notorious image of sexual looseness.[11] For the learned, there might be additional clues. In the *History of Scotland* written in 1582 by George Buchanan, tutor to Mary's son James, Mary Queen of Scots is described, in a suggestive prefiguring of Shakespeare's text, as 'exposed to all the dangers of outrageous fortune'.[12] Moreover, we know from Alastair Fowler's recent work that at one point at least during the composition of *Hamlet* Shakespeare had a Scottish text in mind, for he borrows from Gavin Douglas' *The palis of honoure*.[13]

---

9   Andrew Hadfield, 'Hamlet's Country Matters: The "Scottish Play" within the Play', in *Shakespeare and Scotland*, edited by Willy Maley and Andrew Murphy (Manchester: Manchester University Press, 2004).

10   Alison G. Hayton (now Alison Findlay) suggests that 'Hamlet's ambiguous status as "son" to the ghost, and to the present king, gives a key to his changeable behaviour in the play' ('"The King my father?": Paternity in *Hamlet*', *Hamlet Studies*, Vol. 9, nos 1 and 2 [Summer and Winter 1987], pp. 53–64, p. 53. R.W. Desai makes a similar case for the unknowability of Hamlet's paternity, and suggests, interestingly, that Hamlet's final ability to act comes in the name of Old Hamlet as King (as he undoubtedly was) rather than in that of his problematic identity as father (Rupin W. Desai, '*Hamlet* and Paternity', *The Upstart Crow*, 3 [Fall, 1980], pp. 97–106). See also Sohmer, 'Certain Speculations on *Hamlet*, the Calendar, and Martin Luther'. Sohmer offers a fascinating, if highly speculative, discussion both of Hamlet's possible bastardy as a parallel to Martin Luther's, and also of Luther references in the play in general, pointing, in particular, to the pun which Harry Levin first saw in 'The Diet of Worms'.

11   A good example of such an image is reproduced in Antonia Fraser, *Mary, Queen of Scots* (London: Weidenfeld and Nicolson, 1969), between pp. 368 and 369.

12   Quoted in Paula Louise Scalingi, 'The Scepter or the Distaff: The Question of Female Sovereignty, 1516–1607', *The Historian* 41 (1978), pp. 59–75, p. 74.

13   See Alastair Fowler, 'Two Notes on *Hamlet*', in *New Essays on Hamlet*, edited by John Manning and Mark Thornton Burnett (New York: AMS Press, 1994), pp. 3–10, p. 4.

When the Prince of Denmark takes his journey to England as an alleged cure for his apparent madness, then, we may well remember that his story, too, seems to reach across the water to that of the mad Bothwell, the guilty queen, and her unhappy son. Though this is too dangerous a correspondence to be openly suggested, the idea of exploring the relationship between the guilt of the royal mother and the apparently arrested development of the son would nevertheless have been of profound interest to an English audience imminently expecting the accession to their throne of the son of Mary, Queen of Scots, especially when the final scene of the play draws such attention to the whole issue of succession, and the question of fitness for it. When Hamlet, speaking of the young players who 'exclaim against their own succession' (II.ii.349), asks 'How are they escotted?' (II.ii.344), we may perhaps want to hear a pun on the Scots as well as an unusual English word.

However, *Hamlet* is also interested in how it should most appropriately speak of these things, something which is highlighted by the presence of not just a play-within-a-play but also the outer play's discussion of the state of contemporary theatre and its twin reflections, in the shape of the Pyrrhus speech and 'The Murder of Gonzago', on the style and rhetoric of older modes of drama. *Hamlet*, in short, is a play which is interested in what modes of representation are appropriate for the events it depicts as well as in the events themselves, and it is not surprising, therefore, that its recollection of Roman events should be accompanied by a sustained interest in Roman modes of representation. As well as Hamlet's praise of 'Aeneas' tale to Dido' (II.ii.442–3), he interrupts Polonius with 'My lord, I have news to tell you. When Roscius was an actor in Rome –' (II.ii.386–7), while Polonius in turn assures him that as far as the players are concerned, 'Seneca cannot be too heavy, nor Plautus too light' (II.ii.395–6). The reference to Seneca is particularly noteworthy because it evokes not just a particular author but an entire aesthetic and indeed a philosophy – one specifically at odds with the Christian schema in which *Hamlet* is so heavily invested. It is perhaps not surprising that Hamlet counters Polonius's reference to Seneca with 'O Jephthah, judge of Israel, what a treasure hadst thou!' (II.ii.399–400), for *Hamlet* does stage a contest between the Judaeo-Christian *modus operandi* and the classical – a contest which raises other issues such as the question of old versus new and whether violence should be visible, as on the (at least nominally Christian) early modern stage, or concealed, as on the classical one. P. Jeffrey Ford suggests that 'from as early as *Titus Andronicus*, Shakespeare's Roman plays treat, as a thematic concern, the effect of bloody spectacles on those who observe them' and that this is because 'Shakespeare is deliberately linking the effect of the violent stage spectacle with the effect of the violent act of power in the political realm'; I think *Hamlet*, with its numerous references to Rome, is a central part of this ongoing aesthetic and ethical investigation.[14]

Fowler points out the direct dependence of the description of the morn as 'in russet mantle clad' on Douglas's lines on Aurora. On the subject of the play's negotiations with Scottish history, see also Mark Thornton Burnett's own essay in the same collection, '"The Heart of My Mystery": *Hamlet* and Secrets', pp. 21–46, especially pp. 24 and 38.

14   P. Jeffrey Ford, 'Bloody Spectacle in Shakespeare's Roman Plays: The Politics and Aesthetics of Violence', *Iowa State Journal of Research* 54.4 (May 1980), pp. 481–9, pp. 482 and 484.

Although Aristotle in *The Poetics* did not expressly forbid the representation of violence on stage, he was notably scornful about its use, saying that

> Fear and pity may be aroused by spectacular means; but they may also result from the inner structure of the piece, which is the better way, and indicates a superior poet. For the plot ought to be so constructed that, even without the aid of the eye, he who hears the tale told will thrill with horror and melt to pity at what takes place. This is the impression we should receive from hearing the story of the Oedipus. But to produce this effect by the mere spectacle is a less artistic method, and dependent on extraneous aids. Those who employ spectacular means to create a sense not of the terrible but only of the monstrous, are strangers to the purpose of Tragedy; for we must not demand of Tragedy any and every kind of pleasure, but only that which is proper to it.[15]

The result is that both Greek and Roman theatre avoid the representation of violence and rely instead on verbal description of it. Thus in Seneca's *Thyestes*, Act Four consists entirely of a messenger's description of Atreus' slaughter of Thyestes' sons and the resulting banquet (*Thyestes* is an example which might well seem particularly relevant to *Hamlet* since Atreus also plans to use his revenge to test Menelaus' and Agamemnon's feelings about Thyestes and hence whether he is their true father). On the early modern stage, by contrast, there was virtually a competition for each successive play to outdo the last in bloodthirstiness and goriness of spectacle.

This emphasis on onstage violence can be seen particularly in some of the Renaissance Roman plays which have close textual and thematic intersections with *Hamlet*. When Polonius refers to having acted Julius Caesar, there were various real plays to which he could have been perceived as alluding. In the first place, of course, there is Shakespeare's own *Julius Caesar*. This shares with Hamlet a concern about mob behaviour and who the most appropriate ruler would be and some specific verbal echoes, such as Calpurnia's 'ghosts did shriek and squeal about the streets'[16] and Brutus' 'Call Claudius and some other of my men' (IV.iii.240), as well as Brutus' hesitation about committing suicide, from which his ultimate decision to run on a sword technically absolves him.

Ironically, considering that *Julius Caesar* stages political events of such supreme importance and resonance, it is remarkable how little we actually see of them. At an early stage of the play, Brutus says, 'The games are done, and Caesar is returning' (I.ii.178). Clearly, something has been happening offstage, but we have not been allowed to see it. Similarly we have to depend on Casca for our account of Caesar's reception of the offer of the crown:

> If the tag-rag people did not clap him and hiss him, according as he pleased and displeased them, as they use to do the players in the theatre, I am no true man. (I.ii.256–9)

---

15 Aristotle, *Poetics*, translated by S. H. Butcher, Part XIV. Online: http://classics.mit.edu/Aristotle/poetics.mb.text

16 William Shakespeare, *Julius Caesar*, edited by Norman Sanders (Harmondsworth: Penguin, 1967), II.ii.24. All further quotations from the play will be taken from this edition and reference will be given in the text.

Jonathan Goldberg suggests that 'this is the only moment in all of Shakespeare when the backstage area is conceived of as one on which the action onstage depends',[17] but in fact this play offers several such moments, as when Cassius says,

> Go, Pindarus, go higher on that hill;
> My sight was ever thick. Regard Titinius,
> And tell me what thou not'st about the field.   (V.iii.20–22)

Even when Cassius asks something so apparently trivial as 'Will you go see the order of the course?' (I.ii.25) we are aware that there is something of potential interest which we are not being allowed to see. When it comes to death, however, this takes centre stage. For all its heavily advertised debt to classical history, *Julius Caesar* conspicuously departs from classical aesthetic protocols by showing rather than telling many deaths, most notably, and most bloodily, that of Caesar himself.

Another play that Polonius might have been thought to be glancing at was a now lost Latin play called *Caesar Interfectus*, by Richard Eedes, which was performed at Christ Church, Oxford, probably in February 1581/2.[18] Although there has been speculation on the relationship of this to Shakespeare's *Julius Caesar*, its disappearance means it cannot get us very far. More promising is another play on the same theme, and probably from around the same date, the anonymous *Caesar's Revenge*. (This is also sometimes known as *Caesar and Pompey*, but I shall be using the title *Caesar's Revenge* to distinguish it from Chapman's *Caesar and Pompey*.) As early as 1954 Ernest Schanzer suggested this play as a source for *Julius Caesar*,[19] and William Poole has recently argued for an even closer relationship between it and Shakespeare, arguing not only that *Julius Caesar* quotes from *Caesar's Revenge* but that *Caesar's Revenge* in turn quotes from *Venus and Adonis*,[20] while René Weis proposes *Caesar's Revenge* as a source for *Antony and Cleopatra*.[21]

Caesar's Revenge is of particular interest as a point of comparison for *Hamlet* because as Boas notes, 'the situation that arises is akin to that in another of the "revenge" plays, the pre-Shakespearian *Hamlet*. Enmity springs up between Antony and Octavian, Caesar's great-nephew and adopted "son"'.[22] Octavian exhorts himself,

> For Father, Vnkell, Friend, go make thy mone,
> Who all did liue, who all did die in one.

---

17   Jonathan Goldberg, *James I and the Politics of Literature: Jonson, Shakespeare, Donne, and Their Contemporaries* (Baltimore: The Johns Hopkins University Press, 1983), p. 167.

18   See Frederick S. Boas, *University Drama in the Tudor Age* (Oxford: The Clarendon Press, 1914), p. 163.

19   Ernest Schanzer, 'A Neglected Source of "Julius Caesar"', *Notes and Queries* (May, 1954), pp. 196–7, p. 196.

20   William Poole, '*Julius Caesar* and *Caesars Revenge* Again', *Notes and Queries* 49.2 (June 2002), pp. 226–8, p. 228.

21   René Weis, '*Caesar's Revenge*: A Neglected Elizabethan Source of *Antony and Cleopatra*', *Shakespeare Jahrbuch* (1983), pp. 178–86.

22   Boas, *University Drama in the Tudor Age*, p. 276.

But heere I vow these blacke and sable weeds,
The outward signes of inward heauines,
Shall changed be ere long to crimsen hew.[23]

The suggestive conjunction of father / uncle confusion and the black clothing here certainly seems to anticipate *Hamlet*, as too does Cato's observation that prodigies have recently been observed, Cornelia's comparing of herself to Niobe just before her suicide, and Cleopatra's comment that

Ile bring thee to Great Alexanders Tombe,
Where he, whome all the world could not suffice,
In bare six foote of Earth, intombed lies. (II.iii.43–6)

Moreover Caesar, speaking of Hercules, refers to 'Nemean victories' (II.iii.85) and 'Nemean toyles' (II.iii.86); Cassius refers to the first Brutus's feigned idiocy, which might well seem to come very close to Hamlet's; and Brutus uses the phrase 'liuing monuments' (I.i.118). It is notable, too, that Caesar's funeral occupies the same place structurally as Ophelia's, and that his grave, like hers, is strewn with flowers, including 'sweete violets' (I.iv.27), the flower which Laertes hopes will spring from Ophelia's grave. The author of *Caesar's Revenge* certainly seems to have been watching or be remembering Shakespeare, since Caesar laments that, as in *Henry VI*,

Heere lyeth one that's boucher'd by his Sire
And heere the Sonne was his old Fathers death. (I.ii.40–41)

Equally, Pompey's reassurance to Cornelia that 'It is no danger (gentle loue) at all, / Tis but thy feare that doth it so miscall' (I.v.18–19) might well seem to echo Romeo's (similarly ill-founded) reassurance to Juliet. It looks to me as though in *Hamlet* Shakespeare has returned the compliment by in turn recalling *Caesar's Revenge*. It is, then, worth noting that this play, despite its ostentatiously correct classical learning, does include onstage violence, with Caesar and Pompey both being stabbed in front of us and Cornelia and Cato both committing suicide onstage.

An even more violent play is the anonymous *Claudius Tiberius Nero*, published in 1607. Alison Findlay has argued that it was also composed then, since 'The Pope ordered English Catholics not to pledge allegiance to James and in 1606–1607 three anti-Roman plays linking Catholicism with illegitimacy appeared: *The Whore of Babylon* by Dekker, *The Devil's Charter* by Barnabe Barnes, and the anonymous tragedy *Claudius Tiberius Nero*'.[24] However, I suspect, on the grounds of its

---

23 *The tragedie of Caesar and Pompey or Caesars reuenge* (London, 1607), IV.i.8–12. Further reference will be given in the text.

24 Alison Findlay, *Illegitimate power: Bastards in Renaissance Drama* (Manchester: Manchester University Press, 1994), pp. 75–6.

formal, patterned language and extensive pastiching of Kyd[25] and Marlowe,[26] that it may well have been written earlier. *Claudius Tiberius Nero* too seems to recall Shakespeare's early work, with Tiberius' initial refusal to take the crown looking very like the similarly disingenuous one of Richard III,[27] and Sejanus playing the rôle of Buckingham, while Shakespeare might well be seen as again repaying the compliment, since his representation of Hamlet comes close to that of Caligula in *Claudius Tiberius Nero*. There were in any case obvious points of correspondence between the two stories – in Suetonius' *The Twelve Caesars*, Claudius conceals himself behind a curtain after Caligula's assassination but is eventually discovered in much the same manner as Polonius is,[28] and, as discussed above, both Hamlet and Caligula had fathers allegedly poisoned and uncles named Claudius who made incestuous marriages. Similarly Caligula in Suetonius recounts that he had been going to kill Tiberius but put the dagger down,[29] much as Hamlet is poised to kill Claudius until he thinks better of it.

However, the similarities between Hamlet and the Caligula of *Claudius Tiberius Nero* seem particularly pointed. Each is moved to action only when his mother dies, having previously not responded to the provocation offered by the murder of a father, and each consciously adopts a disguise of simple-mindedness. This is something notably not found in other accounts of Caligula such as that in Jonson's *Sejanus* (which was perhaps already in preparation, and in which Shakespeare was to act Tiberius), in which a very different account of Caligula's behaviour is offered:

> *Laco.* But how comes Macro
> So'in trust and favour with Caligula?
> *Pomponius.* O, sir, he has a wife, and the young prince
> An appetite. He can look up, and spy
> Flies in the roof when there are fleas i'bed,
> And hath a learnèd nose to'assure his sleeps.
> Who, to be favoured of the rising sun,
> Would not lend little of his waning moon?[30]

---

25   See for instance I.i.34–5, 49–52, 56, 60, 95–6. 210 ff; V.iv.65ff; V.v.13, I.iii.47ff, II.ii.104–5, III.iii.200ff, II.iii.83ff, II.ii.137ff, and IV.ii.145. I quote from the version of the play edited by my student Sharon McDonnell as part of the 'Editing a Renaissance Play' module on the MA in English Studies (Renaissance Literature) at Sheffield Hallam University, and available online at http://extra.shu.ac.uk/emls/iemls/resources.html

26   See for instance II.iii.50ff and 125ff and III.i.55–6.

27   Paul Dean also suggests that Sejanus' wooing of Livia is indebted to Richard's of Lady Anne in *Richard III* ('"The Tragedy of Tiberius" [1607]: Debts to Shakespeare', *Notes and Queries* 31.2 [June, 1984], pp. 213–14).

28   Suetonius, *The Twelve Caesars*, translated by Robert Graves (Harmondsworth: Penguin, 1957), p. 186.

29   Suetonius, *Twelve Caesars*, p. 154.

30   Ben Jonson, *Sejanus*, edited by Philip Ayres (Manchester: Manchester University Press, 1990), IV.514–21. Although not licensed until 1604, *Sejanus* seems to have been in preparation for at least two years before that; when it was eventually performed, both Shakespeare and Burbage acted in it.

There are also other similarities between *Hamlet* and *Claudius Tiberius Nero*. In *Claudius Tiberius Nero* the ghost of Germanicus appears to Tiberius in an orchard, the location of Old Hamlet's death; Germanicus recounts prodigies that have recently occurred in Rome (III.i.1–32), as Horatio does; Julia says her love for Tiberius is more than Hecuba's for all her sons (I.iii.100–102), while Caligula, in the rather incoherent final speech of the play, actually accuses Tiberius of having killed Priam (V.x.70–71), both allusions which come close to the Pyrrhus speech of *Hamlet*. Livia jumps into a well, as Hamlet leaps into a grave and Ophelia to her death by drowning. (There is a further parallel between Livia and Ophelia in that Livia is the wife of Nero and Ophelia seemed destined to become the wife of Hamlet, who has tried so hard not to identify with Nero.) There are references to the chameleon and its habit of eating air (II.ii.74–5) and to Troy (III.iii.121), mention of 'Nemean' (III.iv.26), and Pelion and Ossa (V.i.32), as well as the recurrence of the words 'crammed' (V.v.70), found in *Hamlet* in 'Excellent, i'faith, of the chameleon's dish. I eat the air, promise-crammed. You cannot feed capons so' (III.ii.93–4).

Amongst *Claudius Tiberius Nero*'s many violent onstage deaths, some are particularly notable: Piso poisons Germanicus' mural crown; Sejanus is given a burning one; Sejanus stabs Spado, then Tiberius stabs four messengers; Agrippina is force-fed on stage and then strangled, although in Suetonius she was merely flogged and sent into exile; Drusus and Nero eat each other's arms and die of indigestion; and Julius Celsus chokes himself with his fetters onstage. Here, then, is a *Hamlet*-related Roman play showing onstage violence with a vengeance. Indeed of the many Roman plays of the period, only the *Jvlivs Caesar* of William Alexander, also first published in 1607, resolutely eschews violence. Here, the death of Caesar takes place offstage and is related by a suitably classical Nuntius (V.i.100–123). For the rest, the onstage representation of violence seems to be firmly established as a staple ingredient of the recipe for entertainment which Renaissance plays about Rome offer to their audiences, in marked contrast to the representational practices of Rome itself.

Hamlet itself mounts a virtual competition between staging and description as alternative modes of representation – a competition which clearly implies an analogous debate about the extent to which drama should attempt to represent the world beyond the stage, and incite the audience to take an interest therein, and so highlights the question of the political resonance of plays focused on or alluding to the Caesars. *Hamlet* repeatedly contrasts the aesthetic and emotional effect of what is heard with the effect of what is seen. The Pyrrhus speech, in true classical fashion, relies entirely on verbal description, while 'The Murder of Gonzago', which is told partly in the dumbshow of the earlier English stage, relies largely on spectacle. (It also acts almost as a comment on what the remnants of the ancient world have become in the modern one, since as Linda Kay Hoff points out, 'the Gonzago playlet is related to Rome through Julius Caesar's descendants, the ducal Gonzaga dynasty, which claimed descent from the Roman Caesars'.)[31] Moreover, such language as is used in 'The Murder of Gonzago' seems to be deployed primarily for allusive rather than affective purposes, since it is so openly a parody of Greene's play *Alphonsus, King of Aragon*; it is on its visual element that it relies for its emotional effect.

---

31   Linda Kay Hoff, *Hamlet's Choice* (Lampeter: The Edwin Mellen Press, 1990), p. 297.

Part of this contest between the two modes of representation and experience is the way in which *Hamlet* repeatedly pits the idea of reliance on the evidence of hearing against the idea of reliance on the evidence of sight. There are numerous references to ears, many of which are directly or indirectly connected with the murder of Hamlet's father and the actions that are taken as a result of it, and many of which, too, are associated with violence; as Reina Green observes, 'There are more references to ears than in any of Shakespeare's other plays and those ears are most often at risk of some form of violence'.[32] This is not a unique pattern: Mark Robson points out that in general 'In Shakespeare's works, the ear is treated with an ambivalence that cannot be simply idiomatic', but he also observes that 'Among Shakespeare's texts, *Hamlet* and *Venus and Adonis* thematise the problems posed by orality in clear ways',[33] and this is is certainly seen in the play's consistent representation of ears as vulnerable.

At a very early stage in the play, Barnardo says to Horatio,

> Sit down awhile,
> And let us once again assail your ears,
> That are so fortified against our story,
> What we have two nights seen. (I.i.33–6)

Later, when Horatio himself is preparing to tell the same story to Hamlet, Hamlet dismisses his preamble with

> I would not hear your enemy say so,
> Nor shall you do my ear that violence
> To make it truster of your own report
> Against yourself. (I.ii.170–73)

The Ghost himself declares that

> the whole ear of Denmark
> Is by a forged process of my death
> Rankly abus'd. (I.v.36–8)

He tells of how Claudius 'in the porches of my ears did pour / The leperous distilment' (I.v.63–4), and this idea of violence against ears spreads outwards as the Player King speaks of how

> *Then senseless Ilium,*
> Seeming to feel this blow, with flaming top
> Stoops to his base, and with a hideous crash
> *Takes prisoner Pyrrhus' ear.* (II.ii.470–73)

---

32   Reina Green, 'Poisoned Ears and Parental Advice in *Hamlet*', *Early Modern Literary Studies* 11.3 (January, 2006). Online: http://extra.shu.ac.uk/emls/11-3/greeham2.htm

33   Mark Robson, 'Looking with ears, hearing with eyes: Shakespeare and the ear of the early modern', *Early Modern Literary Studies* 7.1 (May, 2001). Online: http://extra.shu.ac.uk/emls/07-1/robsears.htm

Ears are also associated with danger when Laertes warns Ophelia 'Then weigh what loss your honour may sustain / If with too credent ear you list his songs' (I.iii.29–30), and when Polonius effectively condemns himself to death by announcing that 'I'll be plac'd, so please you, in the ear / Of all their conference' (III.ii.185–6), and it is notable that it is *hearing* rather than *seeing* Polonius which causes Hamlet to stab him:

> In his lawless fit,
> Behind the arras hearing something stir,
> Whips out his rapier, cries 'A rat, a rat'. (IV.i.8–10)

Violence is again done on ears when Gertrude laments that 'These words like daggers enter in my ears' (III.iv.95), and when Claudius speaks of how Laertes 'wants not buzzers to infect his ear / With pestilent speeches of his father's death' (IV.v.90–91).

Although so much of the evidence in the play is apprehended through the ear, however, there is also a very considerable insistence on the reliability of sight. Horatio when he sees the Ghost declares,

> Before my God, I might not this believe
> Without the sensible and true avouch
> Of mine own eyes. (I.i.59–61)

Claudius, in contrast to his brother's association with the ear, is particularly linked to eyes. In his opening speech, he speaks of how he is celebrating his marriage 'With an auspicious and a dropping eye' (I.ii.11), and says to Hamlet, 'And we beseech you bend you to remain / Here in the cheer and comfort of our eye' (I.ii.115–16). Hamlet himself is notably ambivalent in his attitude to the evidence of the eye. On the one hand, he is wary of things associated with eyes, dismissing 'the fruitful river in the eye' (I.ii.80) as a trivial signifier of his grief, declaring 'But I have that within which passes show' (I.ii.85), and saying scornfully that his mother remarried 'Ere yet the salt of most unrighteous tears / Had left the flushing in her galled eyes' (I.ii.154–5), but he is also impressed by the evidence that the eye affords:

> I prithee, when thou seest that act afoot,
> Even with the very comment of thy soul
> Observe my uncle. If his occulted guilt
> Do not itself unkennel in one speech,
> It is a damned ghost that we have seen,
> And my imaginations are as foul
> As Vulcan's stithy. Give him heedful note;
> For I mine eyes will rivet to his face,
> And after we will both our judgments join
> In censure of his seeming. (III.ii.78–87)

Having been unconvinced by the tale which he has heard from the Ghost, Hamlet can apparently rely only on the visual evidence which his eyes will read in Claudius' seeing face.

In a number of places in the play, these clashing aesthetics come into direct conflict. On two occasions, for instance, a verbal description of the Ghost is interrupted by the actual appearance of the Ghost.[34] Moreover, Hamlet juggles the evidence of eyes against that of ears when he says that

> I have heard
> That guilty creatures sitting at a play
> Have, by the very cunning of the scene,
> Been struck so to the soul that presently
> They have proclaim'd their malefactions. (II.ii.584–8)

This is something he has heard, but in itself it is something which relies on eyes. A similar balancing of one against the other comes in his declaration that

> O, it offends me to the soul to hear a robustious periwig-pated fellow tear a passion to tatters, to very rags, to split the ears of the groundlings, who for the most part are capable of nothing but inexplicable dumb-shows and noise. (III.ii.8–12)

Most notably, he says,

> O, there be players that I have seen play – and heard others praise, and that highly – not to speak it profanely, that neither having th'accent of Christians, nor the gait of Christian, pagan, nor man, have so strutted and bellowed that I have thought some of Nature's journeymen had made men, and not made them well, they imitated humanity so abominably. (III.ii.28–35)

Hamlet has *heard* others praise these, but when he has *seen* them, he has disagreed. Ears clash with eyes again, if only metaphorically and by association, when he says to his mother, 'Here is your husband, like a mildew'd ear / Blasting his wholesome brother. Have you eyes?' (III.iv.64–5). Finally, he accuses her of having

> Eyes without feeling, feeling without sight,
> Ears without hands or eyes, smelling sans all,
> Or but a sickly part of one true sense
> Could not so mope. (III.iv.78–81)

What is heard and what is seen can, it seems, work together on occasion, but can also be dangerously at odds.

This tension between hearing and seeing is precisely analogous to the competition between classical and early modern modes of representation, and raises the question not only of whether violence should be seen or only heard, but also of the wider relationship between the classical past and the present, and of how the present should view the principles and protocols of the past – and, consequently, of whether and to what extent plays about the Caesarian past are to be considered applicable to the present. It is particularly noteworthy in this respect that many of both Hamlet's

---

34 I am indebted for this observation to Paul Smith of the British Council, Mumbai division, at the international seminar on Shakespeare and violence at the University of Pune, India, at which an earlier version of this chapter was first presented.

and the play's references to classical mythology are specifically associated with his father, as for instance when Hamlet refers to Old Hamlet as 'Hyperion to a satyr' (I.ii.140) and calls his uncle 'no more like my father / Than I to Hercules' (I.ii.152–3), or observes to Horatio of Claudius,

> If his occulted guilt
> Do not itself unkennel in one speech,
> It is a damned ghost that we have seen,
> And my imaginations are as foul
> As Vulcan's stithy. (III.ii.80–84)

The Ghost itself speaks of 'Lethe wharf' (I.v.33), and Horatio's reference to 'the most high and palmy state of Rome' follows directly on the heels of Barnardo's mention of 'the King / That was and is the question of these wars' (I.i.113–14), while it is the crowing of the cock, which Marcellus explicitly identifies with Christianity (I.i.160–69), which forces the spirit to leave. In Hamlet's conversation with his mother, Old Hamlet becomes virtually a one-man pantheon of the classical deities:

> See what a grace was seated on this brow,
> Hyperion's curls, the front of Jove himself,
> An eye like Mars to threaten and command,
> A station like the herald Mercury
> New-lighted on a heaven-kissing hill,
> A combination and a form indeed
> Where every god did seem to set his seal
> To give the world assurance of a man. (III.iv.55–62)

Hamlet's classicisation of his father is all the more striking because the other main character to be haunted by the memory of Old Hamlet, Claudius, remembers him in strictly Judaeo-Christian terms, alluding directly to the biblical story of Cain and Abel when he says that his crime 'hath the primal eldest curse upon't – / A brother's murder' (III.iii.35–7). In Hamlet's mind, however, his father is firmly associated with the classical world.

As well as associating the classical world with his father, however, Hamlet also associates it with violence, as when he says

> Let not ever
> The soul of Nero enter this firm bosom;
> Let me be cruel, not unnatural.
> I will speak daggers to her, but use none. (III.iii.384–7)

To be possessed by the soul of Nero would automatically entail the use of violence. The other characters make a similar link between violence and the Caesarian past: when Horatio declares that 'I am more an antique Roman than a Dane. / Here's yet some liquor left' (V.ii.346–7), he equates *Romanitas* with suicide, and when Polonius recalls that 'I did enact Julius Caesar. I was killed i'th'Capitol' (III.ii.102), he too associates Rome – and a Caesar in particular – primarily with violence. Nor is this an inappropriate association: Heywood in his *Apology for Actors* recounts an anecdote of Julius Caesar playing the protagonist in *Hercules Furens* and becoming so carried away that he killed one of his own servants who was playing the antagonist.[35]

The world of the Caesars, then, is figured as twofold in the play: doubly representing authority and anteriority – both figuratively and literally paternal – it also encodes a mode of enacting and yet simultaneously, in Aristotelian theory, containing violence. This is something of obvious concern in a play which famously contains nine deaths, and which can indeed be seen as something of a meditation on the public display of violence and whether it functions, as early modern English rulers seemed to think, as a necessary tool in the maintenance of public discipline and the proper governance of a kingdom, or is a mark of barbarity.

As with classical mythology, it is again remarkable how many of the play's references to violence are linked directly to Old Hamlet. The keynote is struck in Horatio's initial description of him:

> Such was the very armour he had on
> When he th'ambitious Norway combated.
> So frown'd he once, when in an angry parle
> He smote the sledded Polacks on the ice.   (I.i.63–6)

Old Hamlet was someone who wore armour, who 'frown'd', and who 'smote'. He continues to be portrayed as someone who is both violent in himself – 'our valiant Hamlet....Did slay this Fortinbras' (I.i.87–9) – and also provokes violence in others, as Marcellus observes that their reaction to the Ghost's appearance is 'To offer it the show of violence' (I.i.149). Claudius by contrast is primarily associated with violence which is either victimless or invisible. He commands that

> No jocund health that Denmark drinks today
> But the great cannon to the clouds shall tell.   (I.ii.125–6)

For Claudius, the discharge of a cannon marks mirth and celebration rather than dealing death. A precisely similar note is sounded in his hope that

> [So envious slander],[36]
> Whose whisper o'er the world's diameter,
> As level as the cannon to his blank,
> Transports his poison'd shot, may miss our name
> And hit the woundless air.   (IV.i.40–44)

When it comes to actual or public violence, Claudius is dismissive: he calls Laertes' fencing ability the one of all of his qualities 'in my regard, / Of the unworthiest siege' (IV.vii.74–5) and 'A very ribbon in the cap of youth' (IV.vii.76).

---

35   Paola Pugliatti, *Beggary and Theatre in Early Modern England* (Aldershot: Ashgate, 2003), p. 81. Ronan remarks on the actual prevalence of casual violence in ancient Rome (*'Antike Roman'*, p. 127).

36   There is a lacuna in the text here; 'So envious slander' is the conjectural emendation which appears in Arden 2 and has been generally adopted.

Most notably, even when Claudius is himself guilty of real violence, it is invisible. His poisoning of his brother went unnoticed, and when he wishes Hamlet disposed of he assures Laertes that

> I will work him
> To an exploit, now ripe in my device,
> Under the which he shall not choose but fall;
> And for his death no wind of blame shall breathe,
> But even his mother shall uncharge the practice
> And call it accident. (IV.vii.62–6)

Although he is in other respects monstrous and reprehensible, it is not Claudius who is implicated in setting the tone for the disturbing level of casual violence which passes as normal in Denmark, as is suggested by Polonius's instructions to Reynaldo that in his monitoring of Laertes' behaviour he need not concern himself with 'drinking, fencing, swearing, / Quarrelling, drabbing' because these are merely 'companions noted and most known / To youth and liberty' (II.i.25–6, 23–4). This casual acceptance of bad behaviour is, it seems, the legacy of Old Hamlet's court. Moreover, Claudius's diplomatic intervention settles the Fortinbras affair without violence, avoiding unnecessary bloodshed, and he is also masterful in his defusing of Laertes' anger, neutralising the threat of immediate and unconsidered murder with the bland

> No place indeed should murder sanctuarize;
> Revenge should have no bounds. But good Laertes,
> Will you do this, keep close within your chamber. (IV.vii.126–8)

It is unsurprising that Andrew Hadfield provocatively argues that

> it would be a crude reading of the play that saw Claudius's rule as entirely negative. There is a pointed contrast between the bloody and violent military world represented in the opening scene and the revelry at court represented in the second... Modern kingship has started to impose order on a lawless and anarchic kingdom. The tragedy is in fact precipitated by exposing the king's crime rather than by keeping it concealed.[37]

Implicit here is the suggestion that private, hidden violence may possess mitigating features that public, staged violence does not.

In the light of this idea, it might well prove profitable to consider *Hamlet* in connection with a rather different early modern play about ancient Rome, R. A.'s *The Valiant Welshman*, published in 1615 but certainly written earlier. This is a play which is full of echoes of *Hamlet*, something which is unsurprising if, as is sometimes supposed, 'R. A.' was Robert Armin, Shakespeare's fool.[38] There are

---

37 Hadfield, 'Hamlet's Country Matters'.

38 Alexander S. Liddie surveys the arguments for and against this in his edition of the known Armin play *The History of the Two Maids of More-Clacke* (New York: Garland, 1979), and concludes that the odds are about three to one against Armin's authorship of *The Valiant Welshman* (preface, p. 2). However, *The Two Maids'* parody of *Hamlet*, especially in scene xv, is not dissimilar to that in *The Valiant Welshman*.

several allusions to *Hamlet* so close as to be almost quotations. At the outset, Fortune declares,This Stage and Theater of mortall men,

> Whose acts and scenes diuisible by me,
> Sometime present a swelling Tragedy
> Of discontented men.[39]

Bardh says that Caradoc

> Fights like a Nemean Lyon,
> Or like those Giants, that to cope vvith Ioue,
> Hurl'd Ossa vpon Peleon.   (II.ii.13–15)

And Caradoc himself declares,

> And, if there be, as Heathen men affirme,
> Some godlike sparks in mans diuining soule,
> Then my propheticke spirite tels me true.   (III.ii.8–10)

Caradoc also speaks to his sister Uoada of 'The duty and the care that euer since / My reason could distinguish...' (IV.i.25–6), gives her a pearl which he explicitly compares to one which might be drunk (IV.i.31–3), and observes that 'There's danger in delay' (IV.i.106); finally, he challenges Codigune to a single combat on the basis of which all the property of both will fall to the victor, and it is explicitly stated in the stage directions that when Codigune accepts his offer, 'They fight at Poleaxe' (III. iii.58 s.d.), a possible reading of *Hamlet* I.i.66. *The Valiant Welshman* also contains references to Pyrrhus (I.i.15, and Bardh regrets that Cassandra did not foresee the treason as she did at Troy [II.ii.32–5]), Hercules (I.iv.23), Julius Caesar (I.iii.52), and the hobby horse (II.i.45–6). Like *Caesar's Revenge*, too, this play contains an Octavian, in this case the father of the hero Caradoc, as well as a Cornwall and a Gloster, who commits suicide and is then the subject of an inquest very closely modelled on the gravediggers' conversation in *Hamlet*, while Caradoc, like Hamlet, laments not so much that his father Octauian is dead as that he died 'Bearing a packet of such ponderous sinnes, / Would racke the Axel-tree of heauen to beare' (III.ii.59–60). Most notably, the play is set in the time of the Emperor Claudius, and it is, therefore, suggestive for my discussion that this Claudius is ultimately an honourable figure who acknowledges and honours his debt to Caradoc. This play not only glamourises the heroic single-combat performance of Caradoc but also explicitly refers to the idea that a degree of controlled violence is a necessary by-product of ruling, when Monmouth says dismissively, 'Reade Machiauell: / Princes that would aspire, must mocke at hell' (I.iii.94–5). Since 'R. A.' was obviously steeped in the language and ethos of Shakespearean drama, we should perhaps take some note of his apparent conviction that a character with some of the traits of Claudius can in some ways be read as a positive figure. According to Suetonius, after all, the historical Emperor Claudius was a better emperor than his predecessors

---

39 R. A., *The Valiant Welshman* (London: 1663), I.i.3–6. All further references will be given in the text.

in many respects, except that, like his Shakespearean namesake, he was unfortunate and ill-advised in his marriages.

The final intertextual allusion I want to consider in connection with the rôle of violence in the state is a very suggestive intersection between *Hamlet* and *The Rape of Lucrece* (indeed Andrew Hadfield suggests that the entire plot of *Hamlet* 'is ... in essence a variation of the story of the killing of Tarquin').[40] In a long ekphrastic passage, Lucrece is led to a sustained meditation on her own grief by means of contemplating Hecuba's:

> To this well-painted piece is Lucrece come,
> To find a face where all distress is stelled.
> Many she sees where cares have carvèd some,
> But none where all distress and dolour dwelled;
> Till she despairing Hecuba beheld,
> Staring on Priam's wounds with her old eyes,
> Which bleeding under Pyrrhus' proud foot lies.[41]

Robert S. Miola points out that *ekphrasis* also features importantly in *Titus Andronicus* – 'As in *Lucrece*, the sequence of events leading to the attainment of revenge features an *ekphrasis*. The work of art described is not an imaginary depiction of Troy, but the tale of Tereus, Philomela, and Procne'[42] – suggesting that *Titus* shares with *Hamlet* and *Lucrece* a Rome-conditioned impulse to meditate on the aesthetics and effects of representational modes.

Notably, the narrative teleology of *The Rape of Lucrece* drives towards the replacement of the Tarquins through the initiative of Brutus, who, like Hamlet,

> with the Romans was esteemèd so
> As silly jeering idiots are with kings,
> For sportive words and utt'ring foolish things. (1811–13)

Lucrece, too, pits the power of eyes – deciding to kill herself, Lucrece addresses the sun as 'O eye of eyes' (l. 1088) – against that of ears, with the narrator of the poem noting that 'For by our ears our hearts oft tainted be' (l. 38), and it comes very close to *Hamlet* when Lucretius and Collatine compete in sorrow over the body of Lucrece as Hamlet and Laertes do over Ophelia's, and when Lucrece foreshadows the Ghost's words about the thorns in Gertrude's bosom as she apostrophises Philomel:

> And whiles against a thorn thou bear'st thy part,
> To keep thy sharp woes waking, wretched I,
> To imitate thee well, against my heart
> Will fix a sharp knife to affright mine eye. (ll. 1135–8)

---

40 Andrew Hadfield, '"The power and rights of the crown in *Hamlet* and *King Lear*: "The king – the king's to blame', *Review of English Studies* 54 (2003), pp. 566–86, p. 577.

41 William Shakespeare, *The Rape of Lucrece*, in *The Poems*, edited by John Roe (Cambridge: Cambridge University Press, 1992), 1443–9.

42 Robert S. Miola, *Shakespeare's Rome* (Cambridge: Cambridge University Press), p. 59.

Such echoes highlight the fact that Lucrece and Hamlet both remember the politic use of supposed folly and both use the Pyrrhus / Hecuba story as a prompt to action and to emotional clarification of their own situations, leading, in Lucrece's case, to her decision to perform on herself an act of violence which, while tragic, is also purgative, since it leads directly to the expulsion of the Tarquins and therefore militates against the possibility of further future violence in Rome.

This is, I think, very similar to the conclusion ultimately reached by *Hamlet*. Like *The Rape of Lucrece*, *Hamlet* too hovers imaginatively over the end of a dynasty, since it seems so clearly to reflect on the cultural moment of imminent transition from Elizabeth to James. To reflect on James in the context of a play which is reminiscent of the Caesars does double cultural duty, since the persona James most persistently adopted would be that of the Emperor Augustus, as part of his determined attempt to present himself primarily as a peacemaker. Although this is principally a phenomenon postdating *Hamlet*, its main lines had already been adumbrated in James's Scottish reign, and Shakespeare's play might well therefore be seen as asking which James really is – a prince of peace, or a threatening Fortinbras? And can there, indeed, be such a thing as a prince of peace in a fallen world, or was Machiavelli, in his praise of that modern-day Caesar Cesare Borgia, right, and must violence inevitably accompany strong and successful rule? Certainly Horatio, whose judgement Hamlet himself certifies as the best in the play (and whose name identifies him with the gallant defender of Rome against Lars Porsena in his quest to restore the Tarquins) seems to think so, for, hearing of how Hamlet unhesitatingly sent Rosencrantz and Guildenstern to their deaths, he exclaims, 'Why, what a king is this!' (V.ii.62), as if the ability to order executions were the fundamental mark of a king. *Hamlet* the play, then, seems in its metatheatrical and extradiegetic references to take something of the same course as Hamlet the prince: exploring both the path of avoiding violence and the path of using it, it ultimately seems to endorse its use in limited circumstances because one act of violence can prevent more. In so doing, I think, it offers both an implicit criticism of the incoming James VI and I, whose agenda of ceasing the war with Spain was so directly at odds with Henry IV's advice to his son about the utility of foreign wars, and a declaration of solidarity with the collective cultural enterprise of the early modern stage, which, unlike its Roman predecessor, did not shrink from the overt use of violence to explore the issues it wished to address. For both of these projects, *Hamlet* finds allusion to the Caesars to be a natural, flexible, and richly suggestive language. So too, although in very different ways, does the group of plays to which I now want to turn, Marlowe's *Tamburlaine the Great* and the many plays which imitate it.

Chapter Three

Tamburlaine and Julius Caesar

In this chapter, I propose to explore a number of early modern texts which imaginatively connect Julius Caesar and Marlowe's Tamburlaine. Occurring across a number of texts, this link proves to be a rich and sustained one, serving to underline both the perceived correspondences between Roman past and Renaissance present and also the potential strains and difficulties generated by mapping the one onto the other. These strains arise because Tamburlaine himself was a dangerously ambivalent figure, being both a military leader of the kind sorely needed by an England which was, in the year when Marlowe wrote the play,[1] about to face the Spanish Armada, but also a threatening Scythian Other. To see Tamburlaine in Roman terms helps us to register both his success and his relevance to early modern England; to see *Romanitas* in Tamburlainian terms helps us to understand the ways in which it was both a profoundly authorising and also a profoundly estranging discourse for early modern English culture. The conjunction of the two allows for an ironic, subversive interrogation of the extent to which Rome mattered to early modern England, and of how much weight could still be attached to the idea of the *translatio imperii*, which helped underpin the cultural authority of monarchy.

Pairing Tamburlaine and Julius Caesar also has a second, corollary effect. Drama of this period is often interested in registering not only the impact of the classical world but also the ways in which that influence was inflected and modulated during the early modern era. Of particular interest was the shift in power and interest from the Mediterranean world to the newly unfolding horizons of the north and east. This was something which was of great interest to Elizabethan England, not least because, as Daniel Vitkus points out, 'Elizabeth I was pursuing a policy of commercial and military alliance with the Ottoman sultanate under Amurath III at the time that Marlowe wrote the *Tamburlaine* plays', but it was also disturbing, since 'For Londoners, acknowledging the centrality of the Mediterranean in geography, in history, and in the international economy, required an acknowledgement of English isolation, belatedness, and dependency'.[2] Deanne Williams suggests that a similar dynamic was beginning to attach itself to the story of Dido, on which Marlowe had almost certainly already written his play. She argues of the Siena Sieve portrait that

---

1   We cannot certainly date the composition of *Tamburlaine the Great*, Part One, but we know that Part Two was on stage by November 1587, and had almost certainly been written in the wake of the success of Part One earlier that year.

2   Daniel Vitkus, *Turning Turk: English Theater and the Multicultural Mediterranean. 1570–1630* (Basingstoke: Palgrave, 2003), pp. 59 and 39.

Contemporary Italian or English viewers would have read in the portrait's depiction of Dido an allusion to the ongoing contention between the Ottoman and Holy Roman Empires over Tunis...Throughout the sixteenth century...Tunis shifted between Hapsburg and Muslim rule, and it was finally, definitively, claimed by the Ottomans in 1574. In the early 1580s, at the time of the Sieve portrait, Elizabeth was supporting the Ottoman claim to Tunis by virtue of England's longstanding and escalating enmity with the Holy Roman Empire.[3]

In *The Winter's Tale*, as I shall explore, Shakespeare is clearly interested in the ways in which the centre of economic power had gravitated in a different direction, from Caesar to the Czar. *Tamburlaine the Great* combines these two concerns, offering us a world in which we must register the whole triad of 'Caesar, Kaiser and Vizier'.[4] It calls our attention not only to the most notorious of all the Czars, Ivan the Terrible (who in 1547, following the lead already set the Bulgarians since 913, became the first Russian ruler to use the title of 'czar of the whole Rus' as opposed to the previous nomenclature of 'Grand Duke of the whole Rus', thus explicitly labelling himself as Caesar), but also to the Ottoman Empire, which threatened the security of Christian Europe on many fronts.

The relationship between Romanitas and the Ottoman Empire was complicated. Until 1453, Constantinople had been the last remaining bastion of the Roman world. As Daniel Goffman points out, 'In European lore, Constantinople was the great successor to Rome. Its immense walls and access to both overseas and land-based hinterlands preserved Christendom during times of extreme danger',[5] and David Riggs suggests that one credible reading of Marlowe's play would be that 'The God of Revelation sent Tamburlaine to rescue Constantinople from the Turks'.[6] However, the Turks in turn regarded themselves as the legitimate inheritors of the Romans. Sultan Mehmed 'admired and tried to emulate Alexander the Great, Julius Caesar, and Augustus',[7] and Francisco Balbo di Correggio, an Italian soldier who fought in the Great Siege of Malta in 1565 and published an account of it in Spanish in 1568, cites Ali Pasha as encouraging the Turks to besiege Malta on the grounds that 'There would come a time when we should take that fertile land, Sicily, the granary of the Romans who once ruled where now – praise be to Allah and to His Prophet! – it is we who rule'.[8] Most notably, Süleyman the Magnificent 'sought consciously

---

3   Deanne Williams, 'Dido, Queen of England', *English Literary History* 73 (2006), pp. 31–59, p. 42.

4   This is the reading proposed by the Arden 3 edition of *Merry Wives* (a play which remembers Marlowe at several points) for the mysterious 'Caesar, Kaiser and Pheazer' of F (William Shakespeare, *The Merry Wives of Windsor*, edited by Giorgio Melchiori [London: Thomas Nelson & Sons, 2000], I.iii.9).

5   Daniel Goffman, *The Ottoman Empire and Early Modern Europe* (Cambridge: Cambridge University Press, 2002), p. 12.

6   David Riggs, *The World of Christopher Marlowe* (London: Faber and Faber, 2004), p. 209.

7   Nancy Bisaha, *Creating East and West: Renaissance Humanists and the Ottoman Turks* (Philadelphia: University of Pennsylvania Press, 2004), p. 88.

8   Francisco Balbo di Correggio, *The Siege of Malta*, translated by Ernle Bradford (Harmondsworth: Penguin, 1965), p. 33.

and deliberately to vie with the Holy Roman Emperor and the Pope as imperial successor to the Roman Empire as well as to link himself with the civilizations of Greece, Persia, and Arabia'[9] and maintained that he alone continued to embody the might and traditions of imperial Rome, which he, in a radically alternative version of the traditional *translatio imperii*, saw as having come down to him through the Byzantine Empire. This led him to style himself Caesar and to draw on Caesarian motifs in his iconography: a brass dish commemorating the 1537 Siege of Corfu by the Turks, for instance, juxtaposes images of the siege with a Triumph of Caesar derived from woodcuts by Jacobus Argoratensis,[10] and as Goffman points out, Süleyman also adopted 'the crown and sceptre – regalia associated with Roman and Catholic imperial traditions'.[11] Erasmus tacitly accepted the equation when he declared in 1530 that 'Even if the Turk (heaven forbid!) should rule over us...we would be committing a sin if we were to deny him the respect due to Caesar'.[12] There is thus a savage irony to the scene which occurs in both Faust-books and which Empson argued must have been censored from *Doctor Faustus*, in which Faustus appeared 'dressed as pope...but easily mistaken for Mahomet':[13] if such a scene had been included in Marlowe's original play, it would indeed have had to be censored because of what it reveals about the slipperiness and instability of the ideological oppositions on which the political structure of Renaissance Europe depended.

The suggestion that the Turks might be the true heirs of the Roman Empire had particularly disturbing resonances because of the debate about the Turks' ancestry. As Nancy Bisaha points out,

> Some humanists, such as Aeneas Silvius Piccolomini and Francesco Filelfo, attempted to trace the origins of the Turkish people back to ancient times. Aeneas was particularly keen on dispelling the myth that the Turks were descendants of the Trojans, rather than the rough-and-tumble Scythians...Aeneas makes this argument in a few texts, but it is best articulated in his *Cosmographia* (c. 1458).[14]

When he became Pope Pius II, for instance, Aeneas Silvius Piccolomini explicitly referred to the Turks as descendants of the Scythians in a letter to Mehmed II. However, Giovanni Maria Filelfo's *Amyris*, commissioned by an Italian merchant whose father had been friendly with Sultan Murad II, built on 'the medieval and Renaissance myth claiming the Turks as heirs of the Trojans' and 'invokes the fall of Troy as just cause for Mehmed's conquest of Constantinople and other Greek areas'. Drawing on the fact that the term 'Teucri' was often used to denote a connection between Turks and Trojans on the grounds that '*Teucri* was an ancient name stemming from Teucer

---

9   Goffman, *The Ottoman Empire and Early Modern Europe*, p. 107.

10   J.M. Rogers and R. M. Ward, *Süleyman the Magnificent* (London: British Museum, 1988), pp. 112–13.

11   Goffman, *The Ottoman Empire and Early Modern Europe*, p. 107.

12   Antonia Fraser, *The Gunpowder Plot: Terror and Faith in 1605* (London: Arrow, 1999), p. 105.

13   William Empson, *Faustus and the Censor: The English Faust-book and Marlowe's Doctor Faustus*, edited by John Henry Jones (Oxford: Basil Blackwell, 1987), p. 62.

14   Bisaha, *Creating East and West*, p. 75.

and the Trojans', *Amyris* entirely exculpates the Trojans and places all the blame for the war on the Greeks.[15]

Marlowe's two plays about *Tamburlaine the Great* make full play of these uncertainties and tensions about where Caesarian power now resided. In both the *Tamburlaine* plays, a Turk represents the principal threat to a Tamburlaine who is loosely associated with Russia, and in both attention is drawn to the instability of the very terms Russia and Turkey, since both countries straddle Europe and Asia and threaten continually to riddle the distinction between the two continents. At the same time, though, Tamburlaine himself was sometimes understood as a Turk: Joseph Hall in 'Virgidemiarum', written in 1597–8, referred to 'the Turkish *Tamberlaine*'.[16] Like its mobile and liminal hero, then, *Tamburlaine the Great* is poised uneasily between registering both the continuing significance and the increasing marginalisation of the cultural inheritance of the classical world and, even more radically, the shifting contours of the world which had replaced it. The same dynamic is also explored in many of the subsequent plays which develop provocative pairings of the figures of Tamburlaine and Caesar.

Halfway through the first of the two plays about him, Marlowe's Tamburlaine declares that

> My camp is like to Julius Caesar's host,
> That never fought but had the victory.[17]

Indeed when Tamburlaine declares that 'The god of war resigns his room to me' (Part One, V.i.451) he could well be punning on the standard early modern pronunciation of Rome as 'room', and suggesting that the Roman Mars has now transferred his preferred seat of power. Marlowe's conception of Tamburlaine is clearly partly Caesarian in origin, since, as John Gillies points out, 'Marlowe...alludes admiringly to Lucan's Caesar in *Tamburlaine* [at Part One, III.iii.154]. One may indeed speculate that he was attracted to the first book of the *Pharsalia* for the same reason that he was attracted to the Tamerlane story'; Gillies further observes that the *Tamburlaine* plays repeatedly reveal their debt to Rome by being full of triumphs,[18] a point also made by Anthony Miller: 'No early modern English text makes more comprehensive or more historically informed use of triumph than Marlowe's *Tamburlaine* plays, nor does any treat the triumph with such a disconcerting combination of bedazzlement and

---

15 Bisaha, *Creating East and West*, pp. 89 and 90.

16 Millar MacLure, ed., *Marlowe: The Critical Heritage 1588–1896* (London: Routledge, 1979), p. 41.

17 Christopher Marlowe, *Tamburlaine the Great*, edited by J. S. Cunningham (Manchester: Manchester University Press, 1981), Part One, III.iii.152–3. All further quotations from the play will be taken from this edition and reference will be given in the text.

18 John Gillies, 'Marlowe, the *Timur* Myth, and the Motives of Geography', in *Playing the Globe: Genre and Geography in English Renaissance Drama*, edited by John Gillies and Virginia Mason Vaughan (Cranbury, N.J.: Associated University Presses, 1998), pp. 203–29, pp. 211 and 212. On the links between the Lucan translation and *Tamburlaine* see also Riggs, *The World of Christopher Marlowe*, pp. 172 and 188.

scepticism'.[19] Similarly, declaring that 'No author's plays are more Romanized than Marlowe's', Clifford Ronan argues that 'Romanized Tamburlaine's conquistadorial boasting springs from a deeper understanding of Senecan imperial geographic rant' and that 'Marlowe's Conqueror Play, though set in the late Medieval Middle East, is conceived in partially Roman terms'.[20]

If Tamburlaine is like Julius Caesar, many early modern representations of the Caesars allude to Tamburlaine. Clifford Ronan sees the depiction of Rome in Lodge's *The Wounds of Civil War* as inflected by *Tamburlaine*,[21] and in George Chapman's *Caesar and Pompey*, Caesar echoes Tamburlaine's use of colour to signal his intentions when he orders,

> Hang out of my tent
> My Crimsine coat of armes, to giue my souldiers
> That euer-sure signe of resolu'd-for fight.[22]

Shortly afterwards, Anthony confirms,

> Heark, your souldiers shoute
> For ioy to see your bloody Cote of Armes
> Assure their fight this morning. (III.264–6)

That Chapman is remembering his friend Marlowe in this play is clear from the reference to one of the most striking images of *Tamburlaine*, when Pompey speaks of 'my *Genius* shewing me clearly / (As in a mirror)' (IV.117–118), just as Tamburlaine is introduced in the introduction as offering us a 'tragic glass' (Part One, Prologue, 7). Robert Logan suggests Tamburlaine's presence too in *Antony and Cleopatra*,[23] while Judas in John Fletcher's Roman play *Bonduca* cries to the other Romans: 'Awake, ye men of Memphis!'.[24] Since they are nowhere near Memphis, this exclamation can only possibly make sense in the context of a recollection of *Tamburlaine*.

Other plays too clearly signpost the linkage. In the anonymous *Claudius Tiberius Nero* (c. 1607) Drusus uses clearly Tamburlainian language when he declares,

> The orient does shine in warlike steel,
> And bloody streamers, wavèd in the air,

---

19 Anthony Miller, *Roman Triumphs and Early Modern English Culture* (Basingstoke: Palgrave, 2001), p. 83.

20 Clifford Ronan, *'Antike Roman': Power Symbology and the Roman Play in Early Modern England, 1585–1635* (Athens: The University of Georgia Press, 1995), pp. 156, 38 and 115.

21 Ronan, *'Antike Roman'*, p. 118.

22 George Chapman, *Caesar and Pompey* (London, 1631), III.253–5. Subsequent references will be given in the text.

23 See Robert A. Logan, *Shakespeare's Marlowe: The Influence of Christopher Marlowe on Shakespeare's Artistry* (Burlington: Ashgate, 2007), pp. 174–5.

24 John Fletcher, *Bonduca*, in *Beaumont and Fletcher*, vol. II, edited by J. St Loe Strachey (London: Ernest Benn, 1950), II.iv. p. 150.

By their reflections dye the plains in red,
As ominous unto destructive wars,
As are the blazing comets in the East.[25]

In another anonymous play about the Caesars, the 1590s university play *Caesar's Revenge*, the echoes of Tamburlaine are still more sustained. Caesar says to Cleopatra,

Not onely Aegipt but all Africa,
Will I subject to Cleopatras name.
Thy rule shall stretch from vnknowne Zanziber,
Vnto those Sandes where high erected poastes []
Of great Alcides, do vp hold his name,
The sunne burnt Indians, from the east shall bring:
Their pretious store of pure refined gould,
The laboring worme shall weaue the Africke twiste,
And to exceed the pompe of Persian Queene,
The Sea shall pay the tribute of his pearles,
For to adorne thy goulden yellow lockes,
Which in their curled knots, my thoughts do hold,
Thoughtes captiud to thy beauties conquering power.[26]

The idea of Persia is geographically quite alien in this reference to Africa; it surely derives from the importance of Persia in *Tamburlaine the Great*, Part One, where, as Matthew Dimmock remarks, 'the eponymous hero is closely identified with Persia',[27] just as the speech as a whole is clearly based on Tamburlaine's words to Zenocrate at the close of Part One:

To gratify thee, sweet Zenocrate,
Egyptians, Moors, and men of Asia,
From Barbary unto the Western Inde,
Shall pay a yearly tribute to thy sire;
And from the bounds of Afric to the banks
Of Ganges shall his mighty arm extend.   (V.i.517–22)

Later Cicero too describes Caesar in terms which directly echo the language used of and by Tamburlaine:

Caesar although of high aspiring thoughtes,
And vncontrould ambitious Maiesty,

25   *Claudius Tiberius Nero*, II.iii.127–31. I quote from the version of the play edited by my student Sharon McDonnell as part of the 'Editing a Renaissance Play' module on the MA in English Studies (Renaissance Literature) at Sheffield Hallam University, and available online at http://extra.shu.ac.uk/emls/iemls/resources.html

26   *The tragedie of Caesar and Pompey or Caesars reuenge* (London, 1607), I.vi.29–41. Further reference will be given in the text. The original text had an erroneous full stop after 'poastes' (l.32).

27   Matthew Dimmock, *New Turkes: Dramatizing Islam and the Ottomans in Early Modern England* (Aldershot: Ashgate, 2005), p. 140.

Yet is of nature faire and courteous,
You see hee commeth conqueror of the East.   (II.iv.81–4)

And Caesar himself says,

Leaue to lament braue Romans, loe I come,
Like to the God of battell, mad with rage,
To die their riuers with vermilion red:
Ile fill Armenians playnes and Medians hils,
With carkases of bastard Scithian broode,
And there proud Princes will I bring to Rome,
Chained in fetters to my charriot wheeles.   (III.iv.5–11)

Caesar morphs in and out of the Tamburlaine-persona here, as he first echoes Tamburlaine's use of red banners, then scorns Tamburlaine's ethnic identity of Scythian, and finally proposes to imitate Tamburlaine's notorious treatment of captive kings.

The pairing also occurs in other plays not directly focused on or featuring the Caesars. In George Peele's *The Battle of Alcazar*, we hear:

Tamburlaine, triumph not, for thou must die.
As Philip did, Caesar, and Caesar's peers.[28]

Robert Greene's *The Comicall Historie of Alphonsus, King of Aragon* also evokes both Tamburlaine and Julius Caesar. Carinus tells his son Alphonsus,

go with happie fate,
And soone returne vnto thy fathers Cell,
With such a traine as Iulius Caesar came
To noble Rome, when as he had atchiu'd
The mightie Monarch of the triple world.[29]

This rubs shoulders with rhetoric clearly derived from Tamburlaine, as when Belinus declares,

Thus farre my Lords wee trained haue our Campe,
For to encounter haughtie Arragon,
Who with a mightie power of stragling mates,
Hath trayterously assayled this our land,
And burning Townes and sacking Cities faire,
Doth play the diuell where some ere he comes.   (I.266–71)

Tamburlaine was notorious both for sacking towns and for being conceived as diabolical, with the Soldan refusing to fear him 'were he devil, as he is no man'

---

28   George Peele, *The Battle of Alcazar*, in *The Stukeley Plays*, edited by Charles Edelman (Manchester: Manchester University Press, 2005), I.2.36–7. All further quotations from the play will be taken from this edition and reference will be given in the text.

29   Robert Greene, *The comicall historie of Alphonsus, King of Aragon* (London: 1599), I.160–64. All further references will be given in the text.

(I.i.42). Furthermore, Alphonsus crowns three of his followers on stage (III.60 ff); and Amurack appears as an unexpected opponent just as Bajazeth does, actually has a follower called Bajazeth, and even mentions 'mightie Tamberlaine' (IV.326–7).

In all of these plays, the figure of Tamburlaine seems to operate fairly crudely as a simple signifier for ideas of grandeur and aggression. This is, however, by no means the only possible use of him. In *Caesar's Revenge*, Tamburlaine becomes above all a figure associated with dramatic shifts in the *locus* of power. Initially, Caesar himself is associated with Tamburlaine, but later in the play, as Caesar's fortunes ebb, Tamburlainian attributes are explicitly transferred away from him and onto other characters when Cassius declares 'Looke how our troups in Sun-bright armes do shine' (V.i.115) and Brutus laments

> What hideous sightes appalle my greeued soule,
> As when Orestes after mother slaine.
> Not being yet at Scithian Alters purged... (V.i.191–3)

It is also notable here that all the characters to whom Tamburlainian attributes accrue ultimately die. Tamburlaine seems therefore to have a further function as a yardstick by which their successive failures can be measured. Rick Bowers' researches have shown us that in some parts of the country at least, Tamburlaine was a popular figure, associated with success, since parents called their sons after him; indeed in 1618 Thomas Coryat refers to the popularity of Tamburlaine in a letter written from Agra,[30] while in 1629 R. M.'s *Micrologia* attested to the continuing popularity of the play by observing that when Bridewell inmates are made to clean the streets, 'as they passe, the people scoffing say, / "Holla, ye pampered jades of Asia!"'. In the anonymous *A Pleasant Conceited Historie, called The Taming of a Shrew* (1594), Tamburlaine and Caesar rub shoulders again, and here they are explicitly used to measure success. Ferando says,

> And care not thou swete *Kate* how I be clad,
> Thou shalt haue garments wrought of Median silke,
> Enchast with pretious Iewells fecht from far,
> By Italian Marchants that with Russian stemes,
> Plous vp huge forrowes in the *Terren Maine*.[31]

Very shortly after this, Aurelius declares,

> My fortune now I doo account as great
> As earst did Caesar when he conquered most.

Once again, Caesar and Tamburlaine are evoked as twin benchmarks of success (and it is notable that here, as in *Tamburlaine*, where Tamburlaine's first acquisition is Zenocrate, the conquest of a woman is implicitly equated with the conquest of territory). In *Caesar's Revenge*, while many characters can sound like Tamburlaine

---

30 Rick Bowers, 'Tamburlaine in Ludlow', *Notes and Queries* 243 (1998): 361–3, 362.
31 *A Pleasant Conceited Historie, called The Taming of a Shrew* (London, 1594), C4r.

at times, none can match up to the full scale of his achievement, and the classical world is thus seen as a dying and fragmented force.

Tamburlaine does not, however, simply represent success in *Caesar's Revenge*: he stands above all for a change in fortune, a shift of power away from its traditional base to a new man. This, too, is something he shares with early modern uses of Caesar, most notably in Marlowe's own handling of the motif. In *The Jew of Malta*, Caesar, like Tamburlaine, figures primarily uninherited power, might without right: 'What right had Caesar to the empery?'.[32] In *Edward II*, the Caesar / Tamburlaine linkage attaches itself to the social climber Gaveston, who declares,

> It shall suffice me to enjoy your love,
> Which whiles I have, I think myself as great
> As Caesar riding in the Roman street
> With captive kings at his triumphant car. (I.i.170–73)

Most persistently, Caesarian imagery accrues to the Guise in *The Massacre at Paris*. He declares,

> As ancient Romans over their captive lords,
> So will I triumph over this wanton king,
> And he shall follow my proud chariot's wheels.[33]

Warned of his death, the Guise declares 'Yet Caesar shall go forth' (Scene Twenty-One, 68), before concluding 'Thus Caesar did go forth, and thus he died' (Scene Twenty-One, 90) – lines which Shakespeare was later to remember when it came to composing *Julius Caesar*. In each of these cases, Tamburlaine is used by Marlowe to figure a shift in power from a place where it has long been established to a place to which it is now moving. Similarly Richard Harvey's *Philadelphvs, or A Defence of Brutes, and the Brutans History*, printed by John Wolfe in 1593, although not a play, also evokes the figure of Tamburlaine as an emblem of mobility, this time in answer to George Buchanan's objection to the *translatio imperii* story on the grounds of the impossibility of Brutus's having travelled from Rome to London. In the preface rebutting Buchanan, Harvey testily exclaims,

> Truly I would *Tamerlane* were euen now here, to answere your *Ocean* argument: he could tell you, that his *multitude* of *rude Scythians* and *shepheardes* could do more Actes than all the fine gay troopes and rankes of *Baiazete*, that is no good consequent which you bring forth, as if the *Albane shepheardes* and *clownes* might not be as valiant in vanquishing *the Alpes*, as the *Carthagininian* souldiers.[34]

---

32   Christopher Marlowe, *The Jew of Malta*, in *Christopher Marlowe: The Complete Plays*, edited by Mark Thornton Burnett (London: Everyman, 1999), Prologue, 19.

33   Christopher Marlowe, *The Massacre at Paris*, in *Christopher Marlowe: The Complete Plays*, edited by Mark Thornton Burnett (London: Everyman, 1999), Scene Twenty-One, 53–5. All further quotations from the play will be taken from this edition and reference will be given in the text.

34   Richard Harvey, *Philadelphvs, or A Defence of Brutes, and the Brutans History* (London: John Wolfe, 1593), Preface, p. 5.

Here, Tamburlaine is explicitly a figure who authorises us to believe in the possibility of travel and the transfer of power. The same pattern can be found in other plays. In *Henry VI*, Part One, Henry V, a military hero whose rhetoric, in Shakespeare's later play about him, will prove to be distinctly Tamburlainian, is directly compared to Julius Caesar in Gloucester's apostrophe to him:

> Henry the Fifth, thy ghost I invocate:
> Prosper this realm, keep it from civil broils,
> Combat with adverse planets in the heavens!
> A far more glorious star thy soul will make
> Than Julius Caesar or bright —[35]

Gloucester is interrupted by news of the loss of almost the whole of northern France, so we never learn who else it is that Henry might have been compared with, but the conquests of Tamburlaine are repeatedly alluded to in the subsequent plays which feature or remember Henry V. Julius Caesar also recurs, and both figures are evoked not in connection with the consolidation of power, but with the loss of it, as it leaches from an old site to a new one.[36] The Duke of Suffolk in *Henry the Sixth*, Part Two laments that

> Great men oft die by vile besonians:
> A Roman sworder and bandetto slave
> Murdered sweet Tully; Brutus' bastard hand
> Stabbed Julius Caesar; savage islanders
> Pompey the Great; and Suffolk dies by pirates.[37]

Finally in the third part Henry soliloquises 'No bending knee will call thee Caesar now',[38] and Queen Margaret when her son is killed laments,

> They that stabbed Caesar shed no blood at all,
> Did not offend, nor were not worthy blame,
> If this foul deed were by to equal it:
> He was a man; this, in respect, a child.   (5.5.53–6)

---

35   William Shakespeare, *Henry VI, Part One*, edited by John Dover Wilson (Cambridge: Cambridge University Press, 1952), I.i.47–51. All subsequent quotations from the play will be taken from this edition and reference will be given in the text. James Shapiro has recently suggested that Tacitus' account of the reign of Nero might have been in Shakespeare's mind while writing *Henry V*, since at one point in Tacitus a leader walks disguised amongst his soldiers (James Shapiro, *1599: A Year in the Life of William Shakespeare* [London: Faber and Faber, 2005], p. 141).

36   Ronan (*'Antike Roman'*, p. 119) notes the many references to Rome in the *Henriad* and attributes them to Shakespeare planning *Julius Caesar* while he was writing the Henry plays.

37   William Shakespeare, *Henry VI, Part Two*, edited by John Dover Wilson (Cambridge: Cambridge University Press, 1968), 4.1.134–8. All further quotations from the play will be taken from this edition and reference will be given in the text.

38   William Shakespeare, *Henry VI, Part Three*, edited by John Dover Wilson (Cambridge: Cambridge University Press, 1968), 3.1.18. All further quotations from the play will be taken from this edition and reference will be given in the text.

Again, the emphasis is on the fragmentation of Caesar, whose attributes are mentioned by or distributed among many characters rather than focused on one – and, by analogy, with the fragmentation and instability of centres of power.

The motif is also found in *Henry V* itself, a play which has many notable similarities with *Tamburlaine*: Henry's rhetoric and ruthlessness before Harfleur closely parallel the similarly threatening ferocity and tactics of Tamburlaine, and Graham Holderness sees further parallels between the two kings, commenting that 'Pistol's main function in Shakespeare's play is to parody, by projecting a Marlovian megalomania, the king's tendency to dramatize himself as the old-fashioned epic hero' and that, in the Olivier film at least, where there is an interpolation from Marlowe, 'evidently it *is* passing brave to be a king and ride in triumph through Persepolis'.[39] Finally, both *Henry V* and *Tamburlaine Part One* perform an unusual manoeuvre at the close when their subject matter of war in each case gives way to the conventionally comic finale of marriage – a marriage which in each case uses the bestowal of a daughter to bond a king to his conqueror. That Marlowe was in Shakespeare's mind when writing the Henriad is, moreover, sufficiently illustrated by Pistol's celebrated parody of Tamburlaine, while Exeter's warning to the French not to 'hide the crown'[40] is reminiscent of Mycetes' unsuccessful attempt to do just that,[41] and Henry's insistence on giving all praise to God is uneasily overshadowed by its echo of the hypocritical Ferneze's conclusion of *The Jew of Malta* with the richly ironic lines

---

39   Graham Holderness, *Shakespeare Recycled* (Hemel Hempstead: Harvester Wheatsheaf, 1992), pp. 189 and 190. Holderness also discusses the Brechtian nature of Olivier's production, which ironically introduces a German element into an anti-German film. On similarities between *Henry V* and *Tamburlaine*, see James Shapiro, *Rival Playwrights: Marlowe, Jonson, Shakespeare* (New York: Columbia University Press, 1991), p. 85; Robert Egan, 'A Muse of Fire: Henry V in the Light of Tamburlaine', *Modern Language Quarterly*, 29 (1968), pp. 15–28, and Roy Battenhouse, 'The Relation of Henry V to Tamburlaine', *Shakespeare Survey*, 27 (1974), pp. 71–9, pp. 76 ff. Lisa Jardine (*Reading Shakespeare Historically* [London: Routledge, 1996], p. 11) also compares Henry's wooing to Tamburlaine's. Michael Neill compares the two figures in passing ('Broken English and Broken Irish: Nation, Language, and the Optic of Power in Shakespeare's Histories', *Shakespeare Quarterly*, 45 [1994], pp. 10–28, p. 22), and Joel B. Altman heads one of the sections of his essay on *Henry V* 'Playing the Tamburlaine' ('"Vile Participation": The Amplification of Violence in the Theater of *Henry V*', *Shakespeare Quarterly* 42 [1991], pp. 1–32, p. 13. Gary Taylor also refers to a Henry who 'was *performing* the part of a Tamburlaine' in his 1994 Oxford World's Classics edition of the play (p. 50). On the suggestion that *Tamburlaine* in turn may have been influenced by *The First English Life of King Henry the Fifth*, see Andrew Hadfield, 'Tamburlaine as the "Scourge of God" and *The First English Life of King Henry the Fifth*', *Notes and Queries* 50.4 (December, 2003), pp. 399–400.

40   William Shakespeare, *Henry V*, edited by Gary Taylor (Oxford: Oxford University Press, 1994), 2.4.9. All further quotations from the play will be taken from this edition and reference will be given in the text.

41   Laurie Maguire also suggests a parallel between Hotspur and Lady Percy and Tamburlaine and Zenocrate ('"Household Kates": Chez Petruchio, Percy and Plantagenet', in S.P. Cerasano and Marion Wynne-Davies, eds, *Gloriana's Face* [Hemel Hempstead: Harvester Wheatsheaf, 1992], pp. 129–65, p. 146).

So march away, and let due praise be given
Neither to fate nor fortune, but to heaven.   (V.v.122–3)

It seems, therefore, that Shakespeare has recourse to Marlowe principally to expose the darker side of his hero, and, ultimately, the ephemerality of his conquests.

Henry V also remembers figures associated with the Caesar story. The Constable of France says of Henry that 'you shall find his vanities forespent / Were but the outside of the Roman Brutus' (II.iv.36–7), and Fluellen wants to follow 'the *Roman disciplines*' (3.3.17–18), thinks Pistol 'is as valiant a man as Mark Antony' (3.6.13), and advises that

> If you would take the pains but to examine the wars of Pompey the Great, you shall find, I warrant you, that there is no tiddle-taddle nor pibble-babble in Pompey's camp. (4.1.68–72)

Most notably, the final chorus tells of how

> The Mayor and all his brethren, in best sort,
> Like to the senators of th'antique Rome
> With the plebeians swarming at their heels,
> Go forth and fetch their conqu'ring Caesar in –
> As, by a lower but high-loving likelihood,
> Were now the General of our gracious Empress –
> As in good time he may – from Ireland coming,
> Bringing rebellion broachèd on his sword,
> How many would the peaceful city quit
> To welcome him!   (5.0.25–34)

In the light of later events, this apparent paralleling of Caesar with the Earl of Essex,[42] the man who would go on to lead the only armed rebellion against Elizabeth I, would surely have come to look unfortunate, and to reveal how dangerous and explosive the application of Caesarian imagery to contemporary events could be. This was all the more so because Henry himself is a military leader who, like both Tamburlaine and Julius Caesar, fails to leave a secure succession. In Shakespeare's attempt to portray him in a positive light (while glossing over potentially negative features such as his devout Catholicism), Julius Caesar and Tamburlaine both serve as useful negative exemplars, for the extent to which Henry does *not* map onto them allows us to register him instead as Christian, compassionate, and English. At the same time, though, the closing Chorus ironically reminds us that his conquests were both less in scope and and also less durable than theirs: England was no longer the continental

---

42   It is sometimes argued that this refers not to Essex but to his successor in Ireland, Mountjoy, but the lines are generally accepted as referring to Essex (see for instance James P. Bednarz, 'When did Shakespeare write the choruses of *Henry V*', *Notes and Queries* 53.4 (December, 2006), pp. 486–9). James Shapiro, who sees the lines in *Henry V* as a certain allusion to Essex, points out that Essex's cousin Sir Francis Bacon also conceived the earl in Caesarian terms (Shapiro, *1599*, p. 145).

power that it had once been, and indeed by the time Shakespeare wrote, it no longer had a foothold in France at all.

The figure of Tamburlaine is also used to reflect on England and its territorial extent in *Locrine*, a play which, in its present form, is probably wholly or partly by Greene. The traces of Greene in the play are abundantly apparent. The parallels between *Locrine* and Greene's *Selimus* have already been so extensively remarked upon that I do not propose to dwell on them here,[43] but there are also links between *Locrine* and other Greene plays which seem to have escaped observation, and at least some of them are centred on a connection to Tamburlaine. *Locrine* contains typically Greenian echoes of Marlowe's mighty line, particularly as it had manifested itself in *Tamburlaine*. The stylistic similarity is clearly audible in lines like Thrasimachus'

> I, in the name of all, protest to you,
> That we will boldly enterprise the same,
> Were it to enter black *Tartarus*,
> Where triple *Cerberus* with his venomous throte,
> Scarreth the ghoasts with high resounding noise.[44]

This is obviously an echo of 'the Scythian Tamburlaine / Threat'ning the world with high astounding terms' (Prologue, ll. 4–5), while Strumbo ludicrously terms the powerful Thrasimachus 'an abhominable chieftaine' (II.iv.53) and refers to his enemies as 'the Shitens, the Scythians – what do you call them?' (II.iv.62–3).

Locrine focuses on what happens when *Romanitas* has been transplanted to Britain by means of the *translatio imperii*. Marlowe himself had cast a very sceptical eye on the dynamics of the *translatio imperii* in *Dido, Queen of Carthage*; *Locrine* at least gestures towards nullifying the whole idea of it by apparently showing the complete eradication of the entire progeny of Brutus.[45] In this cynical view, *Locrine* (which may well, like *Tamburlaine*, have in its original form grown out of the machinations surrounding the Babington plot)[46] makes pointed and strategic use both of *Tamburlaine* and of what it suggests about the receding power of the classical world. So far from being, as Peter Berek has it, one of Tamburlaine's 'weak sons',[47]

---

43   See for instance Peter Berek, '*Locrine* Revised, *Selimus*, and Early Responses to *Tamburlaine*', *Research Opportunities in Renaissance Drama* 23 [1980], pp. 33–54.

44   W. S., *The lamentable tragedie of Locrine* (London, 1595), I.i.73–8. All further references will be given in the text.

45   For the debate about the precise route taken by lineal descent from Brutus, see John E. Curran, Jr, *Roman Invasions: The British History, Protestant Anti-Romanism, and the Historical Imagination in England, 1530–1660* (Newark: University of Delaware Press, 2002), pp. 137–8.

46   There is clearly some sort of relationship between *Locrine* as we now have it and the work called *Estrild*. The Babington conspirator Charles Tilney is said to have written, although this is on the basis of a note which was unfortunately first brought to light by the known forger John Payne Collier. For the debate on its genuineness, see Baldwin Maxwell, *Studies in the Shakespearean Apocrypha* (New York: King's Crown Press, 1956), pp. 205–6, note 31.

47   Peter Berek, '*Tamburlaine*'s Weak Sons: Imitation as Interpretation Before 1593', *Renaissance Drama* 13 (1982), pp. 55–82.

Locrine is actually a strong son in its ability to deploy Tamburlaine in this respect (indeed Berek himself concedes it some artistic force when he declares that 'the comic scenes...parody the main plot in a manner similar to that found in the comic scenes of *Doctor Faustus*').[48] *Locrine* is a story which clearly belongs to the world of epic, but the gods are entirely absent, something which recalls both the failure of God to appear in *Doctor Faustus* and Greene's own allegation, in the preface to *Perimedes the Blacksmith*, that the perspective of *Tamburlaine the Great* was an atheist one. Humber apostrophises Jove for aid but receives none; he hopes Strumbo may be Mercury, but is unceremoniously disabused (IV.ii.73 ff). The ghost of Albanact does appear, but never actually does anything (except once strike Strumbo on the hand); it only comments. This notably secularised perspective is reinforced by the euhemerising depiction of the death of Sabren: although Guendoline does declare that the stream shall be named after Sabren, there is no suggestion, as there is in most other versions of the story, that she has been turned into a nymph presiding over the eponymous River Severn (V.iv.247). This represents the opposite extreme to the other play on which *Locrine* clearly draws, which is *A Midsummer Night's Dream* with its busily populated cast of fairies. *Locrine*, then, can be seen as playing a clever game in its use of Tamburlaine, a figure so strongly associated both with Caesar and with challenges to the gods, in its ruthless dismissal of the rôles of both Romans and gods in British affairs, and its quasi-Tacitean espousal of an accident- rather than a destiny-led view of history in which the Romans ultimately proved irrelevant to what Britain became.

Locrine reflects directly on what Britain has become when, early in the play, the dying Brutus speaks of

> This heart, my lords, this neare appalled heart,
> That was a terror to the bordring lands. (I.i.20–21)

Throughout the latter part of the sixteenth century, the notoriously lawless Anglo-Scottish Border loomed large in the internal affairs of both countries. Greene seems to use a very similar phrase elsewhere: in *George a Greene*, which is very probably though not certainly his,[49] the earl of Kendal orders,

> Well, hye thee to Wakefield, bid the Towne
> To send me all prouision that I want;
> Least I, like martiall Tamberlaine, lay waste
> Their bordering Countries.[50]

---

48 Berek, '*Locrine* Revised', p. 36.

49 According to Sir George Buc, Shakespeare told him that the author of *George a Greene* was a minister who had also played the pinner. However, Buc also recorded below this that 'Ed. Iuby saith that this play was made by Ro. Gree[ne]', and there are certainly stylistic similarities with Greene's work (Alan H. Nelson, 'George Buc, William Shakespeare, and the Folger *George a Greene*', *Shakespeare Quarterly* 49.1 [Spring 1998], pp. 74–83, p. 74).

50 Robert Greene, *A Pleasant Conceyted Comedie of* George a Greene, *the Pinner of Wakefield* (London, 1599), p. 2. All further references will be given in the text.

Moreover, Strumbo in *Locrine* lives in Caithness, where part of *George a Greene* had been set. Since Tamburlaine himself was a figure so radically linked with disputed borders and the demarcation of territory, it is ironically appropriate to find him here policing the bitterly disputed Anglo-Scottish Border,[51] and it adds a further layer of potential referentiality to Tamburlaine's use as a figure to mark shifts of power.

The same idea is found in another play which couples Tamburlaine and Caesar, the anonymous university play *Pathomachia: Or: The Battell of Affections* (not published until 1630 though written earlier, maybe c. 1616). In this Pride claims to be the person who 'help't the *Giants* to heape vp their Babylonish Mountaines against *Iupiter*; which ayded *Alexander*, *Iulius Caesar*, *Traiane*, and *Tamberlaine*', as well as to have assisted 'infinite...Authors of Heresies and Schismes' (I.i), and Tamburlaine is mentioned twice more, firstly when Malice says to Pride: 'Your selfe may conduct the Reare-ward: For so did *Tamberlaine* the Prince of the Tartars' (I.v), and secondly when Pride declares, 'I could wish that Madame Hypocrisie be sent for...for *Tamberlaine* one of my good Minions was wont to say, that this was a Cloake long enough to couer the whole World' (II.v), while there is also an implicit allusion to *Tamburlaine the Great*, Part Two in Veracitie's remark that Lust comes from 'the dead Sea called the Asphaltick Lake' (IV.v). *Pathomachia* too has a political point to make, for at the end Love says, 'yet is Ioy the mightier, as the Persians were aboue the Medes, the Romanes aboue the Sabines, the English aboue the Scots' (V.i), with clear malice aforethought against the Stuarts. Once again, Tamburlaine the disturber of borders ironically polices the Border, something which, by the time this play was published in 1630, raises some disturbing questions about the security of national identities in Charles I's kingdoms, and allows us to see how coupling Tamburlaine and Julius Caesar need not be simply a yoking of two figures connoting greatness, but can also serve as ironic interrogation of the meanings and uses of *romanitas*, and hence of the *translatio imperii* itself, in early modern England. After all, as *Locrine* reminds us, Albanact, Locrine and Camber, the three sons of Brutus, supposedly set up the three separate and distinct kingdoms of Albania (Scotland), Logres (England), and Cambria (Wales); now the rule of the Stuarts threatened to obliterate those distinctions, in ways which many did not welcome.

Tamburlaine the Great, then, does not engage only with what Caesarian rule has meant in the past; it also turns the spotlight on its meaning in Marlowe's own world. It does not, however, confine its attention just to Britain, because indeed part of its point is that it is no longer just Britain that matters. Tamburlaine not only presides over the decay and destruction of the classical world (most notably in the shape of the emblematically-named Olympia); he also ensures a thoroughgoing reorientation of the direction of trade and exploration from the Old World to the New. In particular, the play directs us to the growing importance of Asia, and the

---

51 Alan Shepard points out that even before Marlowe, '"Tamerlane" was in use as a ready prop, an eastern hero borrowed by western writers eager to promote various nationalist causes' including 'defence of the coastline and other borders' (*Marlowe's Soldiers: Rhetorics of Masculinity in the Age of the Armada* [Aldershot: Ashgate, 2002], p. 21). It is certainly as a nationalist – indeed jingoistic – icon that he features in the Dutch Church libel, which threatened death to immigrants from the Netherlands in London and was signed 'per Tamburlaine'.

challenge that it posed to the traditional polarities of trade, travel, and the sense of the civil. In Philip Massinger's *Believe As You List*, Hanno declares that 'the tribute Rome receiues from Asia, is / her chiefe supportance' (II.ii.22–3). The *Tamburlaine the Great* plays chart a situation where this polarity has been totally reversed. In *Believe As You List*, a Roman speaks scornfully of 'poore Asiaticqs' (I.ii.63); but in *Tamburlaine the Great*, 'Asiatics' have commandered both the iconography and the military status of Rome and are on course not only to dominate the world, as Rome once did, but to destabilise the classificatory terms which Rome used for categorising and controlling that world. In using Caesarian imagery for the figure of his Tamburlaine, Marlowe deploys a discourse which allows him to reflect on the ways in which the classical world which authorised the Renaissance's conception of itself has given place to the modern one. Tamburlaine, ever on the move himself, neatly tropes this shift of power.

In this context of shifting centres of cultural gravity, two facts about Tamburlaine become particularly important. In the first place, he is referred to in Part One as 'the rogue of Volga' (Part One, IV.i.4) by Zenocrate's father, the Soldan.[52] This touches on a crucial question for the period, and one which became of growing importance as, thanks to the efforts of the Muscovy Company, Russia emerged as an increasingly key trading partner for England, which was that of what Russia's cultural and geographical identity actually was. As John Michael Archer points out, 'Russia was traditionally divided between Europe and Northern Asia'; Richard Eden declared that 'if a ryght line bee drawen from the mouthes of Tanais [the river Don] to the springes of the same, Moscouia shalbe found to bee in Asia and not in Europe'. Archer notes that 'Lake Maeotis or the Tanais river (the Don) were often said to demarcate Asia from Europe. After 1452 the Volga competed with the Don for this role, confirming Russia's status as an in-between nation'.[53] This was an area on which the 'civilising' attention of the Romans had been heavily concentrated: in the *Aeneid*, Anchises says of Augustus 'Even now, before he comes to them, the Caspian kingdom and the land round Lake Maeotis tremble at prophecies of his coming, and the sevenfold mouth of the Nile knows confusion and alarm'.[54] Marlowe registers the significance of this demarcation between Europe and Asia in *Edward II*, when Isabella says,

> Ah sweet sir John, even to the utmost verge
> Of Europe, or the shore of Tanaïs,
> Will we with thee to Hainault, so we will.   (IV.ii.29–31)

---

52   On the importance of rivers in the imaginary of *Tamburlaine the Great*, see Gillies, 'Marlowe, the *Timur* Myth, and the Motives of Geography', pp. 214–15.

53   John Michael Archer, *Old Worlds: Egypt, Southwest Asia, India, and Russia in Early Modern English Writing* (Stanford: Stanford University Press, 2001), pp. 102, 105, and 108. John Gillies notes that 'If for no other reason, Marlowe's familiarity with the ancient boundary discourse may be assumed on the basis of his translation of the first book of Lucan's *Pharsalia*' (Gillies, 'Marlowe, the *Timur* Myth, and the Motives of Geography', p. 210); in *Tamburlaine*, then, the Volga may well have something of the function of the Rubicon.

54   Virgil, *The Aeneid*, translated by W. F. Jackson Knight (Harmondsworth: Middlesex, 1958), p. 171.

It is, therefore, suggestive that Tamburlaine himself should position his preferred display of power absolutely on one of these two crucial border lines, when he promises Zenocrate that she shall

> scale the icy mountains' lofty tops,
> Which with thy beauty will be soon resolved;
> My martial prizes, with five hundred men,
> Won on the fifty-headed Volga's waves,
> Shall all we offer to Zenocrate. (Part One, I.ii.101–4)

This may also recall the descriptions of the use of reindeer-drawn sledges to cross ice and snow and of horse-racing on the ice in Olaus Magnus' 1555 bestseller, *The Description of the Northern Peoples*.[55] That Marlowe had at least looked at Magnus, even if he had not struggled through all the Latin, is, I think, suggested by the description in Part Two of *Tamburlaine the Great*, where Orcanes declares that

> Though from the shortest northern parallel,
> Vast Gruntland, compassed with the frozen sea,
> Inhabited with tall and sturdy men,
> Giants as big as hugy Polypheme,
> Millions of soldiers cut the Arctic line,
> Bringing the strength of Europe to these arms,
> Our Turkey blades shall glide through all their throats
> And make this champion mead a bloody fen. (Part Two, I.i.25–32)

In general, Greenland was commonly supposed to be inhabited by pygmies rather than giants, but Marlowe may have been influenced here by Magnus, who talks about Greenland being inhabited by pygmies but includes an illustration which, since its point is purely one of scale, could as well represent a giant and a normal man as a pygmy and a giant to anyone who looked only at the picture rather than the text.[56] Finally, Tamburlaine's hair is said to be amber in colour (Part One, II.i.23), and in Olaus Magnus amber was clearly identified as coming solely from the North and the Baltic.[57] Marlowe seems, then, to have been thinking of Tamburlaine very much in northern terms.

It is therefore not surprising that Richard Wilson has influentially proposed that 'it cannot be chance that Marlowe's epic of "the rogue of Volga"...should project what Burghley described as "the great end of dealing with the Muscovite: discovery of a passage into Asia"',[58] while Matthew Dimmock suggests that

---

55   Olaus Magnus, *Description of the Northern Peoples* [1555], translated by Peter Fisher and Humphrey Higgens (London: The Hakluyt Society, 1996), 3 vols, vol. 1, pp. 18 and 56–7.

56   Magnus, *Description of the Northern Peoples*, vol. 1, pp. 104–5.

57   Magnus, *Description of the Northern Peoples*, vol. 2, pp. 593–4.

58   Richard Wilson, 'Visible Bullets: Tamburlaine and Ivan the Terrible', *English Literary History* 62.1 (1995), pp. 47–68, p. 50.

English attempts to find a contintental route through Russia to the spice trade and "Asia the lesse" pioneered by explorer-traders like Anthonie Jenkinson and recorded by Hakluyt present an appreciation of the way in which mercantile significance was mapped and offer a context for the geo-political dimension of the play as a whole.[59]

Like Russia itself in the period, however, Tamburlaine is an ambiguous figure. The historical Timur, who originated from Uzbekistan, waged war with Russia, conquering and sacking the Russian cities of Astrakhan, Sarai and Bolgar in 1395; Marlowe's Tamburlaine, similarly, both is and is not Russian. His identity is certainly unclear when he says

> And Christian merchants that with Russian stems
> Plough up huge furrows in the Caspian Sea
> Shall vail to us as lords of all the lake.   (Part One, I.ii.193–5)

Does he object to the use of Russian ships here because they have been captured from their original owners – in which case he implicitly aligns himself with the Russians – or because they are in collusion, and hence his opponents? Moreover, the defining characteristic of Russian identity in the period was slavery;[60] Tamburlaine both threatens Zenocrate and her companions with slavery (Part One, I.ii.255) and conversely proposes to 'enlarge / Those Christian captives whom you keep as slaves' (Part One, III.iii.46–7). He is, then, poised liminally between being Russian and being not-Russian, and this may alert us to the ways in which Russia in the English Renaissance imagination is both itself and a gateway to somewhere else.

The second point of note is that Tamburlaine is repeatedly identified as a Scythian. He shares the savage manners attributed to Scythians, and also their legendary interest in gold,[61] in which he has the dead body of Zenocrate encased, as we see when her hearse is brought in:

> Now, eyes, enjoy your latest benefit,
> And when my soul hath virtue of your sight,
> Pierce through the coffin and the sheet of gold.   (Part Two, V.iii.225–7)

Scythianness too had a northern valency. The modern editor of Olaus Magnus' work remarks that

> Edmund Spenser had certainly read it (though he seems not to have remembered it very clearly), for in *A View of the Present State of Ireland*, written about 1596, he several times mentions Olaus's ancient Goths, taking them to be Scythians and finding numerous resemblances between them and the Irish.[62]

---

59   Dimmock, *New Turkes*, p. 136.

60   See Archer, *Old Worlds*, p. 111.

61   See François Hartog, *The Mirror of Herodotus: The Representation of the Other in the Writing of History*, translated by Janet Lloyd (Berkeley: University of California Press, 1988), p. 21, on the ritual importance of gold in Scythian culture. It is also mentioned in Magnus, *Description of the Northern Peoples*, vol. 2, p. 363.

62   Magnus, *Description of the Northern Peoples*, vol. 1, introduction, p. lxxi.

More specifically, Scythiannness was identified with Russia. Archer observes that 'The nomadic Scythians of Herodotus' fourth book are buried at the foundation of the early modern discourse of Russia in Western Europe',[63] and it is certainly notable that there are a number of significant parallels between the Scythian Tamburlaine and the Russian Czar Ivan the Terrible – both killed their sons, both lost beloved wives whose memories were subsequently fetishised, and Richard Wilson suggests that Tamburlaine's weaponry finds a close analogue 'in the arsenal of Ivan'. Indeed the English envoy Jerome Horsey directly compared Ivan both to a Scythian and to a Roman emperor: '"This Heliogabalus," as Horsey reported him...was "a right Scythian"'.[64]

The issue of Scythianness was central to the vexed question of where Europe ended and Asia began, not least since, as François Hartog notes, in *Prometheus Bound* the Scythians live by Lake Maeotis,[65] one of the two traditional boundary markers between Europe and Asia. Although Herodotus had placed Scythia in Europe, Hartog contends that part of what was understood as making its denizens 'Scythian' is that they disregarded the distinction between Asia and Europe. They also troubled other polarities: Archer suggests that 'The Scythians, youngest of all peoples in Herodotus, represent anti-antiquity, and barbarous Russia a sort of anti-Renaissance to the English traders who stumbled across it in the mid-sixteenth century. Yet early modern Russia also offered a paradigm of territorial empire and commercial control to the English'.[66]

Marlowe's representation of Scythianness, at once the epitome of barbarism and what the English audience sees in the play's 'tragic glass', is even more conflicted than his representation of Russianness, with the tensions it generates being clearly played out when Theridamas incredulously demands, 'Are these resolvèd noble Scythians?' (Part One, I.ii.224; some editions italicise 'Scythians' to make the point clearer). Thus Tamburlaine is poised liminally not only between being Russian and being non-Russian but also, and concomitantly, between being Asian and being European. The figure of Tamburlaine thus proves to embody in himself the tensions and contradictions associated with the European-Asian borderline.

The geographical allegiances of his enemies are equally uncertain. If the *Tamburlaine* plays trouble the question of where Europe is in relation to Asia, they do so even more when it comes to the question of what Asia itself actually consisted of. For Marlowe, Asia seems to be less a stable, monolithic entity than a place which can be seen very differently if viewed from different perspectives. Indeed so polyvalent is it in his writing that it is not always clear where he thought Asia was, or what he thought it comprised. Particularly unclear is whether Asia, as Marlowe understands it, includes India, even though India on Ortelius's map is firmly within Asia. However, as Shankar Raman explains, 'a quick glance at a Renaissance map suggests that answering the simple question "Where is India?" presupposes

---

63 Archer, *Old Worlds*, p. 102.
64 Wilson, 'Visible Bullets', pp. 58 and 47.
65 Hartog, *The Mirror of Herodotus*, p. 13.
66 Archer, *Old Worlds*, p. 103.

a later relation to the world that was only then beginning to emerge'.[67] At times in *Tamburlaine the Great*, India seems not to lie in Asia. Even after he has conquered Asia, Tamburlaine seems to refer to full domination of India as something still in the future, when he says to Bajazeth after he has conquered him,

> I'll make the kings of India, ere I die,
> Offer their mines, to sue for peace, to me,
> And dig for treasure to appease my wrath.   (Part One, III.iii.263–5)

Despite the fact that the historical Timur the Lame successfully invaded India in 1398, Raman suggests of Tamburlaine's 'unconquered' speech that 'Behind Tamburlaine's frustration clearly lurks the tale of Alexander's encounter with India'.[68]

At other times, however, India does appear to be understood as part of Asia. Orcanes in Part Two says that

> From Scythia to the oriental plage
> Of India, where raging Lantchidol
> Beats on the regions with his boisterous blows,
> That never seamen yet discoverèd:
> All Asia is in arms with Tamburlaine.   (Part Two, I.i.73–7)

Perhaps most confusingly of all, one of the things most firmly associated with India was *sati*. John Michael Archer notes that 'In the fourteenth century, *sati* was one of the first things Niccolo Conti mentioned upon recounting his entry into India' and that Cesare Federici's 1587 acccount of travels in India, published in Venice and translated into English the following year, also dwells on *sati*.[69] In Marlowe's play, however, the practice of *sati* is dislocated geographically away from India and onto Olympia, who comes from Balsera (probably near Anatolia)[70] and has a name clearly identifying her as classical, when she burns the bodies of her husband and son and tries to follow them into the fire:

> Take pity of a lady's ruthful tears,
> That humbly craves upon her knees to stay
> And cast her body in the burning flame
> That feeds upon her son's and husband's flesh.   (Part Two, III.iv.68–71)

India, then, seems to be surprisingly mobile in *Tamburlaine the Great*, and perhaps some of the reason for that can be found in Cosroe's declaration that a major contributory factor to his discontent is that

---

67   Shankar Raman, *Framing "India": The Colonial Imaginary in Early Modern Culture* (Stanford: Stanford University Press, 2002), p. 2.

68   Raman, *Framing "India"*, p. 93.

69   Archer, *Old Worlds*, pp. 170 and 172. See also Pompa Banerjee, *Burning Women: Widows, Witches, and Early Modern European Travelers in India* (Basingstoke: Palgrave, 2003).

70   As has been noted by Marlowe's editors, Balsera seems to be a misreading of Passera, which Ortelius has en route from Soria to Natolia. He does have a Balsera, near Basra, but that seems not to be what is intended here.

Men from the farthest equinoctial line
Have swarmed in troops into the Eastern India,
Lading their ships with gold and precious stones,
And made them spoils from all our provinces. (Part One, I.i.119–22)

Again, Marlowe is at his favourite trick of inverting traditional perspectives here, for which actually *is* 'the farthest equinoctial line' depends, of course, on which perspective one is looking from.

There is also ambiguity about Persia, and this would have been particularly noteworthy for Marlowe's original audience because 'Persia was the primary gateway through which the luxury goods arrived from further east on their way to the Mediterranean and Europe, having been moved along the "silk road" and other important trade routes';[71] indeed in Thomas Campion's 1614 masque for the wedding of Robert Carr and Frances Howard, Asia wears 'a Persian Ladies habit', as if the two were synonymous.[72] As Matthew Dimmock notes, in *Tamburlaine the Great* 'the well known contemporary division between the Ottoman Empire and Persia is emphasized, curiously, in favour of Persia'. Dimmock attributes this to the fact that 'The Ottoman-Persian conflict had simmered intermittently throughout the sixteenth century', in ways which the English hoped that it would be useful to them: as he points out, 'Tamburlaine's conquests were considered by many contemporary authorities to be the origin of the present Ottoman / Persian conflict', and he suggests that

> By focusing on the Persian and demonizing the Ottoman, Marlowe crucially inverts the prevailing tenets of late Elizabethan foreign policy, which, although interested in the conflict, sought primarily to supply the continual Ottoman demand for arms and armaments with which to combat the Persians and subsequently to draw the Ottomans away from such a war and into a militant anti-Spanish coalition following the conquest of Portugal in 1580.[73]

Certainly Persia is much stressed by Marlowe. Early in Part One, Cosroe declares,

Ah Menaphon, I pass not for his threats:
The plot is laid by Persian noblemen
And captains of the Median garrisons
To crown me emperor of Asia. (Part One, I.i.109–12)

Here it seems that Persia is so much the heartland of Asia that the Asian empire is in the gift of Persian noblemen. An analogous assumption underpins Usumcasane's confidence that

For as, when Jove did thrust old Saturn down,
Neptune and Dis gained each of them a crown,

---

71 Vitkus, *Turning Turk*, p. 71.

72 Paulina Kewes, 'Contemporary Europe in Elizabethan and Early Stuart Drama', in *Shakespeare and Renaissance Europe*, edited by Andrew Hadfield and Paul Hammond (London: Thomson Learning, 2005), pp. 150–92, p. 163.

73 Dimmock, *New Turkes*, pp. 137, 139 and 141.

So do we hope to reign in Asia
If Tamburlaine be placed in Persia. (Part One, II.vii.36–9)

Here, as if in deliberate chiasmus with Cosroe's formulation, Persia is the key to Asia.

At other times, however, Persia seems to be conceived of as distinct and separate from Asia. Meander says to Mycetes that Tamburlaine is

Hoping, misled by dreaming prophecies,
To reign in Asia, and with barbarous arms
To make himself the monarch of the East.
But ere he march in Asia, or display
His vagrant ensign in the Persian fields... (Part One, I.i.40–45)

Mycetes appears to distinguish here between 'Asia' and 'the Persian fields'. Ortygius too seems to regard the two as separate when he says,

And in assurance of desired success
We here do crown thee monarch of the East,
Emperor of Asia and of Persia. (Part One, I.ii.167–9)

Whatever the relationship between Asia and Persia in the *Tamburlaine the Great* plays, though, it is quite clear that Asia, surprisingly, does *not* include Turkey, which is consistently associated with Africa. This is made quite plain when Bajazeth, in his capacity as Turkish emperor, orders Tamburlaine 'Not once to set his foot in Africa' (Part One, III.i.28). Later, Bajazeth, despite his title of 'the Turk', underlines still further his identification with Africa:

Bassoes and janizaries of my guard,
Attend upon the person of your lord,
The greatest potentate of Africa. (Part One, III.iii.61–3)

Not only does Marlowe's Asia look different from different vantage points, then, but it also differs significantly from conventional representations and understandings of the term. Consequently, *Tamburlaine the Great* pits a liminal and dangerously mobile Scythian against a representative of an unstable Asia in ways which challenge and arguably disable any sense of a securely plotted grasp of geographical polarities and orientations.

It is in this context that Tamburlaine the Great looks both closest to and most in contrast with Caesar. Caesar and Tamburlaine were both colonisers, and like Caesar's, Tamburlaine's plans too are directed ultimately towards Britain, culminating in

Keeping in awe the Bay of Portingale
And all the ocean by the British shore:
And by this means I'll win the world at last. (Part One, III.iii.258–60)

Both too are noted for literally reconfiguring the territories they conquer by renaming them after themselves. William Camden recorded in his 'The Smaller Ilands in the British Ocean',

Under these lieth Southward Caesarea, whereof Antonine hath written, scarce twelve miles distant from Alderney, which name the Frenchmen now have clipped so short as the Spaniards have Caesaraugusta in Spaine: for they call it Gearzey, like as *Cherburgh* for *Caesarisburgus* and *Saragose* for *Caesaraugusta*.[74]

Here Caesar is clearly marked as a figure who has stamped his name on territories as far apart as Cherbourg and Zaragoza. Tamburlaine, meanwhile, declares,

> I will confute those blind geographers
> That make a triple region in the world,
> Excluding regions which I mean to trace,
> And with this pen reduce them to a map,
> Calling the provinces, cities and towns
> After my name and thine, Zenocrate.   (Part One, IV.iv.81–6)

The all-important difference is in the trajectory of conquest in relation to the polarities of savagery and civility. The spread of Rome was understood in the early modern period as the spread of civility; Tamburlaine, by contrast, is associated with savagery. The close association between the two figures in so many early modern texts thus powerfully underlines the extent to which the values of the classical are seen as giving away to a newly configured and distinctly alarming world, in which attention must be paid to emerging centres of power which are very different from those where power traditionally resided. This will be seen even more clearly in the play to which I will next turn, *The Winter's Tale*.

---

74 William Camden, 'The Smaller Ilands in the British Ocean', in *Britannia*, translated by Philemon Holland (1607). Online: http://e3.uci.edu/%7Epapyri/cambrit/isleseng.html#1

Chapter Four

Pocahontas and *The Winter's Tale*

In this chapter, I want to argue what is on the face of it a ludicrous claim: that Shakespeare's play *The Winter's Tale* can profitably be read in the light of the story of the Algonquian princess Pocahontas. The reason that this seems ludicrous is quite simply that *The Winter's Tale* was almost certainly written before Shakespeare can have heard of Pocahontas, and in any case, everyone knows that it is *The Tempest* which is interested in the New World, not *The Winter's Tale*, which is located firmly in the classical past.[1] Nevertheless, as many scholars have observed, the classical past and the New World were rarely far apart in early modern thought, and I want to argue that there is not merely an incidental but a structural parallel, with deep roots in early modern thought systems, between the events of *The Winter's Tale* and those surrounding the visit of Pocahontas to London some four or five years after the play was first performed, so that the later of the two events can indeed help us to read the earlier.[2]

The Winter's Tale, in which a young, promising prince dies and his sister goes on to marry, has been related by many scholars to the death of Henry, Prince of Wales, the young, promising son of James VI and I, and the subsequent marriage of his sister Princess Elizabeth (to a man who would ultimately – if briefly – become King of Bohemia). In the general climate of Caesarian association promoted by James, this combination of promising start and early death meant that there was only one possible figure with whom Henry would be inevitably, irresistibly associated – Marcellus, who was the lost heir of Augustus, the Emperor to whom James was in any case so often compared, and whose loss is mourned in Virgil's *Aeneid*, where Anchises declares that 'No other boy of our Ilian clan shall uplift the hopes of his Latin ancestors so high, and in none of her sons shall the future land of Romulus take such pride'.[3] What is much more surprising is that both Virgilian and Henrician imagery are also accruing at much the same time to the Algonquian princess Pocahontas. I suggest that both the American princess and the Anglo-Scottish Prince of Wales could be troped in Virgilian terms because each in their own way symbolised both

---

1   For instance, at a round table at the 2005 Shakespeare Association of America meeting in Bermuda on 'Is *The Tempest* a New World Play', three of the four panellists answered unequivocally in the affirmative.

2   There are possible signs of an earlier interest on Shakespeare's part in the fruits of voyages. Christopher Newport, who was on the *Sea Venture* and is mentioned on the title page of *Newes from Virginia*, brought back a pair of crocodiles in 1605, which may be reflected in the mention of crocodiles in *Antony and Cleopatra*.

3   Virgil, *The Aeneid*, translated by W.F. Jackson Knight (Harmondsworth: Middlesex, 1958), p. 173.

the potential and the threat of the shift in power, wealth and authority from the Old World to the New. First, then, Pocahontas.

Pocahontas, daughter of Chief Powhatan, was born in Virginia c. 1595, is famously supposed to have intervened to save the life of Captain John Smith after he was threatened with execution by her father Powhatan, and married the English settler John Rolfe on 5 April 1614 after being rechristened Rebecca.[4] Rebecca Blevins Faery suggests that this name may have been chosen because 'Rebecca was the woman at the well in the Bible, giving the strangers all they needed – water, food, shelter', as Pocahontas had earlier assisted the settlers in Jamestown, and points out that she was also the mother of Esau, the 'red' son who sold his birthright,[5] rather as the son of Pocahontas was later to defend a fort against his mother's people. Rebecca was the third name by which Pocahontas was known during her short life, Pocahontas itself being a nickname meaning something like playful or mischievous one; her original birth name had been Matoaka.

In 1615 Pocahontas gave birth to her only child, Thomas Rolfe, from whom a number of prominent Virginian families subsequently claimed descent.[6] Shortly afterwards she, her husband and her son all sailed for England, on what David Stymeist has recently argued was effectively a promotional tour: 'reports of starvation, disease, and attack by "wild and cruell Pagans"...in Virginia were hardly encouraging', and '[f]ew English settlers took native brides because of the fear of syphilis, a general distrust of aboriginals, the lack of prenuptial chastity among the Algonquins, and the fact one did not improve one's social status through marriage', so

> The final step in the Virginia Company's advertisement of exotic intermarriage was to send Pocahontas and Rolfe on tour along with a dozen Algonquins in London in the summer of 1616. They stayed, at Company expense, at the appropriately named Belle Sauvage Inn. Pocahontas's invitation to sit beside Queen Anne and James I during Ben Jonson's Twelfth Night masque, "The Vision of Delight," was the crowning moment of this visit to England.[7]

However, Pocahontas's health failed during her stay in England, and no sooner had she taken ship for her return journey to America than she had to be brought back to Gravesend, where she died and was buried on 21 March 1617.

The many subsequent retellings of Pocahontas's life, perhaps most notably the Disney film with its 'Native American Barbie' heroine,[8] have encouraged an

---

4   On the meanings and resonances of Pocahontas's baptism, see Erica Fudge, 'Pocahontas's Baptism: Reformed Theology and the Paradox of Desire', *Critical Survey* 11.1 (1999), pp. 15–30.

5   Rebecca Blevins Faery, *Cartographies of Desire: Captivity, Race, and Sex in the Shaping of an American Nation* (Norman: University of Oklahoma Press, 1999), p. 84.

6   See Stuart E. Brown, Jr., Lorraine F. Myers, and Eileen M. Chappell, *Pocahontas' Descendants* (New York: Genealogical Publishing Co., 1985).

7   David Stymeist, '"Strange Wives": Pocahontas in Early Modern Colonial Advertisement', *Mosaic* 35 (2002), pp. 109–25, pp. 111, 119, and 122.

8   See for instance Roxana Preda, 'The Angel in the Ecosystem Revisited: Disney's *Pocahontas* and Postmodern Ethics', in *From Virgin Land to Disney World: Nature and Its*

understanding of the Pocahontas story as essentially a romantic one, even though it poses some difficulty for this version of events that Pocahontas seemed initially to be attracted to John Smith but eventually married John Rolfe. But do we thus misread her story? In the first place, many commentators have argued that the story as John Smith recounts it is not to be relied on, since his account may not be accurate or, if it was, he may not have understood the fundamentally ritual nature of the events in which he participated, which may in fact have been a form of adoption ceremony.[9] In the second, Beth Donaldson argues that

> Pocahontas consistently mediates exchange in ways which mark her as... "cultural broker"...and her place in the defining exchange of gifts between the two cultures illustrates her diplomatic role. More specifically, the gender politics of the English – especially the narrative of romantic love and the notion of women as primarily sexual, irrational, emotional beings – have encouraged historical misreadings which depoliticize Pocahontas's role.[10]

I want to follow Donaldson's lead and argue that excessive attention to Pocahontas' relationships with first John Smith and then John Rolfe have prevented us from noticing a much less visible but culturally no less interesting one with Henry, Prince of Wales, and above all with the mode of relationship between England and America which Prince Henry encouraged and with which he ultimately came virtually to be identified.

The famous 1616 portrait of Pocahontas by Simon van de Passe bears some interesting formal similarities to that of Henry's sister, Elizabeth of Bohemia, by Crispin van de Passe.[11] In some sense this might be expected since Simon was the son of Crispin, but I think the similarities go beyond that. Both show the female figure in a cartouche identifying her as the daughter of a king: indeed if anything Pocahontas' status appears to be the more important here, since her father is identified as an Emperor, and she herself is wearing a hat which closely resembles one worn by Elizabeth's mother, Anne of Denmark, in one of her portraits – [12] an image which is very different from, say, the representation of America in Thomas Campion's 1614 masque for the wedding of Robert Carr and Frances Howard, where the personified

---

Discontents in the USA of Yesterday and Today, edited by Bernd Herzogenrath (Amsterdam: Rodopi, 2001), pp. 317–40, p. 329, though the comparison has been frequently made.

9   See for instance Rayna Green, 'The Pocahontas Perplex', *Massachusetts Review* 16.4 (1975), pp. 698–714, pp. 699–700, on Smith's story being a familiar topos and not necessarily to be believed, and Frederic W. Gleach, 'Pocahontas and Captain John Smith Revisited', in *Actes du Vingt-Cinquième Congrès des Algonquinistes*, edited by William Cowan (Ottawa: Carleton University, 1994), pp. 167–86, on the possibility that the events described by Smith might have had a ritual significance which he failed to grasp.

10   Beth Donaldson, 'Pocahontas as Gift: Gender and Diplomacy on the Anglo-Powhatan Frontier', *Journal of the American Studies Association* 30 (1999), pp. 1–17, p. 2.

11   Reproductions of the two images are available at http://vassun.vassar.edu/~robertso/ Poca/poca.html and http://www.npg.org.uk/live/search/portrait.asp?linkID=mp01455&rNo= 4&role=sit respectively.

12   See Karen Robertson, 'Pocahontas at the Masque', *Signs: A Journal of Women, Culture and Society* 21 (1996), pp. 551–83.

America has on her head 'round brims of many coloured feathers, and in the midst of it a small Crowne'.[13] Both the portrait of Pocahontas and that of Princess Elizabeth, too, show the sitter wearing pearls – river pearls in the case of Pocahontas, a marker of her American origins, but she has a tear pearl dangling from her one visible ear, just as Elizabeth does. Pearls had played an important part in interaction between the Native Americans and the colonists, because Powhatan had sent a pearl chain to John Smith on his first arrival and emissaries to him were expected to wear it as proof of their *bona fides*.[14]

However, there is an even closer iconographical link between this portrait and Elizabeth of Bohemia's late brother, Prince Henry, for Pocahontas's fan is made of ostrich feathers.[15] It is true that despite their African origin, ostriches were associated with the New World: in *The Vision of Delight*, the masque which Pocahontas saw, there are the lines

Your Ostritch, beleeve it, 's no faithfull translator
Of perfect Utopian.[16]

Playing on the association between More's Hythloday and the New World, these words effect a forcible transmigration of the ostrich from its African habitat to a North America to which it is an utter stranger.[17] The presence of ostrich feathers in Pocahontas's fan might also, however, make sense of quite another kind in the context of the three ostrich feathers which formed the badge of the Prince of Wales. The supposed story of their origin was well known in the early modern period – it is, for instance, recounted in the play *Edward III*, of which Shakespeare seems to have written part: they were said to have been taken by the Black Prince from the King of Bohemia at the battle of Crécy, and to have been used ever after as the badge of the Prince of Wales. This alleged origin makes it all the more suggestive that they should accrue not to the iconography of Princess Elizabeth, whose brother wore them as his badge and whose husband was later to claim the throne of Bohemia, but to that of Pocahontas. Why should this be?

When Pocahontas was first captured by Captain Samuel Argall, it was with the agreement of the council of Jamestown, and it was to Jamestown that she was taken. Soon, however, 'The Reverend Alexander Whitaker was given charge of Pocahontas'

---

13   Paulina Kewes, 'Contemporary Europe in Elizabethan and Early Stuart Drama', in *Shakespeare and Renaissance Europe*, edited by Andrew Hadfield and Paul Hammond (London: Thomson Learning, 2005), pp. 150–92, p. 163.

14   David A. Price, *Love and Hate in Jamestown: John Smith, Pocahontas and the Heart of a New Nation* (London: Faber and Faber, 2004), pp. 102 and 159.

15   On the identification as ostrich feathers, see Karen Robertson, 'First Friday Talk'. Online: http://vassun.vassar.edu/~robertso/Poca/First_Friday_Talk1.html.

16   Ben Jonson, *The Vision of Delight*, in C. H. Herford and Percy and Evelyn Simpson, eds, *Ben Jonson*, vol. VII (Oxford: The Clarendon Press, 1941), pp. 72–3.

17   It is true that the rhea is sometimes known as an American ostrich, but the only thing approximating to an occurrence of this recorded by OED before 1676 is 'In certaine places of Chili, were many Abstruses in the Plaines' (*OED* 'ostrich' 2).

religious instruction. He took her to his Henrico home'.[18] The new town of Henrico had been founded by Sir Thomas Dale, who felt that Jamestown was not well sited.[19] Its naming was also a fitting monument to Prince Henry's strong interest in America: in 1607, when still only 13, he had committed himself to the colonisation of Virginia, and one Robert Tindall wrote to him from Jamestown in that year, after the 1607 colonisers had christened their landing point Cape Henry;[20] as William Strachey noted, 'This is the famous Chesapeake Bay, which we have called (in honor of our young Prince) Cape Henry, over against which within the Bay lieth another headland, which we called, in honor of our princely Duke of York, Cape Charles'.[21] In 1610 the prince became Supreme Protector of the newly-founded Company of the Merchant Discoverers of the North-West Passage, and Sir John Holles, writing after the prince's death, recalled that 'all actions profitable or honourable for the kingdom were fomented by him, witness the North West passage, Virginia, Guiana, The Newfoundland, etc., to all which he gave his money as well as his good word'.[22] Even on his deathbed, at his mother's request, some of Ralegh's 'Balsam of Guiana' was administered to Henry and was said to have temporarily restored the power of speech to him.[23] After his death, this interest was continued by his grieving mother: indeed Louis H. Roper relates the presence of Pocahontas at *A Vision of Delight* to Anne's imperial interest in the Jamestown colony,[24] and although John Smith called it 'a Virginia maske', suggesting that she would in any case have been the ideal audience for it,[25] there is little in it beyond the ostrich reference to link it to the New World.[26]

This well-established interest in America proved an important part of the iconographical and thematic repertoire of the collective memorialisation which followed the prince's premature death in late 1612. William Hole, who engraved one of the earliest maps of Virginia in *A True Relation of such occurences as hapned in Virginia* (1608), also did the engraving for the Homer of George Chapman (also

18   William Warren Jenkins, 'The Princess Pocahontas and Three Englishmen Named John', in *No Fairer Land: Studies in Southern Literature Before 1900*, edited by J. Lasley Dameron and James W. Mathews (Troy, N.Y.: Whitston, 1986), pp. 8–20, p. 11.

19   Roy Strong, *Henry, Prince of Wales and England's Lost Renaissance* (London: Thames and Hudson, 1986), p. 62.

20   Price, *Love and Hate in Jamestown*, p. 27.

21   William Strachey, in *A Voyage to Virginia in 1609: Two Narratives: Strachey's "True Reportory", Jourdain's* Discovery of the Bermudas (Charlottesville: University Press of Virginia, 1964), p. 61.

22   Strong, *Henry, Prince of Wales*, pp. 51, 61, and 8.

23   Charles Nicholl, *The Creature in the Map: Sir Walter Ralegh's Quest for El Dorado* (London: Vintage, 1996), p. 288.

24   Louis H. Roper, 'Unmasquing the connections between Jacobean politics and policy: the circle of Anna of Denmark and the beginning of the English empire, 1614–18', in *"High and Mighty Queens" of Early Modern England: Realities and Representations*, edited by Carole Levin, Jo Eldridge Carney, and Debra Barrett-Graves (New York: Palgrave Macmillan, 2003), pp. 45–59, p. 45.

25   Price, *Love and Hate in Jamestown*, p. 178.

26   Jonson, *The Vision of Delight*, pp. 83 and 129.

the author of *A Memorable Masque*, which is set in Virginia), which was dedicated to Henry, and for Chapman's *Epicede*,[27] a lament for the loss of the prince, which refers to how

> The poore Verginian, miserable sayle,
> A long-long-Night-turnd-Day, that liu'd in Hell
> When heaven was lost, when not a teare-wrackt eye,
> Could tell in all that dead time, if they were,
> Sincking or sayling; till a quickning cleere
> Gaue light to saue them by the ruth of Rocks
> At the Bermudas; where the tearing shocks
> And all the Miseries before, more felt
> Then here halfe told; All, All this did not melt
> Those desperate few, still dying more in teares,
> Then this Death, all men, to the Marrow weares.[28]

This refers to the 1609 wreck of *The Sea Venture*, after which John Rolfe's first wife had given birth to a daughter named Bermuda while they were shipwrecked on the island, though the baby soon died,[29] so that this passage in an elegy for Henry has a tiny link to Pocahontas too. Suggestively, the fact that Webster appears to have interrupted *The Duchess of Malfi* in order to write his funeral elegy on Prince Henry[30] may well find reflection in a mention of the Bermudas in that play, in Bosola's words,

> I would sooner swim to the Bermudas on
> Two politicians' rotten bladders, tied
> Together with an intelligencer's heartstring,
> Than depend on so changeable a prince's favour.   (III.ii.269–72)

Webster's elegy and his play appear to have been closely interlinked: Michael Neill, arguing for a relationship between *The Duchess of Malfi* and the elegy for Henry (which he also sees as linked with *The Winter's Tale*), suggests that the wax models of Antonio and the children might have been made by the person responsible for the effigy of Prince Henry used for his funeral procession.[31] In all these texts, then, Henry and his loss are imaginatively associated with the Virginia project. Chapman's reference to the Bermudas might also, however, alert us to the fact that, as so often in writing about the New World, imagings of the Old World are not far away. In *The Tempest*, acted at the wedding of Henry's sister the year after his death, mention of

---

27   Strong, *Henry, Prince of Wales*, p. 130.

28   Chapman, George, 'AN EPICED, OR Funerall Song: On the most disastrous Death, of the High-borne Prince of Men, HENRY Prince of Wales, &c', from *An Epicede or Funerall Song* (1612)], ll. 491–508.

29   Price, *Love and Hate in Jamestown*, p. 134.

30   See for instance M. C. Bradbrook, *John Webster: Citizen and Dramatist* (London: Weidenfeld and Nicolson, 1980), pp. 147 and 163.

31   Michael Neill, 'Monuments and ruins as symbols in *The Duchess of Malfi*', in *Themes in Drama 4: Drama and Symbolism*, edited by James Redmond (Cambridge: Cambridge University Press, 1982), pp. 71–87, pp. 76–7 and p. 85, n. 11.

the Bermudas sits alongside an unacknowledged translation of Aeneas' first remark to Venus, 'O dea certe'[32] – 'Most sure, the goddess' (I.ii.422–3). In memorialisations of Henry, too, the American and the classical themes are equally strong.

Prince Henry was born in Scotland in 1594 and moved to England shortly after his father's accession in 1603. Throughout Prince Henry's life in England there was a strong association between him and the figure of Marcellus, nephew and heir apparent of the Emperor Augustus, who died young and whose loss was lamented in the *Aeneid*. This link was in many ways only to be expected after the prince's early death, but more remarkably, it was already established well before that: in 1606 Sir John Harington translated Book VI of the *Aeneid*, in which Aeneas visits the underworld and sees Marcellus (lines which caused Marcellus's mother Octavia to faint when Virgil read them to her); Harington dedicated the translation to Prince Henry. The comparison took on savagely ironic force after Prince Henry's premature death in 1612, when both Chapman and Webster in their funeral elegies referred to the lost heir as a Marcellus. In Chapman's *An Epicede or Funerall Song*, we are first told, as of Marcellus, that 'Heauen open'd, and but show'd him to our eies, / Then shut againe, and show'd our Miseries' (ll. 13–14) and then directly that

> If yong *Marcellus* had to grace his fall,
> Six hundred Herses at his Funerall;
> Sylla sixe thousand; let Prince *Henry* haue
> Six Millions bring him to his greedy graue.   (ll. 617–20)

Webster similarly in his 'Funeral Elegy' wrote of Henry that

> And as *Marcellus* did two Temples reare
> To *Honour* and to *Vertue*, plac't so neare
> They kist; yet none to *Honours* got accesse,
> But that they past through *Vertues*; So to expresse
> His Worthinesse, none got his Countenance
> But those whom actuall merite did advance.   (ll. 102–7)

Pocahontas too was a figure to whom strong Virgilian resonances accrued, as Christopher Hodgkins has recently discussed:

> the Virgilian legend provided striking parallels, and thus a potent paradigm, for the fledgling Jamestown enterprise: in Book 7 of the *Aeneid* Virgil imagines Latium as a place of sylvan rusticity inhabited by a warrior race under a noble chieftain looking to give his daughter in dynastic marriage to a prophecied foreign prince with whom he will share equal rule. Thus a Virgilian Virginia could recapitulate the master epic, promising another cycle of imperial regeneration, with Rolfe an Aeneas of sorts, Chief Powhatan a transatlantic Latinus, Pocahontas the new Lavinia, and Jamestown yet another Troy.[33]

---

32   William Shakespeare, *The Tempest*, edited by Virginia Mason Vaughan and Alden T. Vaughan (London: Thomas Nelson, 1999), I.ii.422.

33   Christopher Hodgkins, 'The Nubile Savage: Pocahontas as Heathen Convert and Virgilian Bride', *Renaissance Papers* (1998), pp. 81–90, p. 87.

Not for nothing did Michael Drayton, a poet whom King James disliked but whom Prince Henry patronised, write in 1606 an 'Ode to the Virginian Voyage', with the very name of 'Ode' sufficiently indicating the classical framework within which New World exploration was to be considered,[34] while Francisco de Vitoria compared Europeans arriving in America to Trojans arriving in Carthage.[35]

The applicability of the Virgilian paradigm to Pocahontas was underpinned by the fact that, perhaps surprisingly for the historical moment, her status as royalty was, as the Van de Passe portrait shows, taken seriously. When Virginia was first colonised in the reign of Elizabeth, its status was prone to fluctuate. Although the queen herself was represented in at least one engraving as 'Elizabeta D.G. Angliae. Franciae. Hiberniae. et Verginiae Regina', and 'The first part of Edmund Spenser's *The Faerie Queene* was pointedly and unusually dedicated in 1590 to 'Elizabeth by the Grace of God Queen of England, Fraunce and Ireland and of Virginia',[36] she nevertheless bestowed on Ralegh the title 'Lord and Governor of Virginia'.[37] By the Jacobean period, however, Virginia had definitively acquired a status far beyond that of a mere lordship, and its ruler was fully acknowledged as royal. William Strachey referred to 'their subtle King Powhatan',[38] and Hodgkins argues that

> biblicist and classical elements in the developing British imperial imagination fused to make it temporarily possible for an early modern white man to wed a woman of color, bring her home to England, and rather than being ostracized for his miscegenation, to find himself celebrated for it. Indeed, King James I, who eventually welcomed the Powhatan bride to his palaces twice, was according to one account at first perturbed when he learned of the marriage – yet not because of the bride's bloodlines, but rather because Rolfe, a commoner, had without his sovereign's permission wedded the daughter of a foreign prince.[39]

Purchas said of the Virginian princess that she 'did not onely accustome herself to ciuilitie, but still carried her selfe as the Daughter of a King',[40] and before Pocahontas had even met John Rolfe, John Smith had already noted, à propos of the rumours of a marriage between Pocahontas and himself, that 'her marriage could no way have

---

34   See Robert S. Tilton, *Pocahontas: The Evolution of an American Narrative* (Cambridge: Cambridge University Press, 1994), pp. 6 and 50, on Jason and Medea as another classical myth informing the construction of the Pocahontas story, and p. 51 on later writers' perception of Virgilian analogues. Peter Hulme in *Colonial Encounters: Europe and the Native Caribbean 1492–1797* (London: Methuen, 1986) also points to parallels with the *Odyssey* (pp. 153–4).

35   Hulme, *Colonial Encounters*, p. 161.

36   Michael G. Brennan, 'English Contact with Europe', in *Shakespeare and Renaissance Europe*, edited by Andrew Hadfield and Paul Hammond (London: Thomson Learning, 2005), pp. 53–97, p. 64.

37   See Robert Lacey, *Sir Walter Ralegh* (London: Weidenfeld & Nicolson, 1973), between pp. 144–5 and p. 64.

38   Strachey, *A Voyage to Virginia in 1609*, p. 71.

39   Hodgkins, 'The Nubile Savage', p. 81.

40   Rocco Coronato, 'Inducting Pocahontas', *Symbiosis* 2.1 (1998), pp. 24–38, p. 29.

intitled him by any right to the kingdome'.[41] (Almost as if to underline the importance of the classical paradigm in matters American, Smith consistently refers to himself in what Peter Hulme identifies as 'the Caesarian third person',[42] a description of which Smith himself would have acknowledged the justice since he explicitly observed of his own writing that 'Julius Caesar wrote his owne Commentaries'.)[43] Even as Smith implicitly contests the specifics of the Lavinia parallel here, he confirms the basis on which it could rest: Pocahontas is a princess, and even if Algonquian practice is not, as in the *Arabian Nights*, for the king to give away part of the kingdom with the hand of his daughter, that actually makes Algonquin royalty more like English royalty, where the custom did not pertain either.

And that, I think, is what the presence of the ostrich feathers in Pocahontas' fan suggests – that Algonquin royalty is like English royalty, and that the Virginian princess, however exotic she may be, is in some sense a psychological replacement for the Virgilian prince who is gone, something neatly emblematised by the fact that it was Sir Thomas Dale, who chose the name Henrico for the new settlement and 'interestingly referred to the Prince in retrospect as his "glorious Master"', who brought Pocahontas to England.[44] *The Tempest* has often been discussed in the light of New World voyages in general and of the Pocahontas story in particular – Peter Hulme, for instance, remarks that 'The early history of the English colony of Virginia contains one story – perhaps its most famous – that has tantalizing parallels with *The Tempest*'[45] – and it is certainly true that Pocahontas is mentioned in both William Strachey's *Historie of Travaile into Virginia Britannia* (1612) and John Smith's *The Proceedings of the English Colonie in Virginia* (1612), so that Shakespeare could in some sense conceivably have had her in mind when writing *The Tempest* in a way that he could not have done in *The Winter's Tale*. Nevertheless it is my contention that Pocahontas – or more properly what she came to represent in the English colonial imaginary – is in fact better figured in *The Winter's Tale*, where the princess from a new land replaces the lost prince who had died in the old, and where the discourse of the classical mingles so powerfully with that of the trade and exploration which drove the quest for the New World. Indeed in some sense the whole point of Marceluss as conceived in the *Aeneid* is that he is a figure who can be reused: Anchises explains that his is one of the 'souls who are destined to live in the body a second time'.[46]

I do not mean 'figured' in a literal sense, since the testimony of Simon Forman that he saw the play at the Globe on 15 May 1611 means that it must certainly have been written before Shakespeare is likely ever to have heard of Pocahontas; it is true that John Smith returned to England in late 1609, but there is no indication either that he knew Shakespeare or that he spread the story of Pocahontas orally, and indeed the fact that in August 1613 John Chamberlain mentioned the capture

41 Faery, *Cartographies of Desire*, p. 104.
42 Hulme, *Colonial Encounters: Europe and the Native Caribbean 1492–1797*, p. 163.
43 Price, *Love and Hate in Jamestown*, p. 23.
44 Strong, *Henry, Prince of Wales*, p. 62.
45 Hulme, *Colonial Encounters: Europe and the Native Caribbean 1492–1797*, p. 137.
46 Virgil, *The Aeneid*, p. 168.

of Pocahontas in a letter without naming her suggests that he did not.[47] Rather I mean that to read *The Winter's Tale* in the light of the Pocahontas story allows us a lens through which to read the culturally crucial intersection of the Virgilian with the Virginian, and of the New World with the Old. After all, as Rayna Green points out, 'America had a Pocahontas Perplex even before the teenage Princess offered us a real figure to hang the iconography on. The powerfully symbolic Indian woman, as Queen and Princess, has been with us since 1575 when she appeared to stand for the New World';[48] indeed Martin Waldseemüller proposed the name America in his *Cosmographiae introductio* (1507) on the explicit grounds that 'I do not see why anyone should object to its being called after Americus the discoverer, a man of natural wisdom, Land of Americus or America, since both Europe and Asia have derived their names from women'.[49] Of course landscape was often imaged as female – for instance the investiture of Henry as Prince of Wales in 1610 was marked by Samuel Daniel's masque *Tethys' Festival*, in which thirteen river nymphs were represented by ladies of the court – but in the case of America this seems to have been particularly strongly registered: in Fletcher, Field and Massinger's *The Knight of Malta*, for instance, a black woman is asked 'do ye snarle you black jill; she looks li[k]e the Picture of *America*'.[50] Most notably, Virginia itself was inherently and insistently feminised. I suggest that in *The Winter's Tale*, the replacement of Mamillius by Perdita charts a shift from the Old World to the New which, while it may be most neatly emblematised by Pocahontas' arrival in London so soon after the death of Prince Henry, is actually a much more deeply-rooted and far-reaching cultural trend, as the hero-oriented world of Virgil, in which women are either to be spurned or must act as the emblems and spoils of conquest, gives place to that of Virginia, which is structured and underpinned by the importance of the cultural rôle of women as objects of trade and exchange (not least because the perilous foothold that the English held there made native cooperation essential for their survival).

The Winter's Tale, for all its trappings of fairy tale and myth, is profoundly concerned with the logic and language of trade and exchange, even though this is something unusual in non-comic drama, as Daryl Palmer observes.[51] The prominence given to such language serves to associate *The Winter's Tale* very firmly with a group of plays which Daniel Vitkus has identified as responding in very particular and specific terms to the changing military and economic concerns of Renaissance Europe: in Vitkus's formulation, 'In the Mediterranean plays that appeared on the early modern stage, commercial discourse is pervasive'.[52] *The Winter's Tale* is not often thought of as a Mediterranean play, but it opens and closes in Sicily, and that,

---

47   Price, *Love and Hate in Jamestown*, p. 151.

48   Green, 'The Pocahontas Perplex', p. 701.

49   Nicholas Crane, *Mercator: The Man Who Mapped the Planet* [2002] (London: Phoenix, 2003), p. 56.

50   John Fletcher, Nathan Field and Philip Massinger, *The Knight of Malta* (London, 1647), V.ii.108–9.

51   Daryl W. Palmer, *Writing Russia in the Age of Shakespeare* (Aldershot: Ashgate, 2004), pp. xiv–xv.

52   Daniel Vitkus, *Turning Turk: English Theater and the Multicultural Mediterranean. 1570–1630* (Basingstoke: Palgrave, 2003), p. 39.

as *The Jew of Malta* reminds us, was an important bulwark against the Ottoman Turks. Indeed the way in which Shakespeare destabilises the traditional associations of Sicily by displacing the discourse of pastoral, spawned on the island in the idylls of Theocritus, to Bohemia, with which it had no established connection, should serve to remind us that things do not always continue to mean what they once did.

In the opening scene of *The Winter's Tale*, Camillo says in response to Archidamus' praise: 'You pay a great deal too dear for what's given freely'.[53] Camillo's words, as is fitting in this tense scene where Archidamus 'know[s] not what to say' (I.i.13), are poised uneasily between recognising the existence and importance of a market and implying that it is not functioning properly, since things are not being paid for at their correct prices. This hint of ambivalence towards the idea of trade and exchange is, I think, developed further a few lines later, when, for the first time in this rather stilted conversation, we hear a speech of considerable length, as Camillo says:

> Sicilia cannot show himself over-kind to Bohemia. They were trained together in their childhoods, and there rooted betwixt them then such an affection which cannot choose but branch now. Since their more mature dignities and royal necessities made separation of their society, their encounters, though not personal, have been royally attorneyed with interchange of gifts, letters, loving embassies, that they have seemed to be together, though absent; shook hands, as over a vast; and embraced, as it were, from the ends of opposed winds. (I.i.21–31)

It has often been observed that 'branch' here may carry connotations of splitting and diverging as well as of bearing fruit.[54] To modern ears, it may also carry the suggestion of 'branch' as in the branch of a bank, and this is by no means inappropriate, since this speech is all about that underlying principle of banking, the ability of objects – specifically money – to function as tokens of assets rather than as the assets themselves. Indeed the way in which money functions as a sign of the thing is soon to be explicitly articulated by Polixenes:

> Time as long again
> Would be fill'd up, my brother, with our thanks;
> And yet we should, for perpetuity,
> Go hence in debt: and therefore, like a cipher
> (Yet standing in rich place) I multiply
> With one 'We thank you' many thousands moe
> That go before it. (I.ii.3–9)

This is, then, a market economy, as Hermione recognises when she declares that 'Our praises are our wages' (I.ii.94) and as Leontes implies when he asks Mamilius, 'Mine honest friend, / Will you take eggs for money?' (I.ii.160–61). It is a world in

---

53   William Shakespeare, *The Winter's Tale*, edited by J.H.P. Pafford (London: Routledge, 1988), I.i.17–18. All further quotations from the play will be taken from this edition and reference will be given in the text.

54   On economic metaphors in the play, see most notably Stanley Cavell, 'Recounting Gains, Showing Losses: Reading *The Winter's Tale*', pp. 193–221 of *Disowning Knowledge in Six Plays of Shakespeare* (Cambridge: Cambridge University Press, 1987), especially pp. 200–201.

which everyone is engaged in business, from the highest – as we see when Polixenes tells Camillo that 'Thou, having made me businesses, which none without thee can sufficiently manage, must either stay to execute them thyself, or take away with thee the very services thou hast done' (IV.ii.13–17) – to Autolycus, who announces that 'My traffic is sheets' (IV.iii.23) and sings of his wares (IV.iv.170–71), or the Clown busy reckoning his profit and what he is to buy (IV.iii.32–7). It is, in short, a world very like the Jacobean England which was sponsoring voyages to the New World in the hope of profit and exchange: it was for this very reason that Ortelius's wall-map of the world 'included a panel listing the sources of European imports such as gold and silver, precious stones and spices'.[55] William Strachey expressly commented on rates of exchange, complaining that the colony has suffered a great deal from traders hiking their prices: 'I myself have heard the master of a ship say... that unless he might have an East Indian increase, four for one, all charges cleared, he would not part with a can of beer',[56] and Richard Wilson well observes that 'even the Bohemian festival of *The Winter's Tale* is revealed to be "fully integrated into the international economy", with its exchange of wool for commodities like raisins, sugar, and spices'.[57]

At the same time, however, there is also a sense in the play that traffic is somehow tainting. As in *King Lear*, where Cordelia will not say how much she loves her father, quality seems implicitly to be pitted against, and ultimately deemed incompatible with, quantity. This is first suggested when Hermione asks Polixenes,

> Will you go yet?
> Force me to keep you as a prisoner,
> Not like a guest: so you shall pay your fees
> When you depart, and save your thanks?   (I.ii.51–4)

To be a fee-paying guest – someone resident for reasons of traffic rather than affection – is no better than to be a prisoner, who would indeed, in the early modern period, have to pay his fees before he could be released. A similar disdain of the values of the market is seen in Leontes' injunction,

> Hermione,
> How thou lov'st us, show in our brother's welcome;
> Let what is dear in Sicily be cheap:
> Next to thyself, and my young rover, he's
> Apparent to my heart.   (I.ii.173–7)

And Leontes is openly dismissive of those whose primary concern is traffic as he rants that Polixenes is one

> who, if I
> Had servants true about me, that bare eyes
> To see alike mine honour as their profits,

---

55   Crane, *Mercator*, p. 243.

56   Strachey, *A Voyage to Virginia in 1609*, p. 72.

57   Richard Wilson, 'A World Elsewhere: Shakespeare's Sense of an Exit', *Proceedings of the British Academy* 117 (2002), pp. 165–99, p. 171.

Their own particular thrifts, they would do that
Which should undo more doing.   (I.ii.308–12)

Hermione is equally dismissive of the values of trade and exchange when she declares that 'To me can life be no commodity' (III.ii.93).

Ultimately, though, this is a play in which traffic and love must be seen not as opposed, but as linked. Ironically, it is the Clown who reveals the relationship between the two, when he says 'If I were not in love with Mopsa, thou shouldst take no money of me; but being enthralled as I am, it will also be the bondage of certain ribbons and gloves' (IV.iv.233–6). Moreover, though Florizel dismisses Polixenes' surprise at his having bought nothing by declaring 'Old sir, I know / She prizes not such trifles as these are' (IV.iv.357–8), we should note that he is entirely unsuccessful when he tries to pass off Perdita with the lie that 'Good my lord, / She came from Libya' (V.i.155–6): in fact Leontes can name the king of that country, and the reason he can do so is because of its twofold importance. First, there was its rich cultural heritage, most clearly explored in Marlowe's *Dido, Queen of Carthage*, where Dido is queen of Libya, and which Shakespeare is surely recalling in *The Winter's Tale* as well as in *The Tempest*, since Aeneas in Marlowe's play asks 'Who would not undergo all kind of toil / To be well stored with such a winter's tale?'.[58] Second, there was the crucial status of Tripoli in the wars between the Moslem and Christian worlds, and as a source of wealth (when Sir Francis Drake set off to explore the coast of America, he pretended to be headed for Tripoli, since that seemed such a plausible destination).[59] All the world's a fair, and all the men and women merely buyers – and an exotic bride, whether in the shape of Pocahontas or of a Libyan princess, is an economic asset and an emblem of international trade and exploration, as well as a beloved.

In this play, then, there is a tension between the values of the market and what are seen as higher, nobler, money-free values. This arises, I think, because all Shakespeare's late plays, and *The Winter's Tale* in particular, chart a shift in orientation from the classical, typified by a gift economy, to a new trade- and commodity-based one which is explicitly oriented not on the Mediterranean, home of the classical, but on the previously peripheral territories of the Orient, Africa, and the Americas: as Daryl Palmer has it, 'Sailing north for Cathay in 1553, [Sir Hugh] Willoughby gave new meaning to the telling of tales in winter'.[60] The heroes of Homeric epics live in a world where exchange consists primarily in the exchange of gifts – and,

---

58   Christopher Marlowe, *Dido, Queen of Carthage*, in *Christopher Marlowe: The Complete Plays*, edited by Mark Thornton Burnett (London: J. M. Dent, 1999), III.iii.58–9. All further quotations from Marlowe will be taken from this edition and reference will be given in the text. The phrase 'winter's tale' also occurs in Marlowe's *The Jew of Malta* (II. i.24–5), in a balcony scene which Shakespeare certainly remembered in *Romeo and Juliet*.

59   Samuel Bawlf, *The Secret Voyage of Sir Francis Drake* (Harmondsworth: Penguin, 2003), p. 68.

60   Daryl W. Palmer, 'Winter, tyranny and knowledge in *The Winter's Tale*', *Shakespeare Quarterly* 46.3 (Fall 1995), pp. 323–39, p. 323. On the shift in the rôle of gift-giving, see Patricia Fumerton, *Cultural Aesthetics: Renaissance Literature and the Practice of Social Ornament* (Chicago: University of Chicago Press, 1991), pp. 31 and 163.

moreover, generally the same type of gift, with ceremonial tripods, used in ritual, predominating. By contrast, the new economy charted in the late plays depends on the exchange of things intrinsically unlike, causing sharp awareness of the fact that there is no inherent link between the thing and what it represents, and also of the fact that there could be a dangerous imbalance in what is exchanged: during Pocahontas' visit to London, her companion, Tocomoco, first did not recognise James as the king and then was appalled that he had offered no gift, saying to John Smith, 'You gave Powhatan a white dog, which Powhatan fed as himself, but your king gave me nothing, and I am better than your white dog'.[61]

In many ways Shakespeare's last plays can all be seen as charting this loss of the classical world and its accompanying values and certainties. In *Pericles*, the classical patriarch, in the shape of Antiochus, is discredited; in *Cymbeline*, heroic classical Rome blurs uneasily into fragmented modern Italy, home of Machiavelli and notorious site of debauchery;[62] in *The Tempest*, a group of characters whose associations come straight from Virgil are pitted against another group whose links are with Aleppo. But it, is above all, *The Winter's Tale* which pits the old classical economy directly against the new trade-oriented one,[63] and which also creates most strongly the sense of a decline in the power and influence of the classical world, evoking the elegiac sense of loss of which Marcellus was so powerful an emblem. Perdita's name is Latin, but it is Latin for lost, and that neatly emblematises the extent to which the values of the classical world are, indeed, lost and in decline here. That is seen too in the case of Hermione, whose name clearly signals Greek affiliations, but who is

---

61   Price, *Love and Hate in Jamestown*, p. 179.

62   See for instance Jonas Barish, 'Hats, Clocks and Doublets: Some Shakespearean Anachronisms', in *Shakespeare's Universe: Renaissance Ideas and Conventions*, edited by John M. Mucciolo (Aldershot: Scolar Press, 1996), pp. 29–36, p. 34; Northrop Frye, *A Natural Perspective: The Development of Shakespearean Comedy and Romance* (New York: Columbia University Press, 1965), p. 57; Harry Levin, 'Shakespeare's Italians', in *Shakespeare's Italy: Functions of Italian Locations in Renaissance Drama*, edited by Michele Marrapodi, A. J. Hoenselaars, Marcello Capuzzo and L. Falzon Santucci (Manchester: Manchester University Press, 1993), pp.17–29, p. 20; Leah Marcus, *Puzzling Shakespeare: Local Reading and its Discontents* (Berkeley: University of California Press, 1988), p. 126; D. R. C. Marsh, *'The Recurring Miracle': A Study of Cymbeline and the Last Plays* (Lincoln: University of Nebraska Press, 1962), p. 50; Patricia Parker, 'Romance and Empire: Anachronistic *Cymbeline*', in *Unfolded Tales: Essays on Renaissance Romance*, edited by George M. Logan and Gordon Teskey (Ithaca: Cornell University Press, 1989), pp. 189–207, p. 189; Douglas L. Peterson, *Time, Tide and Tempest: A Study of Shakespeare's Romances* (San Marino: The Huntington Library, 1973), pp. 120–21; Clifford Ronan, *'Antike Roman': Power Symbology and the Roman Play in Early Modern England, 1585–1635* (Athens: University of Georgia Press, 1995), p. 30; Kay Stanton, 'Paying Tribute: Shakespeare's *Cymbeline*, the "Woman's Part", and Italy', in *Il Mondo Italiano del Teatro Inglese del Rinascimento*, edited by Michele Marrapodi (Palermo: University of Palermo, 1996), pp. 65–79; and Joan Warchol Ross, '*Cymbeline*'s Debt to Holinshed: The Richness of III.i', in *Shakespeare's Romances Reconsidered*, edited by Carol McGinnis Kay and Henry E. Jacobs (Lincoln: University of Nebraska Press, 1978), pp. 104–12, p. 111.

63   On the switch in orientation to the East, see for instance Lisa Jardine, *Worldly Goods: A New History of the Renaissance* (Basingstoke: Macmillan, 1996).

in fact in Shakespeare's play the daughter of the Emperor of Russia, an important trading partner for England since the setting up of the Muscovy Company, as well as a competitor for some of the same goods: after Barents' charting of Svalbard in 1596, English and Russians seem both to have been involved in hunting and trapping expeditions there from the early 1600s, something which might be of interest in the light of recent speculation that the bear in *The Winter's Tale* was a polar bear.[64] Russia too thus reminds us of the new economic alignments which had challenged the traditional geographic orientations of the classical world, and Russia could, it seems, also be used to signal the antithesis and inversion of traditional Greek values, since in Sidney's *Arcadia* the name of King Basilius, under whose stewardship Arcadia is teetering on the brink of collapse, seems to have been inspired by either that of Ivan the Terrible himself[65] – when speaking of Richard Chancellor, William Warner terms the ruler whom he visited (i.e. Ivan the Terrible) 'Basilius' – or that of his father Vasily, as R. W. Maslen suggests.[66] Russia thus encodes the anti-pastoral, providing yet another ironic deflation of the traditional association of Sicily with the pastoral; moreover, the pointed conferral of the controversial title 'Emperor' rather than 'Duke' on the ruler of Russia[67] recognises the way in which the protocols of the old world order must perforce give place to the political and economic realities of the new. As Olaus Magnus observed, the Duke of Moscow's desire to be called '*Czar Ruski*, meaning the Caesar of Russia' was all part of a classicising project for the nation as a whole, by which the Russians modelled themselves on the Latins:

> The Latins and Rutulians, and, on the other side, the Etruscans and Trojans, persuaded themselves that, if Aeneas and Turnus, for whose sakes the war was undertaken, did not enter into single combat and test their fate to the uttermost by battling with each other, there was no way in which their quarrel could be settled. In a similar fashion the Russians steadfastly declare that, until the individuals concerned, or soldiers they have hired and paid for the purpose, have tested their ultimate fate by embarking on single combat, no sentence can be carried out at all.[68]

The Czar, then, has displaced Caesar.

---

64   See Teresa Grant, 'White Bears in *Mucedorus, The Winter's Tale*, and *Oberon, the Faery Prince*', *Notes and Queries* 48.3 (September 2001), pp. 311–13, and Barbara Ravelhofer, '"Beasts of Recreacion": Henslowe's White Bears', *English Literary Renaissance* 32.2 (2002), pp. 287–323.

65   Robert Ralston Cawley, 'Warner and the Voyagers', *Modern Philology* 20 (1922), pp. 113–47, p. 118.

66   R.W. Maslen, 'Sidneian Geographies', *Sidney Journal* 20.2 (2002), pp. 45–55, p. 46.

67   See Maslen, 'Sidneian Geographies', p. 50, on the importance of this. On the meaning of Russia in the play, see also R. W. Desai, '"What means Sicilia? He something seems unsettled": Sicily, Russia, and Bohemia in *The Winter's Tale*', *Comparative Drama* 30.3 (Fall, 1996), pp. 311–24, p. 315, and Palmer, 'Winter, tyranny and knowledge in *The Winter's Tale*'.

68   Olaus Magnus, *Description of the Northern Peoples* [1555], translated by Peter Fisher and Humphrey Higgens (London: The Hakluyt Society, 1996), 3 vols, vol. 2, pp. 533 and 707.

An even more poignant reminder of the passing of the classical comes in the fact that the Hermione of Greek legend was the daughter of Helen and Menelaus, a heritage at once splendid – since it associates her with the most famous of all Greek myths and makes her a granddaughter of Zeus – and hideously flawed, since it links her with the notorious family turmoil of the House of Atreus: she is the niece by blood of both Agamemnon, Menelaus' brother, and Clytemnestra, Helen's sister, and the cousin of the murdered Iphigenia and the matricidal Orestes. Hermione is thus someone famous primarily for having had famous parents rather than for any doings of her own (she is one of the few members of the House of Atreus after whom no play, either classical or Renaissance, is named), just as her namesake in the play defines herself as falling in between two generations – 'a great king's daughter, / The mother to a hopeful prince' (III.ii.38–9). The mythological Hermione is of the generation that followed the Trojan War, and which itself achieved nothing comparable, and our awareness of these resonances is sharply increased by the fact that others of the characters have names which point in the same direction. Autolycus was the grandfather of Odysseus, celebrated in the *Odyssey* as a trickster; together, he and Hermione thus represent the generations either side of that heroic one which fought the Trojan War.[69] Moreover, Polixenes could be seen as linked to the name of Polyxena, daughter of Priam and beloved of Achilles, and Polyxena in the *Iliad* is another character whose life was cut short without any significant achievement. (Priam also had a son named Polyxenes, whose death in battle is referred to in *Troilus and Cressida*.) Like Marcellus, all these are figures of loss. The classical world, in short, seems a spent force in comparison with the dynamic one of trade.

There are also other reminders in the play of the rôle of trade and of the new geographical orientations it had produced, most notably the shopping list given by Perdita to the Clown: 'Three pound of sugar, five pound of currants, rice – what will this sister of mine do with rice?' (IV.iii.37–9). Nor is this the end of Perdita's requirements; the Clown notes too that 'I must have saffron to colour the warden pies; mace; dates, none – that's out of my note; nutmegs, seven; a race or two of ginger, but that I may beg; four pound of prunes, and as many of raisins o'th'sun' (IV.iii.45–9). The vast majority of these ingredients speak clearly of exotic origins. Rice was used to make puddings, as is clearly evidenced by the 1604 receipt book of Elinor Fettiplace, but the fact that the Clown can be presented as not knowing this suggests the extent to which it was still a luxury item – and it may well be worthy of note that Elinor Fettiplace's recipes were directly associated with travel and exploration, since two of them were contributed by Sir Walter Ralegh, whose elder brother Carew was her uncle by marriage[70] (William and Michael Fettiplace were also among the 1607 Jamestown colonists). Indeed so closely are the items listed by the Clown identified as trade goods that some at least of them were included in the

---

69   Sir Arthur Quiller-Couch famously declared 'I challenge anyone to read the play through, seat himself at table, and write down what Autolycus does to further the plot' ('Shakespeare's Workmanship: *The Winter's Tale*', in *The Winter's Tale: Critical Essays*, edited by Maurice Hunt (New York: Garland, 1995), pp. 82–93, p. 89). Perhaps, though, it is his name that is the principal part of his contribution to the play.

70   See Hilary Spurling, *Elinor Fettiplace's Receipt Book* [1986] (Harmondsworth: Penguin, 1987), p. ix. For a 1604 recipe for rice pudding, see pp. 82–3.

various primers used to teach commercial arithmetic: Lisa Jardine quotes an instance from Venice where one of the sample sums was 'If 1 pound and ½ of saffron is worth 20 ducats and 1/3, what will 1 ounce and ¼ be worth?'.[71] In fact rice had to remain a commodity associated with exploration and the exotic, because its cultivation nearer home was discouraged, as R.E. Huke and E.H. Huke have noted:

> [M]edical geographers in the 16th century played an important role in limiting the adoption of rice as a major crop in the Mediterranean area. During the 16th and early 17th centuries, malaria was a major disease in southern Europe, and it was believed to be spread by the bad air (hence the origin of the name) or swampy areas. Major drainage projects were undertaken in southern Italy, and wetland rice cultivation was discouraged in some regions. In fact, it was absolutely forbidden on the outskirts of a number of large towns. Such measures were a significant barrier to the diffusion of rice in Europe.[72]

As a result of these fears, the cultivation of rice in the New World, where the natives were expendable, was actively encouraged: William Strachey declared himself confident that rice could be grown in Virginia.[73] Raisins too were an important commodity which, this time for climatic reasons, often came from the New World, particularly Mexico.

The Winter's Tale, therefore, is a play where the names of the characters may evoke the classical world, but where the details of their lives, even down to what they eat, insistently remind us of the ways in which the world has changed since the days of the classical past, and of the very different values which pertain as a result. Above all, it reminds us that we no longer live in a gift economy, but in one fundamentally conditioned and structured by the values and locations of the ever-expanding global market. When Shakespeare wrote it, he could not have known that Prince Henry, England's hopeful Virgilian prince, would soon be dead, or that a Virginian princess would shortly afterwards visit London. Nevertheless, the portrait of 'Matoaka als Rebecca, filia potentiss: princ: Powhatan Imp: Virginiae' [Matoaka otherwise Rebecca, daughter of the most potent prince Powhatan, emperor of Virginia] crystallises for us of some of the ways in which it was, in Shakespeare's England, possible for the princess to replace the prince, and the New World the Old, and also shows how potent an emblem for such an idea a Caesarian figure such as Marcellus could provide. In the next play to which I turn, *Antony and Cleopatra*, a fear of change will be even more visible and more disturbing, but this time the cause of the fear will, disturbingly, be closer to home.

---

71   Jardine, *Wordly Goods*, p. 322.

72   R.E. Huke and E.H. Huke, *Rice: Then and Now* (International Rice Research Institute, 1990), available online at http://www.riceweb.org/History.htm

73   Strachey, *A Voyage to Virginia in 1609*, p. 101.

Chapter Five

Cleopatra and the Myth of Scota

A play which very clearly reveals the dangerous and subversive uses to which representations of the Caesars could be put on the early modern stage, and the ways in which they can, thanks to the fact of the Roman invasion of Britain, bear directly on contemporary questions of Britishness, is Shakespeare's *Antony and Cleopatra*. Here, the usual view of the *translatio imperii* is crucially inflected by Shakespeare's apparent awareness of the very different accounts of national origin offered by early modern Scottish writers. The result is that reference to the Caesars and to the idea of descent from the classical world can be used to incriminate James VI and I by associating him with a surprising range of wildly undesirable identities – as a stranger, as an Irishman, and as a gypsy.

Shakespeare's Cleopatra has passed into legend for the variety and evocativeness of the descriptions applied to her by the other characters in the play, but it has been widely overlooked that the first term used of her is 'gypsy',[1] when Philo says,

> Nay, but this dotage of our general's
> O'erflows the measure. Those his goodly eyes,
> That o'er the files and musters of the war
> Have glowed like plated Mars, now bend, now turn
> The office and devotion of their view
> Upon a tawny front. His captain's heart,

---

1   An honourable exception to this is Charles Whitney, 'Charmian's Laughter: Women, Gypsies, and Festive Ambivalence in *Antony and Cleopatra*', *The Upstart Crow* 14 (1994), pp. 67–88. Apart from this, material on the gypsy connotations of the play is thin. A.C. Bradley does remark that 'Shakespeare, it seems clear, imagined Cleopatra as a gipsy', but only in order to suggest that when Antony at 4.x.38 calls her 'this grave charm' it is perhaps because 'her eyes may sometimes have had, like those of some gipsies, a mysterious gravity or solemnity which would exert a spell more potent than her gaiety' ('Shakespeare's *Antony and Cleopatra*' [1905], reprinted in *Antony and Cleopatra: A Selection of Critical Essays*, edited by John Russell Brown [Basingstoke: Macmillan, 1968], pp. 63–87, p. 86, n. 6). L.C. Knights refers in passing to Cleopatra's 'gipsy-like double-dealing' ('The Realism of *Antony and Cleopatra*', reprinted in *Antony and Cleopatra: A Selection of Critical Essays*, edited by John Russell Brown [Basingstoke: Macmillan, 1968], pp. 172–7, p. 175), and John Holloway suggests that '[a]s the play closes, the Cleopatra who chats with the countryman and dresses in her finery, becomes (one might put it) a gipsy in a new sense, and with a deeper meaning… only just behind the stage spectacle of the queen of Egypt in all her glory, is the sense of an outcast from society – gipsy, felon, whatever it may be – baited as the victim of the common people' ('The Action of *Antony and Cleopatra*' [1961], reprinted in *Antony and Cleopatra: A Selection of Critical Essays*, edited by John Russell Brown [Basingstoke: Macmillan, 1968], pp. 178–200, p. 198).

> Which in the scuffles of great fights hath burst
> The buckles on his breast, reneges all temper,
> And is become the bellows and the fan
> To cool a gypsy's lust.[2]

All the descriptive energy here is applied to Antony; Cleopatra is merely dismissed, summed up as a gypsy, as if it were a term that needed no glossing or expansion.

Later, Antony himself laments that

> The hearts
> That spanieled me at heels, to whom I gave
> Their wishes, do discandy, melt their sweets
> On blossoming Caesar; and this pine is barked
> That overtopped them all. Betrayed I am.
> O this false soul of Egypt! This grave charm,
> Whose eye becked forth my wars, and called them home,
> Whose bosom was my crownet, my chief end,
> Like a right gypsy hath at fast and loose
> Beguiled me to the very heart of loss.   (IV.xii.20–29)

As Charles Whitney points out,

> Fast and loose was a gypsy game first described as involving disappearing knots in a handkerchief, but in fact all of Antony's characterizations of Cleopatra between the final defeat in battle and the report of Cleopatra's suicide to him…could be said by one claiming to be the victim of an English gypsy.[3]

Equally suggestive of a gypsy identity for Cleopatra are Antony's 'The witch shall die' (IV.xii.47) and the way in which the soothsayer (accurately) predicts the future during the fortune-telling scene in I.ii, and one might, too, wonder whether Antony's apparent foreknowledge of Fulvia's death might also be gesturing towards the quasi-magical, fortune-telling atmosphere of the Egyptian court. Equally, Cleopatra seems to fear being turned virtually into an attraction at a fair, events with which gypsies were so closely associated, when she demands,

> Shall they hoist me up
> And show me to the shouting varletry
> Of censuring Rome?   (V.ii.55–7)

And towards the close of the play Cleopatra's steward reveals that she has kept back more than half her treasure and so has in effect done a gypsy switch (V.ii.165 ff).[4] Moreover, our sense of the play's setting in Egypt, the country which gave gypsies their name, is not a casual one but is repeatedly reinforced by the accumulation of

---

2   William Shakespeare, *Antony and Cleopatra*, edited by Emrys Jones (Harmondsworth: Penguin, 1977), I.i.1–10. All further quotations from the play will be taken from this edition and reference will be given in the text.

3   Whitney, 'Charmian's Laughter', p. 83.

4   There is no mention of gypsies in Mary Sidney's translation of Garnier's *Antonie*.

local colour and pertinent details, with the last scene actually set in the Renaissance idea of a pyramid, which is, as can be seen in mosaics in St Mark's in Venice and in illustrations from the *Hypnerotomachia Polyphili*, a tall building with shuttered windows.[5]

Public perception of gypsies and their meanings in the early seventeenth-century is, I want to argue, therefore crucial to Shakespeare's representations of his heroine. As early as 1547 Andrew Boorde in his *The Fyrst Boke of the Introduction of Knowledge* had attempted to describe gypsy culture and included samples of Romany. In particular, the idea that gypsies were in fact Egyptians was strongly developed in early modern England. In Ben Jonson's *The Gypsies Metamorphosed*, the Gypsies present themselves as descendants of Ptolemy and of a variety of women named Cleopatra: the Gypsy says of the five little children that he leads, 'Gaze vppon them as on the ofspringe of *Ptolomee*, begotten vppon seuerall *Cleopatra's* in theire seuerall Counties'.[6] The Acts passed against gypsies in 1544, 1554 and 1562 were all titled Egyptians Acts, and it seems suggestive in terms of *Antony and Cleopatra* that the first of these, the 1544 Egyptians Act, imposed a penalty of £40 for '"transporting, bringing or conveying" Egyptians intro the country' – and 'conveying' is exactly what is done to Cleopatra in the famous story of her being carried to Caesar rolled in a mattress, of which Enobarbus reminds us (II.6.70). Gypsies were 'said to be physiologically distinct by virtue of their tawny complexion, and it was commented that they wore "od and phantastique" clothes that were "contrary to other nacions"'.[7] Much was also made of their propensity for palmistry, thievery, and the gypsy switch.

Ideas associated with gypsies were also directly related to some of the most pressing concerns of Shakespeare's own culture. David Mayall points out that

> Concern about the consequences of disease, pestilence, crime and poverty was matched by the threat of sedition and the belief that Rome was sending Papal emissaries to England to provoke a Catholic revival. The link between these fears and itinerancy and nomadism were all too evident to contemporaries. Disease and pestilence were spread by nomadic carriers, various crimes were closely linked to an itinerant way of life, poverty and vagrancy were virtually synonymous, sedition was spread by the itinerant colporteurs, and agents of the Pope were suspected of finding a cloak for their subversion in the camps of travellers and Gypsies.[8]

---

5   Erik Iversen, *The Myth of Egypt and its Hieroglyphics in European Tradition* (Copenhagen: GEC Gad, 1961), Plates 1 a and b and XVI. See also Leslie Hotson, *Shakespeare's Sonnets Dated* (London: Rupert Hart-Davis, 1949), p. 22, for a number of examples of Renaissance texts using the term 'pyramids' to include 'obelisks' and other 'slim spires'.

6   Ben Jonson, *The Gypsies Metamorphosed*, in *Ben Jonson*, edited by C. H. Herford and Percy and Evelyn Simpson (Oxford: The Clarendon Press, 1950), Vol VII, p. 567. All further quotations from *The Gypsies Metamorphosed* will be taken from this edition and reference will be given in the text.

7   David Mayall, *Gypsy Identities 1500–2000: From Egipcyans and Moon-men to the Ethnic Romany* (London: Routledge, 2004), p. 68.

8   Mayall, *Gypsy Identities*, p. 60.

In fact, the Council of Trent had declared in 1563 that gypsies could not be priests, and in 1568 Pope Pius V declared them officially expelled from all the domains of the Catholic church; nevertheless, they were popularly associated with the fear of Catholicism. Moreover, second generation gypsies posed further problems of identity, since '[t]he fact of their English birth meant that they were entitled to certain rights under law which were not available to their "stranger" parents':[9] for instance, the 1562 Egyptians Act specified that gypsies born in England and Wales could remain if they left the company of other gypsies, while in 1596, 97 of the 106 men and women comdemned to death at York for being gypsies were spared after proving that they were born in England. And of course there is a tension implicit in the very terms used as alternative names for gypsies, 'Egyptians' and 'Romany', terms which, coincidentally or not, encapsulate the twin poles of *Antony and Cleopatra*, and thus align themselves with each of the sharply bifurcated national and ethnic identities on which it focuses. Gypsies, then, become a powerful emblem of some major uncertainties besetting personal, national, and religious identities in the period.

Moreover, although all this legislation stresses the foreignness of gypsies to English ethnicities and practices, other aspects of seventeenth-century thought about gypsies brought them eerily close to the self, especially in the light of the changing political situation. In England, national self-esteem was boosted by continued clinging to the myth that the kings of Britain were originally descended from Brutus, great-grandson of Aeneas, via King Arthur. Just across the border, in the homeland of England's new king, Scottish writers had attempted to counter the ideological force of the Anglo-Welsh Brutus / Trojan myth by promulgating the story of Scottish descent from Scota, daughter of Pharaoh, and her husband Gathelus, and as late as 1603 Andrew Melville mentioned this legend in his *A trewe description of the nobill race of the Stewards*.[10] For John of Fordun, as Roger A. Mason remarks, 'the progenitors of the Scottish race were a Greek prince named Gathelus (the Greeks did after all defeat the Trojans!) and the eponymous Scota, daughter of Pharaoh'.[11] So for Fordun the idea of Egyptian origins was not just a myth of origin but an encoding of hostility to the English: as William Matthews remarks, 'For several centuries the Scottish legend and the British one were mortal rivals'.[12] Gypsies are first recorded in Scotland in 1505, and are said to have made their way thence to England with letters of recommendation from both James IV and James V. Both these kings' belief in the Scota story certainly led them to be noticeably pro-gypsy, and gypsies had been allowed to live under their own laws in Scotland since 1540, though anti-gypsy laws were passed there in 1541, and in 1573 they were ordered to desist from a nomadic lifestyle or leave Scotland. The climate was slightly less favourable under

---

9   Mayall, *Gypsy Identities*, p. 71.

10   William Matthews, 'The Egyptians in Scotland: The Political History of a Myth', *Viator* 1 1970), pp. 289–306, p. 306.

11   Roger A. Mason, 'Scotching the Brut: Politics, History and National Myth in Sixteenth-Century Britain', in *Scotland and England 1286–1815*, edited by Roger A. Mason (Edinburgh: John Donald, 1987), pp. 60–84, p. 64.

12   Matthews, 'The Egyptians in Scotland: The Political History of a Myth', p. 290

James VI and I – indeed, Charles Whitney argues that 'both as King of Scotland and of England James put into practice sharp punishment, increasing suppression of gypsies as he did of vagabonds and witches',[13] but what Whitney's main source Macritchie actually says is that James VI began to clamp down on nomadism, but 'what was aimed at...was not the suppression and expulsion of Gypsies *as a race*, but as people living an idle and vagrant life'.[14] Even the hostile James VI and I seems, then, to have had some sense of the traditional kinship of Scots and gypsies, but clearly felt less comfortable about it than his predecessors had done.

Certainly the connection between Scottishness and gypsiness is still being openly made as late as *The Gypsies Metamorphosed*, where the Prologue spoken at Windsor included the lines

As many blessings as there be bones
In *Ptolomees* fingers, and all at ones,
Held vp in an *Andrews* Crosse for the nones,
    Light on you, good Master.   (VII, p. 566)

There are unmistakable signs in *Antony and Cleopatra* of an interest in Scotland, as when Cleopatra in her jealousy of Octavia orders 'Bid you Alexas / Bring me word how tall she is' (II.v.118–19), which has been identified as recalling Elizabeth's cross-questioning of the Scottish ambassador Melville over Mary, Queen of Scots, at the time when it was being tentatively suggested that the latter might marry Elizabeth's own favourite Leicester,[15] or as when Scarus announces that there is 'Room for six scotches more' (IV.vii.10). Maecenas' remark of Caesar, 'When such a spacious mirror's set before him, / He needs must see himself' (V.i.35–6), would in this sense seem to be applicable to James himself. Although a Victorian theatregoer was famously moved by the play to remark 'How very unlike the home life of our own dear queen', Shakespeare's original audience might well have been struck by points of correspondence as much as by differences.

To allude to the contemporary politics of England and Scotland in terms of Egypt and Rome had, as we have seen, a particular force. As we have seen, for Fordun, the idea of Egyptian origins was not just a myth of origin but an encoding of Scottish hostility to the English, and there was certainly opposition on both sides of the border to James's attempt to combine England and Scotland in one British Empire. One of the major strains in the forced merger of England and Scotland arose from the attempt to combine a legal system based on Roman law (as pertained in Scotland) with one which was not, and we are certainly not allowed to forget the strong connections of the individual Roman characters with their wider cultural heritage. Antony in particular openly advertises his continuity with the past when he apostrophises Hercules (IV.xii.43–4), and the fact that he retains the services of

---

13   Whitney, 'Charmian's Laughter', p. 81.

14   David Macritchie, *Scottish Gypsies Under the Stewarts* (Edinburgh: David Douglas, 1894), pp. 72–3. On the general tightening of anti-gypsy legislation under James VI and I, see also Dale B. J. Randall, *Jonson's Gypsies Unmasked: Background and Theme of* The Gypsies Metamorphos'd (Durham, N.C.: Duke University Press, 1975), p. 55.

15   See Elizabeth Jenkins, *Elizabeth the Great* (London: Panther, 1972), pp. 117–18.

his schoolmaster emblematises continuity with the classical culture from which he sprang. Indeed Antony could in many senses be seen as the ultimate embodiment of the Romanness on which the Scottish legal system had modelled itself.

For Antony, however, classical culture is barren and unproductive: Hercules leaves him (IV.iii.17–18); his schoolmaster cannot avail him; and 'The sevenfold shield of Ajax cannot keep / The battery from my heart' (IV.xiv.39–40). Notably, too, Antony turns to the classical past only when distressed, deluded, or under pressure. Falsely imagining that Cleopatra has betrayed him, he cries, 'The shirt of Nessus is upon me. Teach me, / Alcides, thou mine ancestor, thy rage' (IV.xii.43–4); but the rage of Hercules resulted only in the massacring of his innocent wife and children. Similarly Cleopatra cries,

> Help me, my women! O, he's more mad
> Than Telamon for his shield; the boar of Thessaly
> Was never so embossed.   (IV.xiii.1–3)

Here again, as in *Hamlet*, the classical past is associated with wanton destruction. Classicism, it seems, is a spent force – and classicism is what Scotland's system of Roman law was based on, and what the figure of James / Augustus embodies.

Cleopatra, by contrast, is associated strongly with the biblical, and so too is Antony when at his noblest and when closest to her values. While the presence of allusion to Christ's nativity in *Cymbeline* has often been recognised,[16] it has been much less remarked that *Antony and Cleopatra* shows equal signs of such an awareness.[17] There is, however, a host of suggestive allusions to the nativity story. Early in the play, Charmian beseeches the soothsayer, 'Good now, some excellent fortune! Let me be married to three kings in a forenoon and widow them all. Let me have a child at fifty, to whom Herod of Jewry may do homage' (I.ii.27–30). Antony recurs to motifs associated with the nativity when he excuses himself to Octavius Caesar by saying, 'Three kings I had newly feasted' (II.ii.80); Cleopatra pretends the fish she catches are Antony as if she were one of the fishers of men (II.v.10–15); and it is suggested that Cleopatra, like the Pharaoh of the Bible, might be stricken by leprosy (III.x.9–11). Other things also point firmly in the same direction, such as the constant references to trinities and triples, Antony's caution that Cleopatra will have to 'find out new heaven, new earth' (I.i.17), the parallel between Enobarbus and Judas, and Pompey's comment about Caesar getting money (II.i.13–14) (indeed

---

16   Robin Moffet, '*Cymbeline* and the Nativity', *Shakespeare Quarterly* 13 (1962), pp. 207–18, p. 215. See also Arthur Kirsch, *Shakespeare and the Experience of Love* (Cambridge: Cambridge University Press, 1981), p.163, Hugh M. Richmond, 'Shakespeare's Roman Trilogy: The Climax in *Cymbeline*', *Studies in the Literary Imagination* 5 (1972), pp. 129–39, and Alexander Leggatt, 'The Island of Miracles: An Approach to *Cymbeline*', *Shakespeare Survey* 10 (1977), pp. 191–209, p. 207, who calls the nativity something which the play 'cannot show'.

17   Though for a notable exception see Gilberto Sacerdoti, 'Three Kings, Herod of Jewry, and a Child: Apocalypse and Infinity of the World in *Antony and Cleopatra*', in *Italian Studies in Shakespeare and His Contemporaries*, edited by Michele Marrapodi and Giorgio Melchiori (Newark: University of Delaware Press, 1999), pp. 165–84.

the whole play could in one sense be seen as centring on giving unto Caesar the things that are Caesar's). There is also Antony's apparent recollection of the Psalms when he speaks of the hill of Basan (III.xiii.126–8), the parodic Last Supper on the night of Cleopatra's birthday, and Caesar's assurance that 'The time of universal peace is near' (IV.vi.5–7).[18] Moreover, Barbara C. Vincent points out that '[i]n IV.iv, Antony crosses the threshold into the serious comic realm of Christianity. This scene is repeatedly concerned with meaning…[Antony's] meaning is lost on his immediate, pre-Christian audience; only his off-stage audience can find meaning in these biblical *topoi*'.[19]

Shakespeare's emphasis on the synchronicity of classical and Christian stories in this play is not found in the other contemporary or near-contemporary treatments of the Cleopatra story by Samuel Daniel, Samuel Brandon or Mary Sidney. It does, however, tap pretty much directly into a difference pointed out by Paul Yachnin between James and Elizabeth:

> The propagandistic contexts of the two monarchs were opposed: James's was largely classical, Elizabeth's mostly biblical. In its own struggle between classical and biblical modes of expression, *Antony and Cleopatra* registers and critiques this competition between the politicized allusive fields associated with Elizabeth and James.[20]

Moreover, the play itself suggests that the Biblical is its preferred explanatory mode, definitively superseding the classical. John F. Danby suggests that its 'Egypt is the Egypt of the biblical glosses: exile from the spirit, thraldom to the flesh-pots, diminution of human kindness'.[21] The suggestion, therefore, is that the Biblical – the mode associated with Elizabeth and by extension England – is superior to the classical, the mode associated with Scotland and James, and, of course, above all with James's preferred avatar Augustus, the Octavius Caesar of this play.

The representation of both Antony and Cleopatra thus taps into highly charged contemporary debates about national identities and the protocols and psychological cost of the political merger between England and Scotland. Indeed one of the play's major concerns, how one country looks at another, may be imaged here as the cultural clash of Rome and Egypt, but is obviously susceptible of a more general application. Antony tells Lepidus,

> Thus do they, sir: they take the flow o'th'Nile
> By certain scales i'th'pyramid. They know
> By th'height, the lowness, or the mean if dearth

---

18 For comment on the Messianic resonances of this, see for instance Steve Sohmer, *Shakespeare's Mystery Play: The Opening of the Globe theatre, 1599* (Manchester: Manchester University Press, 1999), p. 122.

19 Barbara C. Vincent, 'Shakespeare's "Antony and Cleopatra" and the Rise of Comedy', in *Antony and Cleopatra*, edited by John Drakakis (Basingstoke: Macmillan, 1994), pp. 212–47, p. 234.

20 Paul Yachnin, '"Courtiers of Beauteous Freedom": *Antony and Cleopatra* in its Time', *Renaissance and Reformation* 15 (1991), pp. 1–20, p. 14.

21 John F. Danby, 'Antony and Cleopatra': A Shakespearean Adjustment', in *Antony and Cleopatra*, edited by John Drakakis (Basingstoke: Macmillan, 1994), pp. 33–55, p. 52.

> Or foison follow. The higher Nilus swells,
> The more it promises; as it ebbs, the seedsman
> Upon the slime and ooze scatters his grain,
> And shortly comes to harvest. (II.vii.17–23)

This taps into all the standard discourses of wonder and astonishment at the sight of new lands. But Lepidus is not a rewarding audience, venturing no comment more exciting than 'Nay, certainly, I have heard the Ptolemies' pyramises are very goodly things; without contradiction I have heard that' (II.vii.34–6). Already confident in his own prior hearsay knowledge, Lepidus is not to be educated or gainsaid by any mere personal experience. This is fortunate, though, because Antony's next response, to Lepidus' question about what a crocodile is like, would certainly not have afforded him any useful information on the subject:

> It is shaped, sir, like itself, and it is as broad as it has breadth. It is just so high as it is, and moves with it own organs. It lives by that which nourisheth it, and the elements once out of it, it transmigrates. (II.vii.42–5)

Antony's answer both exposes and disables the basic strategies of travel-writing, because it both refuses to explain one thing in terms of another and simultaneously reveals that that is how new things are normally described – not in terms of themselves but in terms borrowed from the observer's own culture. By implication, therefore, when we listen to Shakespeare telling us about Egypt, what we are actually learning about is his own society.

Shakespeare's Egyptian past, then, might well be seen as not so very different from his own present: as Cicely Palser Havely points out, 'Like Octavius, James Stuart had unified the "three-nooked" world of England, Wales and Scotland',[22] and H. Neville Davies argues that 'it is inconceivable that a dramatist late in 1606, the time when Shakespeare is usually supposed to have been writing or planning his play, could have failed to associate Caesar Augustus and the ruler whose propaganda was making just that connection' – that is, James VI and I.[23] That the story of *Antony and Cleopatra* was in fact always potentially applicable to England was indeed hinted at not only by the fact that Fulke Greville was so alarmed at the possibility that his own version of *Antony and Cleopatra* might be read in terms of the Elizabeth and Essex story that he destroyed it,[24] but also in Sir John Harington's translation of the *Orlando Furioso*, where, in a scene set in Egypt, we encounter a detail which points us straight at the heart of the Elizabethan court:

---

22 Cicely Palser Havely, 'Changing critical perspectives', in *Shakespeare: Texts and Contexts*, edited by Kiernan Ryan (Basingstoke: Macmillan, 2000), pp. 145–53, p. 148.

23 H. Neville Davies, 'Jacobean "Antony and Cleopatra"', in *Antony and Cleopatra*, edited by John Drakakis (Basingstoke: Macmillan, 1994), pp. 126–65, p. 128. He links the play particularly to the visit of James's brother-in-law King Christian of Denmark, who arrived in a ship called the *Tre Kroner*, meaning the Three Crowns.

24 On this well-known episode, see for instance F.J. Levy, 'Hayward, Daniel, and the Beginnings of Politic History in England', *Huntington Library Quarterly* (1987), pp. 1–34, p. 2.

Faire *Cloris* who flies out before the morne,
And sprinkleth aire with smell of fragrant flowres
That in her lovely lap about are borne,
From whence do fall the pleasant April showres;
But *Mercury*, sith she his love did scorne,
Lay with his net in wait not many houres
Till at the last by Nylus banks he caught her,
And there to daunce *la volta* then he taught her.[25]

The reference to the volta, Elizabeth's favourite dance, takes us close to the territory of the description of her by a Jesuit writer as 'the English Cleopatra' (with Ralegh, on this occasion, envisioned as her Antony).[26] And England comes close again to Egypt in the *Orlando Furioso* when we are told of Astolfo

And thus he parteth thence triumphing so,
And led the gyant prisner in a string,
And all about the countrie him doth show,
(A sight that to them all great joy did bring).
To *Memphis* Pyramids he then doth go,
Most famous for the tombe of many a King,
More hie in height then fiftie times Pauls steeple,
Then saw he Cayr so huge and full of people. (XV, 46)

It is also notable that in Spenser's *The Faerie Queene*, Egypt – or at least its fauna – is evoked again when, in Empson's memorable formulation, 'Britomart copulates with the crocodile and thus produces the English Monarchy'.[27]

Other animals mentioned in *Antony and Cleopatra* also point in the direction of Elizabeth's personal iconography: Jason Scott-Warren observes that in his poem 'Against Pius Quintus that excommunicated the Queene' Harington uses 'reference to the bulls of Bashan casting England as the elect nation and Elizabeth, once more, as David'.[28] And Ania Loomba points out that 'As the "precious queen" Cleopatra is deified into the goddess Isis, recalling the attempts to depict Elizabeth I as the Virgin Queen ...both Elizabeth and Cleopatra evoke specifically Renaissance fears of female government'. Indeed Paul Yachnin argues that

The proposed parallels between the Queen of Egypt and the Queen of England have become familiar to students of the play and have been widely accepted, if only because the claims made for their importance in the play have been so modest. The argument runs something

25   Robert McNulty, ed, *Ludovico Ariosto's Orlando Furioso, translated into English Heroical Verse by Sir John Harington* [1591] (Oxford: The Clarendon Press, 1972), XV, p. 43. All further quotations from the poem will be taken from this edition and reference will be given in the text.

26   Lacey, *Sir Walter Ralegh*, p. 54.

27   William Empson, 'Paradoxes in *The Faerie Queene* V and VI', in *The Strengths of Shakespeare's Shrew*, edited by John Haffenden (Sheffield: Sheffield Academic Publications, 1996), p. 112.

28   Jason Scott-Warren, *Sir John Harington and the Book as Gift* (Oxford: Oxford University Press, 2001), p. 143.

like this: details in the characterization of Cleopatra such as her militancy, her likening herself to a milk-maid (Elizabeth had done likewise in a speech before Parliament), her fiery temper, her fondness for travel in a river-barge, her wit, her immense charm, (all prominent aspects in contemporary accounts of Elizabeth) reveal a characteristically Elizabethan handling of classical source-material. It is as if Shakespeare had used what he knew about Elizabeth in order to work towards an understanding of Cleopatra.[29]

There are also similarities between *Antony and Cleopatra* and Marlowe's *Dido, Queen of Carthage*,[30] another play which can be seen as encoding an image of Elizabeth, since Dido's other name was Elissa. There was, too, the fact that on his deathbed in 1583 the Earl of Sussex referred to Elizabeth's first favourite Leicester as 'the Gipsey', while the way in which gypsies' ability to change their appearance led to their being called moon-men also offered parallels with the characteristic discourse of the Elizabethan court,[31] which fêted Elizabeth as Cynthia, goddess of the moon.

Yachnin suggests, however, that the claims made for the importance of the Elizabeth references in the play are modest. This is not always the case, nor need it be so. Drawing on the myth of Scota, I suggest, is a way of subtly incriminating James VI and I by associating him with a myth of origin which was doubly embarrassing and undesirable because it linked him not only with the disreputable and socially undesirable gypsies but also with the Irish. The major Scots myth of origin worked both to align Scotland and Ireland and to label Ireland as foreign, since according to this legend both Hibernia and Iberia were named after Hiber, son of Gathelus and Scota, founders of Scotland.[32] To be Irish was, for many in Renaissance England, to be a barbarian; to be cast as Irish is thus a particularly damaging form of Othering. James himself tried to 'Irish' others, such as the troublesome Graham and Armstrong families whom he banished to Ireland from the Scottish borders; but it was often suggested that there was in fact no difference between the Irish and the Scots. Spenser argued this in *A View of the Present State of Ireland*, where Eudoxus relates the Irish name Ferragh to Pharaoh,[33] and it is found too in William Warner's *Albions England*, which also stresses the common Egyptian elements in the ancestry of both:

Fower Dukes at once, in ciuil broyles, seiunctly after raine.
Neere when, the *Scottes* (who some accuse by Ante-Dates to gain)
Did settle in the Northerne Isles. These people bring their line
From *Cecrops* and that *Pharo*, he that euer did decline
From *Moses* seeking *Hebers* house from *AEgypt* to conuay.

---

29   Yachnin, '"Courtiers of Beauteous Freedom"', pp. 5 and 7. See also Helen Morris, 'Queen Elizabeth I "Shadowed" in Cleopatra', *Huntington Library Quarterly* 32 (1969), pp. 271–8, and Kenneth Muir, 'Elizabeth I, Jodelle, and Cleopatra', *Renaissance Drama* 2 (1969), pp. 197–206.

30   Janet Adelman, *The Common Liar: An Essay on* Antony and Cleopatra (New Haven: Yale University Press, 1973), pp. 177–83.

31   Randall, *Jonson's Gypsies Unmasked*, pp. 65 and 57.

32   Matthews, 'The Egyptians in Scotland: The Political History of a Myth', p. 291.

33   Edmund Spenser, *A View of the State of Ireland*, edited by Andrew Hadfield and Willy Maley (Oxford: Blackwell, 1997), pp. 45–6 and 33.

His daughter *Scota Gathelus* their Duke brought thence away,
When *Pharos* sinne to *Iacobs* seede did neere that Land decay.
And *Cecrops* son brought the[n] from thence (as *Scottes* inforce the same)
The stone that *Iacob* slept vpon, when Angels went and came:
Of it was made their fatall Chaire, of which they beare in hand,
That wheareesoere the same is found, the *Scottes* shal brooke the land:
At *Westminster* that Monument doth now, decaying, stand.
In *Lusitanea Gathelus* did first his kingdome found,
And of his race (of *Scota, Scottes*) when *Spanish Scottes* abound,
Ariue in *Ireland*, and in it a second Empire ground:
And thirdly, when their broodie Race that Isle did ouer-store,
Amongst the Islands *Hebredes* they seeke out dwellings more.
These *Irish*, sometime *Spanish Scots*, of whence our now-*Scottes* bee
Within the Isles of *Albion* thus, whilst *Brutaines* disagree,
Did seat themselves, & nestle too amongst the Mountaine groundes:
What time a *Scythian* people, *Pichtes*, did seaze the middle boundes
Twixt them and vs: & these did prooue to *Brutaine* double woundes.[34]

For Warner, then, the Scots are both Irish and Spanish, and their presence in the British Isles is a 'wound'. Moreover, the linkage is seen as distinctly sinister. In the first place, it lays the Scots open to a charge of cannibalism. This was not an uncommon *canard*: in William Strachey's *The Historie of Travell into Virginia Britania*, for instance, we are assured that if the Romans had not invaded the British might still 'be eating our owne Children, as did the Scots in those dayes', and Strachey cites St Jerome on the Scots: 'when they found in the forrests Heards of Swyne, Beasts, and Cattell, they would cut off the buttocks of the Boies which kept them, and also the womens Paps, and tooke that to be the most deyntie and delicate meate'.[35] In Warner's hands, however, the supposedly cannibalistic propensities of the early Scots are directly linked to their Irishness:

The *Pichts* were fierce and *Scythian*-like: much like the *Irish* now
The *Scots* were then: couragious both: Nor them I disallowe
That write they fed on humane flesh, for so it may be well.   (ll. 62–4)

In the second place, the Scots-Irish linkage seems to be part of a distinctly irreverent overall project on Warner's part, glimpsed most clearly when he says of the deaths of Ferrex and Porrex

And thus from noble *Brute* his line the scepter then did passe:
When of his bloud for to succeede no heire suruiuing was.   (ll. 30–31)

To contest the continuity of the *translatio imperii* in this manner by blithely declaring that the entire progeny of Brutus was eradicated wreaks a devastating blow to the pretensions of all subsequent 'British' kings. The idea that the line of descent from Brutus had been wholly broken is not a totally unique view – it is for instance also

---

34   William Warner, *Albions England* (1602), Book III, chapter XV, ll. 32–53.
35   William Strachey, *The Historie of Travell into Virginia Britania* (1612), edited by Louis B. Wright and Virginia Freund (London: The Hakluyt Society, 1953), pp. 24–5.

found in Thomas Hughes's *The Misfortunes of Arthur*, where we read that 'There lay the hope and braunch of Brute supprest',[36] and it is also the view implied at the end of *Gorboduc*. It was, however, a minority one – compare for instance Thomas Nashe's 'In some places of the world there is no shadow of the sun: *Diebus illis* if it had been so in England, the generation of Brute had died all and some'[37] – and also a risky one to express because of its inevitably anti-establishment overtones, as indeed Elizabeth I's reported displeasure at *Gorboduc* made plain. As Richard Harvey reminds us in the closing paragraph of *Philadelphvs*, 'It is a dangerous position to refuse the offspring of *Brute*'.[38]

The availability of a Scots-Irish link was further inflected by the fact that '[i]n terms of their nomadic lifestyle, there was little to distinguish the Gypsies from the Irish, with both travelling the country in groups'.[39] The connection made between the two groups was by no means an accidental one: Arthur L. Little points out that '[i]n many early modern English texts blackness seeps into Ireland through discursive trickery. And on occasion Irishness makes its way, suspiciously, into early modern English texts on Africa, sometimes to the depreciation of the former'. Little argues that in *Antony and Cleopatra* 'Ireland provides a semiotics for reading Antony's lost Roman self and provides the reason why Egyptianness, like Irishness, must be sacrificed, cut off from Rome (or England) in the pursuit of an already known national and imperial character'.[40] Indeed the connection between Egypt and Ireland was even made by Elizabeth I herself, since she wrote to the 1st Earl of Essex in Ireland 'urging him "not to fester reproachfully in the delights of the English Egypt, where many take greatest delights in holding their noses over the beef pots"'.[41]

Shakespeare too suggests a parallel between the world of his play and 'the English Egypt', and indeed might even be seen as taking a cue from Warner, but he does not make quite the use that might have been expected of it. One of the frequent accusations against the Irish was that of eating 'uncivilly', of being the 'raw' element to England's cooked in a proto-anthropological polarity.[42] In Shakespeare's play, the idea of uncivil eating is foregrounded, but it is associated not with the Egyptian characters but with the 'civilised' Romans. It is Octavius himself, the future Augustus

---

36   Thomas Hughes, *The Misfortunes of Arthur* (London, 1587), IV.ii.232. For others who took this view, see John E. Curran, Jr, *Roman Invasions: The British History, Protestant Anti-Romanism, and the Historical Imagination in England, 1530–1660* (Newark: University of Delaware Press, 2002), pp. 137–8.

37   Thomas Nashe, *The Unfortunate Traveller and Other Works*, edited by J. B. Steane. (Harmondsworth: Penguin, 1972), p. 276.

38   Richard Harvey, *Philadelphvs, or A Defence of Brutes, and the Brutans History* (London: John Wolfe, 1593), p. 107.

39   Mayall, *Gypsy Identities*, p. 72.

40   Arthur L. Little, Jr., *Shakespeare Jungle Fever: National-Imperial Re-Visions of Race, Rape, and Sacrifice* (Stanford: Stanford University Press, 2000), pp. 124 and 125.

41   Sylvia Freedman, *Poor Penelope: Lady Penelope Rich, An Elizabethan Woman* (Bourne End: The Kensal Press, 1983), p. 18.

42   See Andrew Hadfield, '"The naked and the dead": Elizabethan perceptions of Ireland', in *Travel and Drama in Shakespeare's Time*, edited by Jean-Pierre Maquerlot and Michèle Willems (Cambridge: Cambridge University Press, 1996), pp. 32–54, p. 35.

Caesar, who advocates an eating régime which comes very close to the alleged practices of the Irish:

> Antony,
> Leave thy lascivious wassails. When thou once
> Was beaten from Modena, where thou slew'st
> Hirtius and Pansa, consuls, at thy heel
> Did famine follow, whom thou fought'st against,
> Though daintily brought up, with patience more
> Than savages could suffer. Thou didst drink
> The stale of horses and the gilded puddle
> Which beasts would cough at. Thy palate then did deign
> The roughest berry on the rudest hedge.
> Yea, like the stag when snow the pasture sheets,
> The barks of trees thou browsed'st. On the Alps
> It is reported thou didst eat strange flesh,
> Which some did die to look on. And all this -
> It wounds thine honour that I speak it now -
> Was borne so like a soldier that thy cheek
> So much as lanked not. (I.iv.55–71)

Another common accusation against the Irish was that of making undue noise at funerals and of fetishising death. Again, it is Octavius who focuses on and is associated by others with death rather than life. Thidias chillingly tells Cleopatra,

> it would warm his spirits
> To hear from me you had left Antony,
> And put yourself under his shroud,
> The universal landlord. (III.xiii.69–72)

And Octavius' own final statement is,

> She shall be buried by her Antony.
> No grave upon the earth shall clip in it
> A pair so famous. (V.ii.356–8)

There may just conceivably be an ironic reflection here on the fact that James I's own major cultural activity in these years involved tomb-making, since he commissioned the monuments of both his predecessor Elizabeth I and his mother Mary, Queen of Scots.

Given the uninspiring nature of the activities with which Octavius is thus associated, it is little wonder that Cleopatra should declare ''Tis paltry to be Caesar' (V.ii.2); but it is also, clearly, Irish. This is surprising because it ought logically to be the Egyptian Cleopatra rather than the Roman Octavia who is aligned with the Egypto-Scoto-Irish; but Shakespeare has no interest in incriminating Cleopatra. He may laugh at her, but he also lavishes attention on establishing her fascination and affords her the dignity of a death in which she out-Romans the Romans. Above all, he associates her with Elizabeth, and then uses that association to castigate Octavius – and by implication James VI and I who so closely identified himself with

Octavius – as a highly suspect Other, a Scot who is by implication Irish, and gypsy, and foreign. In the next play to which I turn, *Cymbeline*, Shakespeare continues to deploy images of the Caesars, and of Augustus in particular, in the service of this anti-James project, but this time Wales too is called into play.

Chapter Six

The Romans in Wales:
Cymbeline

Shakespeare's last Roman play, *Cymbeline*, returns to the figure of Augustus, but this time Shakespeare takes us to Wales – though he does not, as we shall see forget Scotland – and once again, he uses a narrative which evokes a Caesar to criticise the Stuarts. As Robert S. Miola has pointed out, the Romanness of *Cymbeline* has been often overlooked, but is an important element of the play:

> Because *Cymbeline* little resembles its somber, tragic predecessors and because most of the action takes place in Britain, it has attracted little attention as Shakespeare's last Roman play. Yet Rome is a major locality in the play and opposes Britain.

(Miola also points out that 'the wager strongly resembles the contest recalled in the Argument of *Lucrece*'.)[1] Moreover, as Patrick Cheney observes, 'In *Titus Andronicus* near the beginning of his career (as in *Cymbeline* toward the end), Ovid's most famous book, *The Metamorphoses* features as a stage property',[2] so in both these respects, as well as by its allusions to Augustus, *Cymbeline* takes pains to stress its Romanness. The Welshness of *Cymbeline* has been only slightly less neglected than its status as Roman play; to consider these two aspects together is, however, highly illuminating.

To some extent, Wales is seen as alien in the early modern period, a country which, while legally assimilated to England, was nevertheless not fully part of it. Wales may be both less separate from and more friendly to England than its dangerous neighbour Ireland, but it is also seen, like Ireland, as dangerously vulnerable and penetrable. As Shakespeare's *Richard III* reminded people, in 1485 Henry Tudor had led a successful invasion of England after landing at Milford Haven (this was something repeatedly recurred to in the celebrations surrounding the accession of Henry's great-great-grandson James VI and I), and although this was understood in English historiography as an entirely fortunate event, its meanings were eerily inverted when in 1603 Guy Fawkes travelled to Spain to try to persuade Philip to land at Milford Haven. The Haven is also represented as a point of vulnerability in

---

1   Robert S. Miola, '*Cymbeline*: Shakespeare's Valediction to Rome', in *Roman Images*, edited by Annabel Patterson (Baltimore: The Johns Hopkins University Press, 1984), pp. 51–62, pp. 51 and 52. See also Hugh M. Richmond, 'Shakespeare's Roman Trilogy: The Climax in *Cymbeline*', *Studies in the Literary Imagination* 5 (1972), pp. 129–39.

2   Patrick Cheney, 'Biographical Representations: Marlowe's Life of the Author', in *Shakespeare, Marlowe, Jonson: New Directions in Biography*, edited by Takashi Kozuka and J. R. Mulryne (Aldershot: Ashgate, 2006), pp. 183–204, p. 192.

Peele's *Edward I*.[3] *Cymbeline* acknowledges this alterity by representing its Wales as markedly more rural and more dangerous than its England, yet also as part of it. When Innogen travels to Wales, she finds a pathless wilderness, and people who live in caves. However, these apparent troglodytes prove to be noble, unspoiled, and generous, and are finally revealed as her own kin. John Kerrigan points out that 'The positive qualities of ancient Britain were associated with Wales';[4] in *Cymbeline*, Wales paradoxically marks both the margin and the centre of what Britain needs to be, in that it is the place where the true nature of the Roman tradition can best be discerned. Though Augustus may be hostile to Wales at the moment, he knighted its overlord, and ultimately, the virtues for which he ought to stand prove to be found more readily amongst the inhabitants of Wales than amongst his own men. Most notably, he is forced to accept defeat at Cymbeline's hands, and when Cymbeline agrees to come to terms, he may well appear more Augustan than Augustus himself.

Although not often thought of as an important location for the Romans, Wales was famously well provided with Roman sites – Caerleon, Carmarthen and Caernarfon, with their associations with Merlin and Constantine respectively, being some of the most notable – and was supposed to be the location of one of the two great roads of 'Trojan' Britain: according to Geoffrey of Monmouth, Belinus ordered the construction of two roads of stone and mortar, one from Cornwall to Caithness and one from St Davids to Southampton.[5] Wales was also the place where the descendants of Brutus, in the shape of the Tudors, had supposedly lived on. Wales in *Cymbeline* thus proves to be the truest *locus* of Romanitas, and one to which, Shakespeare seems to be suggesting, we should still be looking for what was best in the Roman ethos.

At the same time, though, he never loses sight of its peripheral position. Evidence of Wales's marginality in the Renaissance is to be found in the titles of William Camden's *Britain, or a Chorographicall Description of the Most Flourishing Kingdomes, England, Scotland, and Ireland* and Raphael Holinshed's *Chronicles of England, Scotlande and Irelande*, from both of which Wales is entirely excluded. This feeling that Wales is somewhere not fully known in the sense that England, Scotland and even Ireland may be is echoed in *Cymbeline* when Cloten says that 'I am near to th'place where they should meet, if Pisanio have mapped it truly',[6] since this so clearly recalls the difficulties and uncertainties which were indeed attendant on the mapping of Wales. As John Kerrigan points out,

---

3   For discussion of this, see Ronald J. Boling, 'Anglo-Welsh Relations in *Cymbeline*', *Shakespeare Quarterly* 51.1 (Spring 2000), pp. 33–66, p. 48. On the vulnerability of Milford Haven and on other invasions of it, see also Terence Hawkes, *Shakespeare in the Present* (London: Routledge, 2002), p. 50.

4   John Kerrigan, 'The Romans in Britain, 1603–1614', in *The Accession of James I: Historical and Cultural Consequences*, edited by Glenn Burgess, Rowland Wymer and Jason Lawrence (Basingstoke: Palgrave, 2006), pp. 113–39, p. 114.

5   Geoffrey of Monmouth, *The History of the Kings of Britain*, translated by Lewis Thorpe (Harmondsworth: Penguin, 1966), p. 93.

6   William Shakespeare, *Cymbeline*, edited by Roger Warren (Oxford: Oxford University Press, 1998), IV.i.1–2. All further quotations from the play will be taken from this edition and reference will be given in the text.

the borders of Wales and the Marches, already redrawn in 1536–1543, remained an issue, and it is no accident that the Jacobean plays about the Romans in Britain coincide with the Four Shire Controversy of 1604–1614, during which border magnates and gentry tried to secure the same exemption from control by the Council in the Marches as had been granted to Cheshire and Bristol in the 1560s.[7]

Moreover, both the country's external and internal boundaries were in any case understood as inherently unstable, as Philip Schwyzer argues:

> The supplement to Ortelius's *Theatrum Orbis Terrarum* published in 1573 included a map drawn by the Welsh physician, philologist and antiquarian Humphrey Lhuyd. Here Wales, or Cambria, is divided into its three traditional regions, Gwynedd, Deheubarth and Powys – none of which had possessed a political existence for several centuries – and the eastern border of Powys is the river Severn.[8]

Distances were also problematic. Norden's 1625 *England. An Intended Gvyde for English Travailers* writes of distances within Wales that

> It is to be considered that by reason of the multitude of Hilles, Mountaines and Dales, and the bending of the Sea, betweene *St. Dauids* and the point neere *Bradsey* [sic] Iland, causing passages and highwayes in many places to curue and crooke, that the distances betweene the Townes, may be something differing from this Table: But not so, but that good vse may be made of it.[9]

Such difficulties in the precise reckoning of distance are echoed when the delirious Innogen asks,

> Yes sir, to Milford Haven, which is the way?
> I thank you; by yon bush? Pray how far thither?
> 'Od's pitikins, can it be six mile yet? (IV.ii.292–4)

Pembrokeshire was particularly problematic to map, not least in the famous incident where its representation on a larger scale than other Welsh counties had led to a doubling of its taxation burden. Unsurprisingly, strenuous attempts were made to compensate for this, leading to still further fluctuations in the county's apparent size: as Ronald Boling points out, 'If Saxton's map enlarges Pembrokeshire as a bulwark against Ireland, [George] Owen's map shrinks it to reduce the military levy for which he is responsible'.[10]

The versatile George Owen of Henllys is a particularly interesting figure to consider in connection with *Cymbeline* for a number of reasons. Firstly, he was an antiquarian whose son married the step-granddaughter of Thomas Phaer, translator

---

7   Kerrigan, 'The Romans in Britain, 1603–1614', p. 115.

8   Philip Schwyzer, 'A Map of Greater Cambria', *Early Modern Literary Studies* 4.2 (September, 1998). Online: http://extra.shu.ac.uk/emls/04-2/schwamap.htm

9   Garrett A. Sullivan, Jr, 'Civilizing Wales: *Cymbeline*, Roads and the Landscapes of Early Modern Britain', *Early Modern Literary Studies* 4.2 (September, 1998). Online: http://extra.shu.ac.uk/emls/04-2/sullshak.htm

10   Boling, 'Anglo-Welsh Relations in *Cymbeline*', p. 41.

of the *Aeneid*, and who was himself the patron of the translator of Gerald of Wales, both projects being part of a collective mid-sixteenth-century Welsh push to rebuff the Brutus-sceptic Polydore Vergil; most importantly, however, it was Owen who, writing on St David's Day, 1608, defended the title of 'Prince of Wales' as part of a drive to encourage James to create Henry Prince of Wales, as did eventually occur in 1610.[11] As John Kerrigan observes, 'It is often said that *Cymbeline* was written to celebrate the investiture in 1610 of Prince Henry, as Prince of Wales (or, more correctly – and the difference was symptomatic – Prince of Wales and of Britain)', the distinction arising from the fact that

> From about 1607 the rights and honours attached to Wales became topics of interest in Henry's circle. Prompted by George Owen of Henllys, the Pembrokeshire historian who argued that the principality had not been abolished under the Acts of Union, the case was made that Wales was uniquely attached to the crown and could be separately governed.[12]

Philip Schwyzer has recently suggested that Shakespeare can be seen as tapping into this debate about the possibility of separate government for England, Scotland and Wales, albeit in *King Lear* rather than *Cymbeline*:

> According to Harry's 1604 *Genealogy*, 'Ragan' and Henwyn, Duke of Cornwall, were James Stuart's direct ancestors. Indeed, their union was of more than average significance, for it was through them that the bloodlines of Locrine, first king of England, and Camber, first ruler of Wales, were reunited. It is not only James's descent from Brutus but the presumption that England and Wales should have a common ruler that is called into question by the untimely deaths of Cornwall and Regan.[13]

I want to suggest that *Cymbeline*, in which the true prince of Britain emerges from Wales, can be seen as part of the same propaganda drive, which aimed simultaneously to aggrandise the popular prince and to elevate the status of Wales – but that it also, in doing so, raises some difficult questions about the nature and terms of Stuart rule as a whole, not least in the way that it marginalises and renders fallible Augustus, James's own preferred persona, and suggests that Augustus is strangely separable from true *Romanitas* rather, as he should, incarnating it.

Despite its unmapped and peripheral status, Wales was also of central importance to early modern England's understanding of itself because of the crucial rôle of Wales in the story of the *translatio imperii*. As a result, Wales is often much lauded. Certainly in Richard Harvey's *Philadelphvs, or A Defence of Brutes, and the Brutans History*, Wales comes in for special praise – 'who can tell the genealogies of *Camber*? how happy is hee in his dwelling places, which no man taketh from him? His loynes are like a springing well: he runneth within his bankes, and is not stopped: surely his Riuer is one of Gods Riuers: his hils are the mountaines of

---

11 B.G. Charles, *George Owen of Henllys: A Welsh Elizabethan* (Aberystwyth: National Library of Wales Press, 1973), pp. 29, 60, and 116.

12 Kerrigan, 'The Romans in Britain, 1603–1614', p. 116.

13 Philip Schwyzer, 'The Jacobean Union Controversy and *King Lear*', in *The Accession of James I: Historical and Cultural Consequences*, edited by Glenn Burgess, Rowland Wymer and Jason Lawrence (Basingstoke: Palgrave, 2006), pp. 34–47, pp. 40–41.

Safety'. Equally, glorification of Wales can clearly be seen as lying behind R. A.'s
The Valiant Welshman, and since this play features Guiderius, it relates closely to
Cymbeline. Above all, Wales is seen as the place where the line of Brutus survives,
and this is certainly stressed in *Cymbeline*, as the very name of Innogen – the wife of
Brutus – signals so unmistakably. As Huw Griffiths observes, Innogen 'can be read
as a personification of the idea of "Britain"'; like the line of Brute, she seems to die
out in Wales but is in fact resurrected there.

It is true that the idea of the *translatio imperii* is very ironically treated in
Cymbeline. The First Gentleman says of Posthumus that

I cannot delve him to the root. His father
Was called Sicilius, who did join his honour
Against the Romans with Cassibelan
But had his titles by Tenantius, whom
He served with glory and admired success,
So gained the sur-addition 'Leonatus';
And had, besides this gentleman in question,
Two other sons who in the wars o'th'time
Died with their swords in hand; for which their father,
Then old and fond of issue, took such sorrow
That he quit being, and his gentle lady,
Big of this gentleman, our theme, deceased
As he was born. The King he takes the babe
To his protection, calls him Posthumus Leonatus. (I.i.28–41)

The whole *translatio* myth is fundamentally dependent on the tracing of descent,
from Brutus back to Silvius to Ascanius and thence to Aeneas; yet the First Gentleman
says of Posthumus, who is later explicitly identified as an Aeneas figure, that 'I
cannot delve him to the root'. He is confident about Posthumus' father (though even
there the direct link may well seem less secure than usual because of Posthumus'
posthumous birth), but not only has that father changed the name by which he
was initially known, he has not transmitted his doing so directly – it was, the First
Gentleman says, the king who named Posthumus 'Leonatus', clearly implying that
he was not already called that even though his father had been. There is also the
question of the two elder sons, who seem to have been introduced to the narrative
for no visible purpose other than effectively to emblematise the idea of dynastic
red herrings (or to give the whole thing the feel of fairy tale rather than history by
making Posthumus the youngest son of three). The genealogical situation is further
complicated by the fact that when the direct line of Brutus died out with Ferrex
and Porrex, the person through whom it was ultimately transmitted was actually
called Cloto, or in some versions, Cloten: Richard Harvey makes this very clear,
stressing the crucial rôle of Cloto, Duke of Cornwall, Brutus' nephew, as the man
who 'began the second family of the *Brutan* kings, and begat *Mulmucie*',[14] from
whom Cymbeline proudly claims descent (3.i.54) while in Geoffrey of Monmouth
Dunvallo Molmutius, the son of Cloten King of Cornwall, takes up the kingship

---

14 Harvey, *Philadelphvs*, p. 34.

after the death of Ferrex and Porrex.[15] In a play which gives the name of Cloten to its villain, then, the Brutus story can never be simple.

Even more ironic is Belarius' reference to

> This Polydore,
> The heir of Cymbeline and Britain, who
> The King his father called Guiderius.   (III.iii.86–8)

As John E. Curran has pointed out, the world of *Cymbeline* represents Britain at a time which sophisticated Renaissance historiography, discarding the authority of Geoffrey of Monmouth, was increasingly insisting was crude and primitive, when to be British was essentially to be brutish, with no indigenous history or traditions worthy the name. This idea is powerfully encapsulated in the play in the name of Polydore, since Polydore Vergil was Geoffrey's first serious critic.[16] (Moreover, since Polydore Vergil himself was of Italian origin with a name that recalls Roman antecedents, this would thus add another layer of irony to the play's strongly developed debate about Italian origins and the interpenetration of Rome and Italy, to which I shall return below.)[17] Curran concludes that 'I take it as a general tendency in *Cymbeline* for Shakespeare to be fairly immune to the spell of Geoffrey and actually to advocate moving on from him', since

> the play calls attention to the Brute myth but then urges us to abandon it. By naming his heroine Imogen after Innogen, the wife of Brutus, and his hero Posthumus, after Aeneas's son, Shakespeare forces the issue of the Brute myth...But once we have called the Brute myth to mind, we see how Shakespeare plays upon it and reveals its complications and absurdities.[18]

Garrett A. Sullivan goes further still to argue that 'the play is deeply invested in repudiating ancient British culture'.[19] To offer Polydore and Guiderius as effectively interchangeable names for the same person does indeed seem to reduce the entire controversy over the Brutus story to a non-event. Equally provocative is the fact that

---

15   Geoffrey of Monmouth, *The History of the Kings of Britain*, p. 88.

16   For details of Vergil's arguments and their contemporary reception, see Richard Koebner, '"The imperial crown of this realm": Henry VIII, Constantine the Great, and Polydore Vergil', *Bulletin of the Institute of Historical Research* 26 (1953), pp. 29–52.

17   See John E. Curran, 'Royalty Unlearned, Honor Untaught: British Savages and Historiographical Change in *Cymbeline*', *Comparative Drama* 31:2 (summer, 1997), pp. 277–303, p. 286. Curran suggests that there are also other names in the play 'denoting the fall of Galfridian mythology' (p. 287), before arguing that 'the plot of the two lovers is designed to teach us how to be readers' (p. 299). On the topicality of such references to the pre-Roman past, see also Leah Marcus, *Puzzling Shakespeare: Local Reading and its Discontents* (Berkeley: University of California Press, 1988), p. 126. Marcus also comments on the problems attendant on reading in the play (p. 140).

18   John E. Curran, Jr, *Roman Invasions: The British History, Protestant Anti-Romanism, and the Historical Imagination in England, 1530–1660* (Cranbury, N.J.: Associated University Presses, 2002), pp. 71 and 116.

19   Sullivan, 'Civilizing Wales'.

Arviragus' identity is vouched for by Belarius' possession of the mantle in which he was wrapped, though it is not actually produced, and Guiderius' by the presence of a mole on his neck (V.iv.360–66) – hardly secure proofs on which to base the succession to the crown, let alone to lay claim to the whole panoply of the *translatio imperii*.

Even if we were to accept the Brutus myth, moreover, that story has internal contradictions, and *Cymbeline* calls attention to these. It is particularly notable that Innogen should say that

> True honest men being heard like false Aeneas
> Were in his time thought false, and Sinon's weeping
> Did scandal many a holy tear, took pity
> From most true wretchedness. So thou, Posthumus,
> Wilt lay the leaven on all proper men.   (III.iv.58–62)

Patricia Parker suggests that we should follow Imogen's lead in seeing Posthumus as a version of Aeneas,[20] whose great-grandson Brutus was the mythical founder of Britain, and Nancy R. Lindheim argues that III.iii begins 'with a clear reference to the *Aeneid*, to Evander's "aude, hospes" speech'.[21] Here, though, we may be deliberately meant to remember that there is more than one tradition about Aeneas, and that he has been so often represented that we cannot be sure what is true or false about him.[22] As Dido says to Aeneas in Marlowe's *Dido, Queen of Carthage*,

> May I entreat thee to discourse at large,
> And truly too, how Troy was overcome?
> For many tales go of that city's fall,
> And scarcely do agree upon one point.
> Some say Antenor did betray the town,
> Others report 'twas Sinon's perjury;
> But all in this, that Troy is overcome,
> And Priam dead. Yet how, we hear no news.[23]

Most notably, in one of those alternative traditions Aeneas was the treacherous betrayer of Troy rather than just a simple escapee from it, so that descent from him would be a matter of shame rather than of honour. In William Alexander's 1607 play *Jvlivs Caesar*, for instance, Juno, describing the aftermath of the fall of Troy, tells how

---

20   Parker, 'Romance and Empire', pp. 190–91.

21   Nancy R. Lindheim, '*King Lear* as Pastoral Tragedy', in *Some Facets of King Lear: Essays in Prismatic Criticism*, edited by Rosalie L. Colie and F.T. Flahiff (London: Heinemann, 1974), pp. 169–84, p. 176.

22   See for instance the extensive discussion in Heather James, *Shakespeare's Troy: Drama, Politics, and the Translation of Empire* (Cambridge: Cambridge University Press, 1997).

23   Christopher Marlowe, *Dido, Queen of Carthage*, in *Christopher Marlowe: The Complete Plays*, edited by Mark Thornton Burnett (London: Everyman, 1999), II.i.106–13.

And yet two traitors who betrayd the rest
O! that the heaven on treason sometime smiles!

Though having worst deserv'd, did chance the best,
More happy th[a]n at home in their exiles.[24]

The two traitors to whom she refers prove to be Antenor and Aeneas, and Juno goes on to say that

Then false *AEneas*, though but borne t'obey,
Did (of a fugitive) become a King:
And some of his neere Tibers streames that stay,
Would all the world to their obedience bring.
Their ravenous Eagles soaring o're all lands,
By violence a mighty prey have wonne.   (I.125–9)

Alexander's play, dating from only a year or two before *Cymbeline*, thus unequivocally presents Aeneas as villain rather than hero.

However, some of the details of the *translatio imperii* story are in fact validated in *Cymbeline*. In the 'Epitomie of the Whole History of England' first found in the 1602 edition of his *Albions England*, William Warner writes,

Returne we now to *Cassiuilan*, yeelding hence, as is aforesaide, Tribute to the *Romaines*. To him succeeded in Raigne his Nephewe *Theomant*, to him *Cymbeline* his sonne: in whose raigne *Calphurnius Agricola* being then heere for the *Romaines*, was borne our Sauiour Christ Iesus: after the ariuall of *Brute* 1107 yeares.

From *Cymbeline* was *Lucius* the fift King. This *Lucius*...was the first of the *Brittish* Kings that by publique Auctoritie intertained the Christian Faith: and was, with his, Baptized about the yeere of our Lord God 188.[25]

Cymbeline chimes exactly with this, having Cloten declare that 'We have yet many among us can grip as hard as Cassibelan' (III.i.39–40) (and also threaten Arviragus that he will 'on the gates of Lud's town set your heads' [IV.ii.101]), and pointedly giving the name of Lucius to its Roman general.[26] And when the First Captain remarks that ''Tis thought the old man and his sons were angels' (V.iii.85), early British history, albeit of a later period than the Romans, is perhaps evoked again, for we may well recall the anecdote of the Pope who confused Angli with Angeli.[27]

Despite the apparent scepticism about the legitimacy of its claim to be the true home of the nobility and cultural authority validated by the *translatio imperii*,

---

24   William Alexander, Earl of Stirling, *Jvlivs Caesar* (1637), I.113–16. Subsequent references will be given in the text.

25   William Warner, *Albions England* [1612] (Hildesheim: Georg Olms Verlag, 1971), p. 553.

26   Though for a counter-view see Curran, *Roman Invasions*, p. 72.

27   Mary Floyd-Wilson, 'Delving to the root: *Cymbeline*, Scotland, and the English race', in *British Identities and English Renaissance Literature*, edited by David J. Baker and Willy Maley (Cambridge: Cambridge University Press, 2002), pp. 101–15, p. 112, also notes this as a possible parallel.

moreover, Wales is nevertheless seen in the play as the one remaining home of true British valour; indeed the Britons, in the shape of the Welsh, are markedly more Roman than the Romans. Garrett Sullivan argues that 'with the possible exception of the two beggars who give Imogen directions, there are no Welsh in the play' and that 'Its separateness also requires that we see that Britain really refers to England, that the court of Cymbeline is seen as an English one',[28] but Philip Schwyzer points to

> the strange moment in *Cymbeline* when the king commands his lord to escort the Roman ambassador as far as the Severn – strange in that the Roman has just requested conduct as far as Milford Haven, and we had thought Cymbeline was king of all Britain. The river clearly has border significance here, though whether it marks the bounds of Geoffrey of Monmouth's Cambria or of William Camden's Silures, we are not quite sure.[29]

It seems, then, that the distinction between 'Welsh' and 'English', insofar as these terms can be said to apply at the time of the play, is secure; however, that between Britons and Romans is surprisingly easily riddled. Posthumus resolves that

> I'll disrobe me
> Of these Italian weeds, and suit myself
> As does a Briton peasant.(V.i.22–4)

Posthumus, a Briton with a Roman name, can not only pass seamlessly between the two identities but, in so doing, displaces the Romans themselves into the position of Italians. Later, Posthumus also recounts how Belarius cried,

> 'Our Britain's harts die flying, not her men.
> To darkness fleet souls that fly backwards. Stand,
> Or we are Romans, and will give you that
> Like beasts which you shun beastly, and may save
> But to look back in frown. Stand, stand.' (V.iii.28)

First Belarius accuses his fellow Britons of not being British enough; second, he declares that he and his supposed sons will morph into Romans, which will, ironically, in fact be a means of demonstrating their superior Britishness. This builds on an episode in Geoffrey of Monmouth, but with rather different inflection. There, Geoffrey ascribes to Guiderius the rebellion staged by Cymbeline in the play and tells how during it the Roman Lelius Hamo 'threw off the armour he was wearing, put on British arms, and began to fight against his own men as though he were a Briton' and used his disguise to kill Guiderius. However, Arviragus redeems the situation by in turn pretending to be Guiderius.[30] For Geoffrey, though, these assumed identities are only the means to an end for assertion of a fundamental, underlying one; something rather less secure is suggested by Belarius' assertion that if the Britons will not stand, then 'we are Romans', rather than, for instance, 'we seem Romans'. Also richly ironic is Innogen's saying to her father Cymbeline of Giacomo, whose name

---

28 Sullivan, 'Civilizing Wales'.
29 Schwyzer, 'A Map of Greater Cambria'.
30 Geoffrey of Monmouth, *The History of the Kings of Britain*, pp. 119–20.

so irresistibly suggests that of James VI and I, that 'He is a Roman, no more kin to me / Than I to your highness' (V.iv.112–13).

If the British are Roman, the Romans themselves are seen in a variety of unflattering lights; indeed Hirota Atsuhiko, pointing that 'The "Roman" forces invading Cymbeline's Britain consist mainly of legions called from Gallia reinforced with Italian gentlemen mobilized in haste', concludes that 'The expansion of Rome has...conveyed the traditional Roman virtues to the farthest periphery of the empire where they can, ironically, defeat Roman armies'.[31] The worst aspect of the Romans' heritage is stressed when Giacomo emerging from the trunk compares himself to Tarquin (II.ii.12), and indeed the Romans seem hardly to be Roman at all when Giacomo speaks of the tapestry in Innogen's bedroom as showing 'the story [of] / Proud Cleopatra when she met her Roman' (II.iv.69–70), as though he himself were something other than Roman – all indictments and denigrations which are, of course, made much more damaging by the fact that Giacomo's name is a version of James. Elsewhere in the play, it is in fact made quite clear that the play's 'Romans' should be thought of primarily as Italian rather than Roman. Thomas G. Olsen observes that 'Everything about Philario's house indicates contemporaneity, not antiquity',[32] while J.S. Lawry comments that '[h]istorically, Shakespeare's South is that of pagan Rome. In its literal effects, it is that of Renaissance Italy',[33] and when Giacomo is identified as 'Siena's brother', it seems quite clear that it is of Renaissance Italy rather than ancient Rome that we are to think.[34]

Most damagingly, the play's Romans are seen as Catholic. This is clearly apparent when Innogen, outraged by Giacomo's attempt to solicit her, explodes that Cymbeline can have no value for his daughter at all

> If he shall think it fit
> A saucy stranger in his court to mart
> As in a Romish stew.   (I.vi.150–52)

The change from the expected 'Roman' to the actual 'Romish' may seem slight, but it speaks volumes. Giacomo himself also implicitly aligns the British Innogen with Protestantism, the opposite pole of Catholicism, when he uses the Calvinist language of election in speaking to her of

> your great judgement
> In the election of a sir so rare
> Which you know cannot err.   (I.vi.174–6)

---

31   Hirota Atsuhiko, 'Forms of Empires: Rome and its Peripheries in *Cymbeline*', *Shakespearean International Yearbook* 4 (2004), pp. 279–93, pp. 280 and 288–9.

32   Thomas G. Olsen, 'Iachimo's "Drug-Damn'd Italy" and the Problem of British National Character in *Cymbeline*', *Shakespeare Yearbook 10: Shakespeare and Italy*, edited by Holger Klein and Michele Marrapodi (Lewiston: Edwin Mellen Press, 1999), pp. 269–96, p. 273.

33   J.S. Lawry, '"Perishing Root and Increasing Vine" in *Cymbeline*', *Shakespeare Studies* 12 (1979), pp. 179–93, p. 182.

34   For an extended discussion of this, see Peter A. Parolin, 'Anachronistic Italy: Cultural alliances and national identity in *Cymbeline*', *Shakespeare Studies* 30 (2002), pp. 188–215.

Innogen too uses similar language of herself when she asks Pisanio,

> Why hast thou gone so far
> To be unbent when thou hast ta'en thy stand,
> Th'elected deer before thee? (III.iv.107–9)

And she is certainly presented as a pefect Christian when she rejects the temptation to suicide on the grounds that

> Against self-slaughter
> There is a prohibition so divine
> That cravens my weak hand. (III.iv.76–7)

This idea would be wildly anachronistic when applied to a woman who lived during the time of the Romans, but in this context it serves to solidify the identity of Innogen as Protestant and hence of her opponents, the Romans, as Catholic.

I think the reason why Shakespeare incriminates his Romans and glorifies his Welsh Britons is to be found in the wider cultural uses that he makes of Wales in this play. As Huw Griffiths has it,

> *Cymbeline* is self-consciously concerned with the idea of "Great Britain." The problematic and contested location of "Great Britain" in the period immediately following James VI of Scotland's accession to the English throne informs the geographies of the play. The peculiarities of its setting are brought about by the remapping of the space of the nation that is entailed in James's accession.[35]

In particular, I think it is worth note that Innogen experiences particular difficulty in finding her way to Milford Haven when she is six miles from it. The specificity of this distance seems suggestive, and there are indeed four places of considerable interest at approximately that distance from Milford Haven. All of them are places that a person on their way to Milford Haven might pass through, and all of them evoke some very significant cultural issues which it would be extremely provocative to consider in connection with *Cymbeline* (indeed I wonder whether one reason that we are not specifically told where Imogen is might be that anyone familiar with the topography would recall all of these places, and that Shakespeare wants all four potential associations to be activated at once).

Firstly there is Picton Castle. George Owen of Henllys, whose map of Pembrokeshire was mentioned above, married the daughter and co-heiress of William Philipps of Picton. She was a niece of Sir John Perrot, who will be discussed below, and Owen joined with Sir James Perrot and Sir John Philipps of Picton in encouraging Robert Holland's translation of James I's *Basilikon Doron*.[36] This seat of a family who were extensively involved in both military preparation and literary patronage might therefore be an appropriate stopping-point for Innogen. Owen's connection with Thomas Phaer alone might make Picton Castle worth a nod, for

---

35 Griffiths, 'The Geographies of Shakespeare's *Cymbeline*', p. 339.
36 Charles, *George Owen of Henllys*, pp. 27 and 117.

Phaer, sometimes now considered the 'Father of English Pediatrics',[37] was in his own time far more famous as a translator of the *Aeneid*, and his translation was well thought of, being, amongst others, praised by Nashe and quoted by Richard Stanyhurst.[38] Phaer was also, by his own account, an experimenter in poisons and antidotes, something with obvious resonance with the sustained motif of poisoning in *Cymbeline*. He had contributed a lament supposedly spoken by Owain Glyndwr to the first edition of *The Mirror for Magistrates*, though this had subsequently been suppressed, and has been credited with producing a ballad, now lost, on the robbery at Gadshill, one of the pranks played by Prince Hal in *Henry IV, Part One*. In 1556 he was appointed 'searcher' or customs officer of the town of Milford Haven, and his 'Report on his perambulation around the coast of Wales' became a major source of knowledge about the town.[39] This classically- and medically-minded figure might well have been in Shakespeare's mind as he dispatched his emblematically Trojan-named heroine to Milford Haven, with a strange drug in her pocket.

A still more interesting candidate than Picton Castle would be Manorbier Castle. This had been the home of Giraldus Cambrensis, Gerald of Wales, who hymns its beauty and superb location. Gerald is an important figure in both the history of Wales, through his family links with the Geraldines and with his grandmother Princess Nest, the 'Helen of Wales', and its historiography, through his careful account of his tour with Archbishop Baldwin. To evoke him taps into the vexed question of the history of colonialism within the British Isles (the Geraldines had initiated the wave of Anglo-Norman settlers in Ireland), a resonant context both for a play concerned with Britain's relationship with Rome – as Garrett Sullivan observes, in *Cymbeline* 'Rome is analogous to Lhuyd's England, engaged in cultural annexation in the name of unity'[40] – and also for one which, as I shall be suggesting, looks too at the later relationship of Britain's constituent parts to each other. Indeed the two ideas are connected: as Willy Maley observes,

> the process of national liberation in an early modern English context involves a repetition of the colonial project, a common feature of postcolonial discourse. This act of repetition – greatly feared and eagerly awaited in equal measure – is implicit in Shakespeare's Roman / British plays.[41]

Any glance at Gerald also steps firmly into the area where history and legend, particularly those of Wales, meet. (Since Gerald was eight years old when Geoffrey of Monmouth died, he also belonged to the generation likely to have felt his influence

---

37   J. Rührar, *Pediatrics of the Past* (1925), quoted in the *DNB*. Despite living in Wales, Phaer was English by birth, and always wrote in that language.

38   Donna B. Hamilton, *Virgil and* The Tempest (Columbus: Ohio State University Press, 1990), pp. 59–60.

39   See W. R. B. Robinson, 'Dr. Thomas Phaer's Report on the Harbours and Customs Adminstration of Wales under Edward VI', *Bullboard of Celtic Studies* (1972), pp. 485–90.

40   Sullivan, 'Civilizing Wales'.

41   Willy Maley, 'Postcolonial Shakespeare: British Identity Formation and *Cymbeline*', in *Shakespeare's Late Plays: New Readings*, edited by Jennifer Richards and James Knowles (Edinburgh: Edinburgh University Press, 1999), pp. 145–57, p. 146.

most fully.) An allusion to Gerald's celebrated grandmother Nest would also be particularly appropriate in this play, for Nest represented a diametrical contrast to Imogen by being a Princess of Britain who really had committed adultery (with both King Henry I and with her cousin Owain ap Cadwgan, son of the Prince of Powys) but who had effectively escaped any punishment for it (though her husband, Gerald de Windsor, killed Owain ap Cadwgan). There would be a certain ironic appropriateness in having Shakespeare's maligned Princess Innogen, on her way to Milford Haven, knock on the door of the daughter of Princess Nest and ask for directions.

It would, however, be equally fitting to have her knock on another door not very far away, that of Carew Castle, home of Nest herself. Carew too has strong connections with earlier periods of Welsh history, as is indeed indicated by the name, which derives from 'caerau', the Welsh word for an old fort: a cross commemorating the death of Maredudd ap Edwin in 1035 is visible from the castle, and it later became the home of Sir Rhys ap Thomas, the South Wales magnate whose decision not to resist the landing of Henry Tudor at Milford Haven had been a major factor in the latter's success (indeed the guidebook to Carew Castle suggests that Rhys may well have entertained Henry there on his march to Bosworth, though no such visit is documented). Most resonantly, an earlier Princess Nest figured prominently in the ancestry of James VI and I, since in legend, Banquo's son 'Fleance, having fled to Wales, married Princess Nesta, and so ensured one of James's two claims to the English throne'.[42] In this account, then, *Cymbeline* looks like the sequel to *Macbeth*, and here would be a very pointed reminder that James simply could not afford to ignore Wales, especially since, as Mary Floyd-Wilson points out, 'The play's inverted chronology unsettles the authority of Britain's chronicle history and taps into the uncertainties already present in Holinshed – the discrepancies between the English and Scottish histories of ancient Britain':[43] in Richard Harvey's *Philadelphvs,* the credibility of the Brutus-sceptic George Buchanan is specifically stated to be less than that of Geoffrey of Monmouth with the rhetorical question 'who is most credible, he or you, a *Monmouth* or a *Scot*',[44] and John Kerrigan notes that 'Welsh intellectuals had particularly tense relations with the Scots. It was resented that Hector Boece, for instance, had argued that Caractacus and Boadicea were Caledonian leaders'.[45]

Any allusion to Princess Nest would also, of course, raise the question of female ancestry in general, something hugely embarrassing to James, whose claim to the throne had been transmitted through his adulterous, Catholic, executed mother Mary, Queen of Scots. As is the case in all Shakespeare's last plays, *Cymbeline* works to exclude the female from the succession. Moreover, other women also suffer in its plot: Leah Marcus argues that 'the wicked queen...can be seen as a demonized

---

42   Emrys Jones, 'Stuart Cymbeline', *Essays in Criticism* 2 (1961), pp. 84–99, p. 97. However, Peter A. Parolin, in 'Anachronistic Italy', argues that the thrust of the play is anti-James, not pro-.

43   Floyd-Wilson, 'Delving to the root', p. 101.

44   Richard Harvey, *Philadelphvs, or A Defence of Brutes, and the Brutans History* (London: John Wolfe, 1593), p. 83 and preface.

45   Kerrigan, 'The Romans in Britain, 1603–1614', p. 116.

version of Queen Elizabeth I',[46] while Jodi Mikalachki reads her more generally within a framework of a 'gendering and sexualizing of the nation [which]...involved both an exclusion of originary female savagery and a masculine embrace of the civility of empire'.[47] However, to evoke the figure of that earlier Princess Nest, wife of Fleance, would introduce a marked note of reverse thrust here, and a powerful reminder that while the question of female ancestry may be tainted and problematic, it cannot so lightly be brushed away: the play would, in effect, be working to remind us both that claims through the female should be distrusted, and that this was the basis of James's claim to England, Wales and Scotland.

By Shakespeare's day, however, Carew Castle was the home of the Perrot family, and particularly of Sir John Perrot, another figure prominent in the history of Ireland – he had been Lord Deputy there – who was also widely rumoured to be the illegitimate son of Henry VIII, and thus the natural half-brother of Elizabeth I. (His sister Jane was also the wife of William Philipps of Picton.) To have a Princess of Britain going into Wales and finding long-lost brothers there begins, in such a context, to look rather double-edged. It might even be seen as hinting at the dangerously subversive possibility that the blood of the Tudor dynasty had not, in fact, entirely died out with Elizabeth. (Indeed Sir John Perrot's descendants were alive and flourishing: his granddaughter Penelope Perrot, for instance, had married Sir William Lower, friend of Thomas Hariot and the first person to record an observation of Halley's Comet, c. 1605.) There was also a possible connection between Carew Castle and Sir George Carew, who owned property in Stratford adjacent to Shakespeare's and married the heiress of the important local Clopton family,[48] which might have served to draw Shakespeare's attention to the location.

The Perrots were an important family with many court connections; one of their members, Sir John's son Sir Thomas, who in 1587, along with George Owen of Henllys, 'raised a militia of five hundred men to defend the Haven from Spain',[49] made a particularly distinguished, albeit runaway, match with Dorothy Devereux, sister of Elizabeth I's favourite the Earl of Essex. (They were the parents of Penelope Perrot.) This marriage probably came about because Essex himself had strong local links. His father – another Lord Deputy of Ireland – had been buried in Carmarthen, and Essex himself had spent much of his youth at nearby Lamphey Palace. This therefore becomes my fourth candidate for the place where Innogen might stop to ask the way.

Although it is now a remote and peaceful spot, Essex's residence there had once made Lamphey an important centre of power and patronage; when he launched his ill-fated rebellion in 1601 a considerable degree of his support came from Wales or had Welsh connections, not least because of his family links with the Perrots and indeed with the Earl of Pembroke himself, whose uncle, Sir Philip Sidney, had been

---

46 Marcus, *Puzzling Shakespeare*, p. 128.

47 Jodi Mikalachki, 'The masculine romance of Roman Britain: *Cymbeline* and early modern English nationalism', *Shakespeare Quarterly* 46.3 (Fall, 1995), pp. 301–22, p. 301.

48 Richard Abrams, 'Meet the Peters', *Early Modern Literary Studies* 8.2 (September 2000). Online: http://extra.shu.ac.uk/emls/08-2/abrapete.html

49 Boling, 'Anglo-Welsh Relations in *Cymbeline*', pp. 48–9.

the first husband of Essex's wife Frances Walsingham; indeed Essex had originally planned to return from his ill-fated mission to Ireland via Milford Haven, in the hope that he could rally supporters to his cause as he marched through Wales.[50] Thus, if Manorbier and Carew spoke primarily of the past, Lamphey had a far more contemporary and pointed resonance. It spoke of Essex, who, though dead, was by no means forgotten, and was indeed the subject of something of a growing cult in the early years of the seventeenth century (for instance, the poet and playwright John Ford, who did not publish a word until five years after Essex's execution, repeatedly referred to the earl in his writings). Ronald J. Boling, discussing *Cymbeline* in the context of Pembrokeshire's soubriquet of 'Little England Beyond Wales', points to precisely this aspect of its history as particularly subversive:

> from London's vantage point Little England had often promoted its own interests independently of and even counter to the crown's. Some members of Little England's ruling class had pursued unauthorized claims in Ireland, some had been international mercenaries of uncertain loyalties, and as recently as Essex's rebellion some had harped on London's fear that Little England might mobilize Welsh or Irish hordes against the crown. Yet while the Irish war kept Pembrokeshire's strategic importance paramount in late-Elizabethan court thinking, O'Neill's surrender and pardon in March 1603 relaxed political tensions in Little England.[51]

Indeed 'During the Tudor era "for at least two generations Pembrokeshire men... intrigued with Scotch [sic] kings, hoping by their aid to establish some form of home rule for Wales with Little England as the seat of Government"'.[52] Peggy Muñoz Simonds suggests that a similar collusion between Wales and Scotland may in fact be embodied in Guiderius and Arviragus, since she argues that they can be read as Wild Men and points out that 'about one fourth of all Scottish noble families employed Wild Men in their coats of arms', while the fight in a lane in which Belarius, Polydore and Cadwal defeat the Romans specifically echoes the legendary history of the Scottish Hay family.[53] This would, then, be another reminder that Anglo-Scottish union cannot be considered in isolation from the question of Wales.

It is, of course, completely unprovable that Shakespeare invites us to contemplate his Imogen at any of the Pembrokeshire locations which I have suggested. But for anyone in the audience who did know the Pembrokeshire area to stop and wonder where Imogen might have passed on her journey might well be a very suggestive exercise, especially given the fact that they are interconnected dynastically. To do so might indeed have been particularly intriguing for the Earl of Pembroke himself, to whom the First Folio was dedicated in terms that imply personal acquaintance and

---

50   James Shapiro, *1599: A Year in the Life of William Shakespeare* (London: Faber and Faber, 2005], p. 295.

51   Boling, 'Anglo-Welsh Relations in *Cymbeline*', p. 34.

52   Boling, 'Anglo-Welsh Relations in *Cymbeline*', p. 41.

53   Peggy Muñoz Simonds, *Myth, Emblem, and Music in Shakespeare's* Cymbeline: *An Iconographic Reconstruction* (Newark: University of Delaware Press, 1992), p. 157. On the Hay connection see also Griffiths, 'The Geographies of Shakespeare's *Cymbeline*', p. 352; Kerrigan, 'The Romans in Britain, 1603–1614', p. 128; and Ros King, *Cymbeline: Constructions of Britain* (Aldershot: Ashgate, 2005), p. 98.

patronage, since on 1 November 1595 his father, the 2ⁿᵈ Earl and the lord lieutenant of Pembrokeshire, wrote to George Owen of Henllys,

> My Good Cousin, I have long expected to have received from you a map of Milford Haven. There is now great occasion to use it and therefore...I most earnestly desire you with all possible speed to send it...I pray you be very careful to make your scale perfect for thereby shall I be able to know the true distance of places which unknown will either make void or make fruitless all our endeavours.[54]

In particular, situating *Cymbeline* firmly in Pembrokeshire might allow us to notice that at least three of these four places in a radius of six miles or so from Milford Haven have very specific connotations of resistance to royal rule in ways which could, at the period when *Cymbeline* was written, very easily be co-opted to serve specifically anti-Stuart purposes. Ultimately, *Cymbeline* reaffirms the centrality of Wales to British rule in the face of the Stuarts, at a time when 'James I's British Union project erased Wales from political discourse altogether'.[55] Having first, as Michael J. Redmond points out, made 'the decision to give Cymbeline two sons and a daughter in defiance of the chronicles' in an obvious glance at James, Shakespeare then 'assigns his villain the name Giacomo, the Italian word for James'.[56] At the same time, he also evokes James's preferred persona of Augustus only to marginalise and trivialise him, and ultimately to suggest that he is a figure wholly peripheral to the survival of proper notions of *Romanitas*. In *Cymbeline*, then, Shakespeare uses a story of the Romans in Wales to suggest that the Scots have at best a tenuous position in England, and that the true traditions of the *translatio imperii* have not been transmitted to them but are instead to be found elsewhere, among the progeny of Brutus. In the group of plays to which I next turn, that note of resistance of Stuart rule will be heard even more strongly.

54 Charles, *George Owen of Henllys*, p. 154.

55 Boling, 'Anglo-Welsh Relations in *Cymbeline*', p. 34.

56 Michael J. Redmond, '"My lord, I fear, has forgot Britain": Rome, Italy, and the (Re)construction of British National Identity', *Shakespeare Yearbook 10: Shakespeare and Italy*, edited by Holger Klein and Michele Marrapodi (Lewiston: Edwin Mellen Press, 1999), pp. 297–313, pp. 307 and 312.

Chapter Seven

He, Claudius

If Roman and British identities blur in *Cymbeline*, they do so even more in Jasper Fisher's *Fvimvs Troes*. Fisher's play offers a complex picture of British identity which is deeply rooted in the enduring myth of British descent from Brutus. Its full title, in its own bizarre typography, is *Fvimvs Troes* AEneid *2. The True Troianes, Being A Story of the* Britaines *valour at the Romanes first invasion*. (Actually the reference to '*AEneid* 2' is misleading: the play's plot, nomenclature, and moral all owe a very great deal more to Geoffrey of Monmouth than to Virgil, although it is from the latter that the resonant phrase 'fvimvs Troes' itself is derived.) The play was, the title-page proclaims, 'Publikely represented by the Gentlemen Students of Magdalen Colledge in Oxford' at an unknown date after 1611. However, it was first published in 1633, a year in which Charles I's Scottish coronation, coupled with his growing political unpopularity, seems to have provoked a collective soul-searching on the subject of national identities. Whatever meanings it may originally have possessed, it certainly takes on new ones in that context, since for all its ostentatious display of the trappings of the classical past, the play also speaks directly to the dominant discourses of the reign of Charles I.

As the play's subtitle of *The True Troianes* suggests, both sides in the conflict devote much energy to establishing who *are* the true Trojans. Ostensibly, the British and the Romans, both claiming descent from Aeneas, are mirror-images of each other, but some word-play of Caesar's neatly suggests the extent to which mirror-imaging is not the same as identity:

> Or is our might
> Answer'd with like, since Troy gainst Troy doth fight?
> Nor can I write now, *I came ouer, and*
> *I ouercame*: Such foes deny such hast.[1]

Caesar's denial here of his own most famous words echoes the similar refusal of the wicked queen in *Cymbeline* to allow that Caesar's phrase applied to Britain. 'A kind of conquest / Caesar made here, but made not here his brag / Of "Came, and saw, and overcame"' says the queen,[2] and John E. Curran has interestingly discussed the way in which her stance aligns her with the Jacobean historians who refused to concede that Polydore Vergil had discredited the Galfridian (that is, derived from Geoffrey

---

1   Jasper Fisher, *Fvimus Troes* (London, 1633), III.iv.17–20.
2   William Shakespeare, *Cymbeline*, edited by J.C. Maxwell (Cambridge: Cambridge University Press, 1968), III.i.22–4.

of Monmouth) idea of a knowable British history predating the Romans.[3] Here, Fisher goes one step further than Shakespeare in daringly having Caesar himself bear witness for the Galfridian case, and the implications of this would not be lost on those for whom the debate between Vergilians and Galfridians was one of the central issues of contemporary historiography. At the same time, however, we are clearly invited to register that the difference between 'I came ouer' and 'I ouercame' does not simply reverse the word order but totally alters the meaning: the same components may produce entirely different results, in an uncanny echo of Caesar's uncertainty about which Trojan-born side is which.

The confusion over who are the true Trojans persists. Hulacus, the mistletoe-bearing, pyramid-hatted druid who might have stepped straight out of the pages of Tacitus, reports that

> Late in a groue by night, a voyce was heard
> To cry aloud, *Take heed, more Troianes come.* (II.iii.45)

This, the first mention of Trojans in the text (as opposed to the title) of the play, immediately sets up a worrying equivalence between self and enemy. Cassibelane's letter to Caesar makes the same point:

> As you from Troy, so we; Our pettigree do claime:
> Why should the branches fight, when as the roote's the same? (II.iv.25)

Cassibelane's logic does not persuade Caesar, however, and that is unsurprising, for his metaphor brings with it the ideological baggage of a very dangerous question: when does descent from an ancestor become so temporally and generationally remote that it ceases to be meaningful? This was a question which, in the year of the play's eventual publication, was particularly provocative, since Charles I's journey northwards for his coronation meant that the question might well be asked about the king himself: when does a Stuart – particularly one who had never lost his Scottish accent[4] – cease to be a Scot? And, by extension, when (if ever) can the Scots – who, while not positively unfriendly in this play, 'gnaw, and suck / Their enemies bones' and are 'Painted like Beares, and VVolues, and brinded Tygers' (II.v.66), and who were excluded by Hadrian's Wall beyond the bounds of the civilised world – become an accepted part of a wider British identity?

In the case of *Fvimvs Troes*, the answer to this burning question is further complicated by the fact that it is not always clear that either the Romans or the Britons really are Trojans: as Caesar will eventually ask, 'Haue wee, or They / The Phrygian powers?' (IV.iv.47). Both the ghosts who enter at the opening and close, Camillus and Brennus, represent other ethnic components in the ancestry of their respective nations, and it is hardly likely to have been from Troy that the mistletoe-

---

3   John E. Curran, 'Royalty Unlearned, Honor Untaught: British Savages and Historiographical Change in *Cymbeline*', *Comparative Drama* 31:2 (summer, 1997), pp. 277–303.

4   J.P. Kenyon, *The Stuarts* [1958] (London: Fontana, 1966), p. 71.

wielding druid derived the rites which are so important to the play's Britons. Camillus explains to Caesar that he is visiting him to

> bid thee take a full Reuenge on this,
> This Nation, which did sacke and burne downe Rome,
> Quenching the coales with blood, and kickt Our ashes,
> Trampling vpon the ruines of our state.   (II.vii.36–9)

'[T]his, / This Nation', he splutters, but can come no closer to naming it than defining it as what it is not: it is *not* Rome, and Britons and Romans are thus not the same race. Caesar is interested to learn this:

> Is this that Northerne route, the Scourge of kingdomes?
> Whose names till now vnknowne, We iudged Gaules;
> Their Tongue and Manners not vnlike.   (II.vii.42–4)

Even the words which appear to be the play's most unproblematic assertion of Trojan identity simultaneously undo it: 'fuimus Troes' translates not as 'we are Trojans' but as 'we *have been* Trojans', leaving open the question of what 'we' are now, and alluding, by the quotation of the wandering Aeneas' words to Dido, to the destruction of Trojan identity and its ensuing modulation into Latinity.

The confusion is even further exacerbated when Caesar assures his men that the Britons 'were not dipt in Styx' (IV.iv.15) – that is, they are not like Achilles, and are thus not like the Greeks besieging Troy – and so by implication are aligned with the Trojans (though the British, ironically, proceed to compare themselves, or at least the Cornish members of their contingent, with the Scythians [IV.iv.23–4]). So, Camillus thinks that the Romans are Latins and that the British are Trojans; Caesar used to think the British were French, but now realises that they are 'a Northern [rout]', and compares his own men with the Greeks. What ish my nation? The meanings of the scene are, moreover, richly complicated by the fact that it is so ironically haunted by the prolepsis of that other scene in Shakespeare's *Julius Caesar* when Caesar himself is the pre-battle ghost – appearing to a man named, of all things, Brutus, who claims to represent the truest and noblest elements of traditional Roman identity.

At least the British know who they are. At the close of the second act, the Chorus sing a song which first, appropriately enough for the Oxford setting of the original performance, hymns the second Troy built on the banks of the Isis, and then celebrates how 'Locrinus eldest sonne / Did drowne the furious Hunne' (II.viii.9–10) before rehearsing, in true Galfridian fashion, the doings of Bladud and Mulmutius. But matters become a little less clear cut when Cassibelane asserts that

> The Nature of our Soyle won't beare a Romane,
> As Irish earth doth poyson poysonous beasts.   (III.i.12–13)

Not only does this simile comprehensively undo the equivalence which he himself has posited between the Britons and the Romans, it forces instead an equivalence, which would normally be anathema to writers of this period, between mainland Britain and Ireland. The issue is complicated even further when the Romans and

Britons actually start to fight, and, as in *Cymbeline*, identities shift and whirl in the heat of the battle. Eulinus dismisses Rollano's claim to Britishness on the grounds of his cowardice (III.i.62–3), while Nennius assures the Romans that they are 'at home: Heere's Campus Martius' (III.ii.14). Most confusingly, Cassibelane envisages the island of Britain as suffering from a collective Achilles' heel (IV.iii.29), thus categorically identifying it not with any of Troy's defenders but with her worst enemy. Britain becomes 'Britany', and we are told of the troubles that torment her that 'More ghastly monster did not spring, / From the Hybernian flood' (IV.vi.5–6) – that is, from Ireland.

In this riot of identities, though, one thing at least is clear: the worst strife of all is internecine. As Belinus remarks, 'No way halfe so quicke / To ruinate kingdomes, as by home-bred strife' (V.ii.8–9). Cassibelane's first act has been, Lear-like, to devolve power in the kingdom:

> Meane while *Androgeus* hold vnto your vse
> Our Lady-City Troynovant, and all
> The Toll and Tribute of delicious Kent;
> Of which each Quarter can maintaine a King.
> Haue you, *Themantius*, Cornewalles Dukedome large,
> Both rich and strong, in metalles and in men.
> I must to Verulams fenced towne repaire,
> And as Protectour for the whole take care.   (I.iii.6–13)

Of course this division will prove to mean trouble, especially when we are reminded of the Lear story by the fact that Hirildas' mistress, who is only once mentioned and never seen, and thus seems to be introduced into the narrative expressly for the purpose of having her name mentioned, is called Cordella (I.iv.108), which seems deliberately designed to echo the name of Cordelia.[5] This has a clear resonance for modern Britain as well as for its ancient counterpart: the constituent parts of the kingdom may be only very loosely a whole, but it is nevertheless clear that if they fail to cohere, the cost will be high.

The uncertainty about the play's date makes it difficult to be sure in what ways its concern with internal factional strife arose from the domestic political difficulties of Charles I. What does seem unmistakable, though, is that the portrayal of Fisher's classical Romans is inflected by a distrust of seventeenth-century Roman Catholicism. After first undoing the distinction between Rome and Egypt which Shakespeare had made so crucial in *Antony and Cleopatra* with the assertion that 'Tyber doth breed as venemous beasts as Nile', the dying hero Nennius prays:

> Graunt Thames and Tyber neuer joyne thair chanells;
> But may a naturall hate deriv'd from vs
> Liue still in our long-trailed progeny.   (III.v.30–32)

Comparing Tiber with Nile retains the classical context which structured the Egypt / Rome distinction, but shifting the comparison to the Thames abruptly imposes a

---

5   There are also two mentions of Sabrina, bringing the play into the same discursive field as Milton's *Comus* the following year.

far more modern one in which the associations of Rome have changed dramatically, and it now represents the home of the Pope. Since Nennius is the king's brother, whose loss is deeply mourned, he can be read as something of a Prince Henry figure, and certainly his words here are squarely in line with the prince's committed anti-Catholicism.[6] This passage, especially when delivered by someone who might have been seen as dignified by association with Prince Henry, would have been so offensive to Henrietta Maria that one must suppose it most likely that the play was originally written before Charles's marriage, but that would not make the sting in 1633 any the less. This play, then, sharply underlines the ways in which remarks ostensibly about ancient Rome could pack a formidable punch when uttered in early modern England.

Particularly useful in this respect was the story of the Emperor Claudius. The scandalous doings of the later Caesars were well known in Renaissance England, through the study of the lives and careers of authors such as Suetonius, Lucan and Seneca, and provided material for a number of plays focusing on a variety of members of the family. Although the Claudius story makes an early appearance in *Hamlet*, it really comes into its own in the reign of Charles I, when perceived parallels between English king and Roman emperor allow it to be used as a powerful trope for the expression of dissent – especially after, as Martin Butler's influential thesis has it, the cessation of Parliament made the theatre the only effective forum for public debate of Charles's rule and policies.[7]

The operation of this paradigm is explicitly theorised in Massinger's *The Roman Actor*, a play which, though not about the Claudius family specifically, is set firmly in ancient Rome and does some of the same cultural work as, I shall argue, plays about Claudius do. This is a play which not only clearly reflects on the Stuart court – Lamia is forced to divorce his wife Domitia, whom the Emperor desires, on the false grounds that he is impotent,[8] just as the Earl of Essex had been forced to divorce Frances Howard so she would be free to marry Robert Carr – but effectively announces that it is doing so when the actors are summoned before the Senate on the charge of satirising a consul, and Aretinus accuses them:

> You are they
> That search into the secrets of the time,
> And, under feign'd names, on the stage, present
> Actions not to be touch'd at; and traduce
> Persons of rank and quality of both sexes,
> And, with satirical and bitter jests,
> Make even the senators ridiculous
> To the plebeians. (I.iii.36–43)

---

6   On the prince's political and religious beliefs, see for instance Roy Strong, *Henry Prince of Wales and England's Lost Renaissance* (London: Thames and Hudson, 1977).

7   Martin Butler, *Theatre and Crisis 1632–1642* (Cambridge: Cambridge University Press, 1984).

8   Philip Massinger, *The Roman Actor*, in *Five Stuart Tragedies*, edited by A.K. McIlwraith (London: Oxford University Press, 1953), I.iii.91. All further quotations from the play will be taken from this edition and reference will be given in the text.

To this Paris replies,

> If any in this reverend assembly,
> Nay, e'en yourself, my lord, that are the image
> Of absent Caesar, feel something in your bosom,
> That puts you in remembrance of things past,
> Or things intended, - 'tis not in us to help it.   (I.iii.136–40)

It is, it seems, a case of 'if the cap fits, wear it' – and in the case of Charles I and the Emperor Claudius, the cap fitted very well indeed.

The ways in which the story of Charles I was perceived to intersect with that of the Emperor Claudius were surprisingly numerous. Even before the young Charles had had a chance to reveal his character, the paradigm was already in place. In the first place, Charles's father James VI and I was often compared with Augustus, including, as I have argued, in Shakespeare's *Antony and Cleopatra*. Secondly, James's popular elder son Prince Henry was closely associated with the idea of reviving the splendours of ancient Rome: Rolf Soellner argues that Chapman wrote his play *Caesar and Pompey* for Prince Henry 'because the Prince was from various sides urged to study Caesar's military accomplishments and even encouraged to think of himself as a future Caesar', something to which 'King James had unwittingly pointed the way when in his *Basilikon Doron*...he recommended to him the study of Caesar's *Commentaries on the Gallic War*. Sir Clement Edmondes promptly dedicated to Henry his *Observations upon the Five First Books of the Commentaries* (1604)'.[9] In due course, this imagery percolated into Charles's: John Peacock notes a number of masques which represent Charles as 'a reincarnation of an antique emperor' and comments on the extent to which these recapitulate imagery earlier used for Henry,[10] and Anthony Miller comments that

> Charles...cultivated and adapted the style and ideology of triumph, one manifestation being his acquisition of Andrea Mantegna's *Triumph of Julius Caesar...The Triumph* was the most prized item in Charles's purchases from the collection of the Gonzaga family at Mantua.[11]

This was also extensively reflected in the drama of the period. As Geoffrey Bullough notes of the anonymous play *The Valiant Welshman*, which tells the story of the heroic Welshman Caradoc and his encounter with the Emperor Claudius, 'The whole play is framed by a Presenter, a Bard raised by Fortune from his tomb, with the help of four harpers who sing the praises of Wales – no doubt because the piece was performed before [Henry,] the Prince of Wales',[12] while Goran Stanivukovic

---

9   Rolf Soellner, 'Chapman's *Caesar and Pompey* and the Fortunes of Prince Henry', *Medieval and Renaissance Drama in England* 2 (1985), pp. 135–51, p. 137.

10   John Peacock, 'The Image of Charles I as a Roman emperor', in *The 1630s: Interdisciplinary essays on culture and politics in the Caroline era*, edited by Ian Atherton and Julie Sanders (Manchester: Manchester University Press, 2006), pp. 50–73, p. 55.

11   Anthony Miller, *Roman Triumphs and Early Modern English Culture* (Basingstoke: Palgrave, 2001), p. 122.

12   Geoffrey Bullough, 'Pre-Conquest Historical Themes in Elizabethan Drama', in *Medieval Literature and Civilization: Studies in Memory of G. N. Garmonsway* (London: The

suggests that in Beaumont and Fletcher's *Bonduca*, 'The character of Hengo may well have been inspired by James's son, Prince Henry, and Hengo's death evokes Henry's'.[13]

Most notably, as we have seen in chapter four, Henry was often referred to as Marcellus, the promising nephew and son-in-law of the Emperor Augustus, who had died at the age of 19 and was greatly mourned. It is true that Marcellus was not the elder brother of Claudius, but rather his uncle on the mother's side (Marcellus having been the brother of Claudius's mother Antonia) and his stepcousin on the father's side (Claudius's father Drusus having been the stepson of Augustus, Marcellus's uncle and father-in-law). Nevertheless, Marcellus had been the heir apparent to the throne to which Claudius ultimately succeeded, so the comparison between Charles and Claudius was readily available for use. It was of course not the only possible paradigm – J. H. M. Salmon notes that 'When Prince Henry died, Sir Simonds d'Ewes heard many compare his demise with the poisoning of Germanicus. The growth of Tacitean influence in preceding years explains the popularity of the image'[14] – nor was it immediately wanted, not least because Elizabeth of Bohemia, sister of Henry and Charles, was so very unlike the promiscuous Livilla, sister of Claudius: Chapman referred to her as 'His Cynthian *Sister*, (our sole earthly Grace)' (l. 574), and the comparison to Elizabeth I, implied here by the reuse of Cynthia, one of the central planks of the late queen's iconography, was often made explicitly. Nevertheless, the usefulness of the Claudian paradigm having once been established, it remained latent. Charles himself might seek to associate himself with other Caesars – John Peacock notes allusions in his portraits to Otho and Alexander Severus, amongst others,[15] with the latter a particularly interesting choice because Alexander Severus was credited with building Hadrian's Wall, and so was an exceptionally useful figure to enable Charles to put some distance between himself and his Scottish roots. Whatever identities he himself might prefer, however, Claudius was always lying in wait for him.

As the death of his elder brother brought Charles more firmly into the public eye, reasons for using that comparison became stronger, not least because the name of another member of the family was by now being applied to his mother, as James Knowles observes: 'by 1613 Anna's relations with the favourite [Buckingham] were strained. Carr and Overbury nicknamed her Agrippina in their coded letters'.[16] Like

---

Athlone Press, 1969), pp. 289–321, p. 300.

13   Goran Stanivukovic, '"The blushing shame of souldiers": the eroticism of heroic masculinity in John Fletcher's *Bonduca*', in *The Image of Manhood in Early Modern Literature: Viewing the Male*, edited by Andrew P. Williams (Westport: Greenwood Press, 1999), pp. 41–54, p. 47.

14   J. H. M. Salmon, 'Seneca and Tacitus in Jacobean England', in *The Mental World of the Jacobean Court*, ed. Linda Levy Peck (Cambridge: Cambridge University Press, 1991), pp. 169–88, p. 177.

15   Peacock, 'The Image of Charles I as a Roman emperor', pp. 50–51.

16   James Knowles, '"To Enlight the Darksome Night, Pale Cinthia Doth Arise": Anna of Denmark, Elizabeth I and the Images of Royalty', in *Women and Culture at the Courts of the Stuart Queens*, edited by Clare McManus (Basingstoke: Palgrave Macmillan, 2003), pp. 21–48, p. 35.

Claudius, Charles had been a sickly and unpromising child. Robert Carey, Earl of Monmouth, who was given the charge of the young Charles, noted in his *Memoirs* that when Henry was still alive and Charles was only Duke of Albany,

> There were many great Ladies suitors for the keeping of the Duke; but when they did see how weak a child he was, and not likely to live, their hearts were down, and none of them were desirous to take charge of him...The Queen, by the approbation of the Lord Chancellor, made choice of my wife to have the care and keeping of the Duke. Those who wished me no good were glad of it, thinking if the Duke should die in our charge, his weakness being such as gave them great cause to suspect it, then it would not be thought fit that we should remain in Court after...The Duke was past four years old, when he was first delivered to my wife; he was not able to go, nor scant stand alone, he was so weak in his joints, and especially his ancles, insomuch as many feared they were out of joint... Many a battle my wife had with the King, but she still prevailed. The King was desirous that the string under his tongue should be cut, for he was so long beginning to speak as he thought he would never have spoke. Then he would have him put in iron boots, to strengthen his sinews and joints; but my wife protested so much against them both, as she got the victory, and the King was fain to yield.[17]

Compare this with what Suetonius says about the Emperor Claudius:

> Nearly the whole of his childhood and youth was so troubled by various diseases that he grew dull-witted and had little physical strength; and on reaching the age at which he should have won a magistracy or chosen a private career, was considered by his family incapable of doing either...Claudius's weak health also accounted for his being muffled in a cloak – an unprecedented sight – while presiding at the gladiatorial games given by Germanicus and himself to honour their father's memory; and, at his coming of age, he was taken up to the Capitol in a litter, about midnight, without the customary solemn procession...Claudius's mother often called him 'a monster: a man whom Mother Nature had begun to work upon but then flung aside'.[18]

Since the name Claudius is also etymologically linked with the Latin word for 'lame', *claudus*, the parallels with the young Charles were inescapable.

When Charles ascended to the throne, other layers of parallelism were added. In the first place, Claudius had been officially declared a god by the Britons; in the fictional version of events offered by Geoffrey of Monmouth, his daughter had married Arviragus, one of the two princes of *Cymbeline*; and his son had historically been named Britannicus in honour of the conquest of Britain. In some accounts, this name was also applied to Claudius himself: William Strachey in *The Historie of Travell into Virginia Britania* refers to 'the Emperor *Claudius*, (who was therefore called Britannicus)'.[19] Claudius was therefore a particularly telling persona to figure the increasingly autocratic king who believed in the divine right of kings and whose

---

17   Robert Carey, Earl of Monmouth, *Memoirs*, reprinted in John Nichols, *Progresses of King James the First* (London, 1828), pp. 460–61.

18   Suetonius, *The Twelve Caesars* (Harmondsworth: Penguin, 1957), p. 183.

19   William Strachey, *The Historie of Travell into Virginia Britania* (1612), edited by Louis B. Wright and Virginia Freund (London: The Hakluyt Society, 1953), p. 24.

father had so unflaggingly promulgated the use of the term 'Britain' rather than 'England'. Secondly, J. H. M. Salmon notes that

> Under Charles I Sejanus [the prime favourite of Claudius's uncle Tiberius] became a popular name of opprobrium for the Duke of Buckingham. Sir John Eliot applied the label to the duke in parliament in 1626, and the king, who was as quick as his father to resent the implication that he resembled Tiberius, sent Eliot to the Tower. In 1628 Pierre Matthieu's biography of Sejanus...appeared in two separate English versions to satirize Buckingham, both of them entitled *The Powerful Favourite or the Life of Aelius Sejanus*.[20]

When Charles married the French Catholic princess Henrietta Maria on 1 May 1625, the need to use the Claudius story became both more urgent and more appropriate, for Henrietta Maria was both feared and distrusted on account of her nationality and religion, which gave rise to popular dissatisfaction with Charles, and also had links of her own with the story of the Caesars. Her father, the legendary Henri IV, had repeatedly deployed Caesarian imagery, and had called the eldest of his bastard sons César. To use Caesarian imagery to attack his daughter was therefore savagely appropriate.

It is not surprising, then, that allusions to the Caesars, and to the Claudius story in particular, in connection with the English royal family are widespread in and after the reign of Charles, or that Henrietta Maria is often associated with her husband in the use of Roman imagery.[21] It is notable, for instance, that in Margaret Cavendish's *The Unnatural Tragedy* a discussion of the reliability of Camden and clear allusions to the civil war are combined with the Fourth Virgin's rhetorical question 'have not some Writers spoke well of *Nero*, and striv'd to have glorify'd him, who was the wickedst of all the Emperours? And have not some Writers done the like for *Claudius*, who was the foolishest of all the Emperours?'.[22] Though herself a staunch Royalist who had been a Maid of Honour to the exiled Henrietta Maria, Margaret Cavendish was under no illusions about the character of both the queen and the late king, and she was particularly bitter about what she saw as the scapegoating of her husband the Marquess of Newcastle after his defeat at the Battle of Marston Moor. Here it is made clear that the terms in which long-dead Caesars are described remain very much live issues. Similarly in William Strode's *The Floating Island*, which was acted by the students of Christchurch before Charles I on 29 August 1636, the conclusion contains the lines

> My Complexion
> Is I confesse the same with *Messaline*'s;
> We might have layn together in one Egg. (p. 29)

The Floating Island is a play which flatters Charles by presenting him as majestic enough to stabilise the previously floating eponymous island, but it is impossible

---

20 Salmon, 'Seneca and Tacitus in Jacobean England', p. 188.

21 On the use of Roman imagery for Henrietta Maria, see Miller, *Roman Triumphs and Early Modern English Culture*, p. 125.

22 Margaret Cavendish, *The Unnatural Tragedy* (London, 1662), xiii, p. 37.

not to hear also a note of criticism slipped in here, as the political situation visibly deteriorated, by the allusion to Claudius's notoriously promiscuous wife Messalina, and indeed by 1643 a pamphlet entitled *The Subject of Supremacie. The Right of Caesar* was openly using the trope of Caesarism as a direct tool to debate contemporary political issues.

Particularly interesting is the presence of the Claudius story in Thomas May's *The Tragedy of Julia Agrippina, Empress of Rome* (1639) and Nathaniel Richards' *The Tragedy of Messalina, the Roman Empress* (1639), both of which slyly suggest an equation between Claudius' two wicked Roman wives, Agrippina Minor and Messalina, and Charles's supposedly wicked Roman Catholic wife. The idea also recurs in the anonymous *Tragedy of Nero*, which may conceivably also be by May. In all of these plays, it is clear that 'Roman' has become a way of referring to 'Roman Catholic', in a code which is cursorily covert but effectively an open secret. The parallel is underlined by the insistent use of anachronisms, such as the mention of the early modern dance lavolta in *Messalina*. (There is also mention of dancing the lavolta in Massinger's *Believe As You List*, something which is undoubtedly part of that play's veiled but pointed political commentary.)[23] To underscore the point, there are two separate references to the lavolta in *Messalina*. The first comes when Silius says to Messalina,

> Ravished in thought, panting, amazed I stand
> At your harmonious speech emphatical.
> Ambitious blood, like to the banks of Nile
> Overflows this orb of man's circumference,
> And points my actions thus their way to ill,
> Aspiring arms' Lavolto when they kill.[24]

The second comes in Montanus' protest to Messalina:

> Keep off, insatiate Empress, I'll no more!
> Poison on monsters, the blood of Nessus
> Dam up thy curtain, gulf-like appetite!
> May Furies fright thy whorish fortitude,
> Dancing Lavoltos in the very act,
> And damn you.   (III.ii.58–62)

In this respect, *Messalina* actually borrows from imagery traditionally used to incriminate Elizabeth I, who was painted dancing the lavolta, rather than Henrietta Maria, and it does so again when it twice refers to Semiramis. On the first occasion, Semiramis is directly alluded to, when Messalina says,

---

23   Philip Massinger, *Believe As You List*, in *The Plays and Poems of Philip Massinger*, edited by Philip Edwards and Colin Gibson (Oxford: The Clarendon Press, 1976), vol. III.

24   Nathaniel Richards, *Messalina*, II.ii.120–25. I quote from the version of the play edited by my student Samantha Gibbs as part of the 'Editing a Renaissance Play' module on the MA in English Studies (Renaissance Literature) at Sheffield Hallam University, and available online at http://extra.shu.ac.uk/emls/iemls/resources.html

wer't my brother
Resembled him we so entirely love,
We'd force him ravish pleasure, if not kill;
Be a Semiramis to sate our will. (III.i.195–8)

On the second, Menester mentions Semiramis' husband Ninus:

Not Ninus
Was e'er more dull, more easily entrapped,
Than Rome's ridiculous Emperor Claudius. (IV.i.14–16)

Although she was a problematic figure, because she was said variously to be the epitome of valour and discretion and a woman crazed with lust, whose passions allegedly extended even to bulls and horses, to have slept with her own son, and to have invented castration,[25] references to Semiramis are frequent in writing of the earlier part of Elizabeth's reign.[26] To that extent, then, these are generic rather than specific terms of abuse for a queen, but they are given a new lease of life by the direct comparison of Ninus with Claudius.

However, Henrietta Maria is more obviously and personally the target when Lepida, Messalina's mother, exclaims

Mors aerumarum quies, mors omnibus finis
Dissolve the glassy pearls of mine eyes,
That Niobe-like I may consume in tears. (II.ii.234–6)

B. N. De Luna has argued that in Jonson's *Cynthia's Revels*, 'The salient feature of Niobe's myth – her tearfulness and her boastfulness about her children – unlock her identity as Mary Queen of Scots, who seems to have cried on slight provocation and who mortally offended "the goddess Diana" (Cynthia-Elizabeth) by her smugness about her offspring'.[27] Since Mary Queen of Scots was Charles I's grandmother, the proposed identification certainly seems salient here, and would be underlined when

---

25   Samuel Butler writes in *Hudibras* that
          Loss of *Virilit[y's]* averr'd
          To be the cause of loss of *Beard*,
          That does (like *Embryo* in the womb)
          Abortive on the Chin become.
          This first a *Woman* did invent,
          In envy of *Mans* ornament.
          Semiramis of *Babylon*,
          Who first of all cut men o'th'*Stone*:
          To mar their *Beards*, and laid foundation
          Of *Sow-geldering* operation. (Second Part, Canto 1, ll. 709–18)

26   See Lisa Hopkins, 'The Dark Side of the Moon: Semiramis and Titania', in *Goddesses and Queens: The Iconography of Elizabeth I*, edited by Annaliese Connolly and Lisa Hopkins (Manchester: Manchester University Press, 2007).

27   B.N. De Luna, *Jonson's Romish Plot: A Study of* Catiline *in its Historical Context* (Oxford: Clarendon Press, 1967), p. 11.

Messalina is sentenced to beheading, as Mary was, and does indeed mount the block on stage before wounding herself with the executioner's sword.

Messalina is an unusually allusive play. There are references to *Hamlet*, when Narcissus exclaims 'O, insatiate / Bawdy villain' (V.i.25–6); to *Othello*, when Claudius cries 'Misery of marriage' (V.i.36); to *Julius Caesar*, when Menester speaks of 'Brave Cassius' and Titinnius' hate to life' (V.ii.157) and when Syllana alludes to 'The burning coals of Portia' (V.ii.273); and also to *The Revenger's Tragedy*, when Narcissus declares 'When the bad bleed, give me that tragedy' (V.ii.15), and to *The White Devil*, when Silius says,

> Like a spent taper, only for a flash
> I do recover to embrace thee, sweet. (V.ii.251–2)

Given this general level of self-reflexiveness, it is impossible not to notice that there are also two very deliberate references to the *translatio imperii*. The first comes when Narcissus says,

>   This put home
> With low submission, making her believe
> By cringes, creepings, and a Sinon's face,
> That all our care is only for her good,
> May work persuasion. (IV.ii.39–43)

Here, the allusion is to Sinon, the legendary betrayer of Troy. The second is in the following exchange:

> *Pallas.* In sign whereof
> From the high top, the temple of god Mars,
> Let a bright burning torch i'th dead of night
> Waft our approach.
> *Narcissus.* Like Sinon's unto Troy. (V.i.95–9)

To harp in this manner on the darker side of the Troy story, in the shape of Sinon's betrayal, in itself does damage to any monarch who traces his descent back to Troy.

The same tactics of incrimination are also deployed in *The Roman Actor*. It is true that Massinger's play never mentions Claudius, although Domitilla alludes to his nephew and his stepson when she says,

>   Nero and Caligula
> Commanded only mischiefs; but our Caesar
> Delights to see 'em. (III.i.107–9)

To a large extent, however, the actual king discussed in *The Roman Actor* is immaterial, because the play itself announces its general applicability when it has Paris refer to 'Caesar, (in whose great name / All kings are comprehended)' (I.iii.53–4). Moreover, *The Roman Actor* gestures very pointedly to a play in which a character called Claudius had figured prominently, and that is *Hamlet*. Domitia says of Paris' acting,

By Caesar's life he weeps! and I forbear
Hardly to keep him company. (III.ii.196–7)

This clearly recalls Hamlet's comment about the tears of the First Player, and language familiar from *Hamlet* is also heard again when Paris as Iphis declares that,

> Niobe,
> Proud of her numerous issue, durst contemn
> Latona's double burthen; but what follow'd?
> She was left a childless mother, and mourn'd to marble.
> The beauty you o'erprize so, time or sickness
> Can change to loath'd deformity; your wealth
> The prey of thieves; queen Hecuba, Troy fir'd,
> Ulysses' bondwoman. (III.ii.253–60)

The Roman Actor also shares with *Hamlet* a profoundly metatheatrical sensibility (something also strongly developed in Massinger's other Roman play *Believe As You List*).[28] Paris declares,

> I once observ'd
> In a tragedy of ours in which a murder
> Was acted to the life, a guilty hearer
> Forc'd by the terror of a wounded conscience
> To make discovery of that which torture
> Could not wring from him. (II.i.89–95)

The plot centring on Parthenius' father is entirely about the potentially enlightening and therapeutic effects of drama on its audience. Finally, Caesar declares,

> Off with my robe, and wreath: since Nero scorn'd not
> The public theatre, we in private may
> Disport ourselves. This cloak and hat, without
> Wearing a beard, or other property,
> Will fit the person. (IV.ii.224–8)

He then proceeds to kill Paris with what appears to be a blunted foil, echoing the situation of the fencing match in *Hamlet*.

This glance towards a play which seemed to encode allusions to English and Scottish history starts to look like a direct strike at the theatrical pretensions of the Caroline court in the light of *The Roman Actor*'s many references to the *translatio imperii*. Lamia prays,

> That this my ravish'd wife may prove as fatal
> To proud Domitian, and her embraces
> Afford him, in the end, as little joy,
> As wanton Helen brought to him of Troy. (I.ii.106–9)

---

28 For comment on the importance of metatheatrical imagery in Shakespeare's Roman plays, see Thomas Betteridge, *Shakespearean Fantasy and Politics* (Hatfield: University of Hertfordshire Press, 2005), pp. 114–19.

Along similar lines, Caesar says to Domitia,

> Kiss me; - again:
> If I now wanted heat of youth, these fires,
> In Priam's veins, would thaw his frozen blood,
> Enabling him to get a second Hector
> For the defence of Troy. (II.i.281–5)

Finally, Domitia says to Paris, 'Kiss closer. Thou art now my Trojan Paris, / And I thy Helen' (IV.ii.103–4). As Rome moved to England, then, so too *The Roman Actor* invites us to refocus our gaze and apply its comments about ancient Rome to contemporary England.

The Tragedy of Nero too points up its contemporary applicability with a stream of references to France (rather than the historically correct form of Gaul), culminating in a mention of Rheims, notorious as the original home of the seminary for English Catholics – the point, of course, being that Henrietta Maria, whom Charles was already envisaging as his bride when *The Tragedy of Nero* was published, was French. The dangerous contemporary applicability of the story is also stressed in *The Tragedy of Julia Agrippina* by an addition which May makes to the usual version of events when he pointedly gives his Agrippina literary ambitions and has her ask Seneca, Vitellius and Pollio to read her Commentaries before she comments disparagingly both on Caesar's Commentaries and on Cicero's qualifications and ability to act as a critic of them, remarking dismissively that

> Had I ruled
> Rome and her Senate then, as now I do,
> Not all th'Orations that e'er Cicero
> Made in the Senate should have saved one hair
> Of an offender, or condemned a mouse. (I.ii)

There is no historical warrant for this, but it might well have made the Roman queen look very like the English queen, who took a close interest in literary circles and to whom authorship of the masque *Florimène* is sometimes attributed.[29] There might well be another parallel apparent in actual performance of the play: 'if English clothes were used, which is most likely, then Agrippina would have to be more extravagantly dressed than the other characters as she is the empress and so she would straight away remind the audience of their queen'.[30]

Also increasingly suggestive would be the parallel between the wilful blindness of the Emperor Claudius to the behaviour of both Messalina and Agrippina and Charles I's stubborn refusal to see the trouble he was headed for. May's play, moreover,

---

29   See Nancy Cotton Pearse, 'Women Playwrights in England: Renaissance Noblewomen', in *Readings in Renaissance Women's Drama*, edited by S.P. Cerasano and Marion Wynne-Davies (London: Routledge, 1998).

30   Thomas May, *The Tragedy of Julia Agrippina*. I quote from the version of the play edited by my student Lyndsey Clarke as part of the 'Editing a Renaissance Play' module on the MA in English Studies (Renaissance Literature) at Sheffield Hallam University, and available online at http://extra.shu.ac.uk/emls/iemls/resources.html

stresses the British links of Claudius by mentioning the presence in Rome of the prisoner Caractacus and having Claudius comment on his own title of Britannicus (I.ii), while Montanus enquires hopefully whether it will become lawful under Nero to eat British oysters (III.v); finally *The Tragedy of Julia Agrippina* takes a nasty crack at not only Charles but his whole family when it has Nero pointedly observe that his mother's lover, the odious power-seeking Pallas, is the 'steward of th'imperial house' (III.vi), the same position as that originally occupied by the Stewarts.

As well as similarities and allusions which are at work in the play, however, one should also note some interesting and telling differences and omissions. Incest and close intermarriage was a recurring theme in the story of the Julio-Claudians, and is prominent in *Hamlet*. It is certainly present in the story of the historical Emperor Claudius: according to Suetonius, Agrippina 'had a niece's privilege of kissing and caressing Claudius, and exercised it with a noticeable effect on his passions'.[31] In *The Tragedy of Agrippina*, though, the marriage between Claudius and his wife Agrippina appears to be entirely platonic, and there is no mention either of Agrippina's allegedly incestuous relations with her son Nero or her brother Caligula. I would suggest that this is because an attack on the queen is one thing, but an attack on the legitimacy of the succession quite another. Though May was later to be a Parliamentarian, *The Tragedy of Julia Agrippina* as a play stops short of advocating actual Republicanism, and notably presents Claudius' son Britannicus as one who would have been a worthy successor if he had ever had a chance to reign. Perhaps because of lingering nostalgia for the Marcellus-like Henry, perhaps because of hope that the baby prince Charles might turn into a second Britannicus, the Claudius story seems to be used not as a vehicle for republicanism but as a mode of criticising one specific Caesar – and for this purpose the closeness of the match between Charles I and Claudius made it a perfect vehicle.

---

31 Suetonius, *The Twelve Caesars*, p. 198.

Conclusion

Britain regarded itself as descended from Rome. However, Renaissance Britain had an eerie double vision of Rome as classical capital of the world and contemporary whore of Babylon. This is dramatised in *Titus Andronicus*, and questions of Romanness are also central to *Hamlet*, a play which, like *Titus*, recalls Marlowe's *Dido, Queen of Carthage* and thus the entire tradition of the *translatio imperii*, but whose hero attends Luther's university. However, Romanness, and above all the Caesars, also mapped onto other issues important to English Renaissance society. Perhaps the primary cultural function of the Romans in Renaissance Britain was to offer a template for the nation and for its relation to the rest of the world. We see this reflected on the stage in the wide range of plays which draw on the idea of the *translatio imperii* and of Britain's Trojan / Roman heritage. The Caesars were particularly useful as models for conquest, and this is the dynamic which is explored in the *Tamburlaine* plays and in those which draw on their motifs. At the same time, though, both *Tamburlaine* and *The Winter's Tale* also reveal fundamental shifts in the world's centres of power which suggest that though Roman rhetoric and models remain influential, the world they now serve is very different from that of the Caesars.

The Romans also provided a protocol for understanding the logic of the internal relationships of Britain's own constituent parts. Spenser regarded the fact that the Romans never visited Ireland as a material factor in what he saw as the savagery of its inhabitants, and it was easy to see Hadrian's Wall as excluding the Scots culturally even more than it did physically. Wales, by contrast, with its status as origin of the Tudors and of their claims to Arthurian / Roman descent, functioned as favourite internal colony, and this explains why, in *Antony and Cleopatra* and *Cymbeline*, we have a pair of plays in which Shakespeare was able to play Scotland and Wales off against each other, with each play working separately but with the same logic to the ultimate incrimination of the Scots in general and James VI and I in particular. This is a motif which reaches its apogee of its relevance in the reign of Charles I, when a series of unfortunate parallels between the English / Scottish king and the Roman emperor Claudius make allusion to the Caesars an explosive technique for probing the legitimacy and effectiveness of his rule. Together, then the plays considered here show the continuing urgency and relevance of stories of the Caesars to Britain's understanding of itself in the late sixteenth and early seventeenth centuries.

Works Cited

Abrams, Richard. 'Meet the Peters', *Early Modern Literary Studies* 8.2 (September 2000). Online: http://extra.shu.ac.uk/emls/08-2/abrapete.html.

Adelman, Janet. *The Common Liar: An Essay on* Antony and Cleopatra. New Haven: Yale University Press, 1973.

Adler, Doris. 'Imaginary Toads in Real Gardens', *English Literary Renaissance* 11.3 (1981): 235–60.

Alexander, William, Earl of Stirling. *Jvlivs Caesar*. London, 1637.

Altman, Joel B. '"Vile Participation": The Amplification of Violence in the Theater of *Henry V*', *Shakespeare Quarterly* 42 (1991): 1–32.

Anonymous. *A Pleasant Conceited Historie, called The Taming of a Shrew*. London, 1594.

——. *Claudius Tiberius Nero*. Ed. Sharon McDonnell. Online: http://extra.shu.ac.uk/emls/iemls/renplays/ctneroindex.html.

——. *The tragedie of Caesar and Pompey or Caesars reuenge*. London, 1607.

——. ('R. A.'). *The valiant Welshman*. London: 1663.

——. ('W. S'.). *The lamentable tragedie of Locrine*. London, 1595.

Archer, John Michael. *Old Worlds: Egypt, Southwest Asia, India, and Russia in Early Modern English Writing*. Stanford: Stanford University Press, 2001.

Aristotle. *Poetics*. Trans. S. H. Butcher. Online: http://classics.mit.edu/Aristotle/poetics.mb.text.

Armin, Robert. *The History of the Two Maids of More-Clacke*. Ed. Alexander S. Liddie. New York: Garland, 1979.

Atsuhiko, Hirota. 'Forms of Empires: Rome and its Peripheries in *Cymbeline*', *Shakespearean International Yearbook* 4 (2004): 279–93.

Balbo di Correggio, Francisco. *The Siege of Malta*. Trans. Ernle Bradford. Harmondsworth: Penguin, 1965.

Banerjee, Pompa. *Burning Women: Widows, Witches, and Early Modern European Travelers in India*. Basingstoke: Palgrave, 2003.

Barish, Jonas. 'Hats, Clocks and Doublets: Some Shakespearean Anachronisms'. In *Shakespeare's Universe: Renaissance Ideas and Conventions*. Ed. John M. Mucciolo. Aldershot: Scolar Press, 1996. 29–36.

Battenhouse, Roy. 'The Relation of Henry V to Tamburlaine', *Shakespeare Survey*, 27 (1974): 71–9.

Bawlf, Samuel. *The Secret Voyage of Sir Francis Drake*. Harmondsworth: Penguin, 2003.

Bednarz, James P. 'When did Shakespeare write the choruses of *Henry V*', *Notes and Queries* 53.4 (December, 2006): 486–9.

Beer, Anna. *Bess: The Life of Lady Ralegh, Wife to Sir Walter*. London: Constable & Robinson, 2004.

Berek, Peter. '*Locrine* Revised, *Selimus*, and Early Responses to *Tamburlaine*', *Research Opportunities in Renaissance Drama* 23 (1980): 33–54.

——. '*Tamburlaine*'s Weak Sons: Imitation as Interpretation Before 1593', *Renaissance Drama* 13 (1982): 55–82.

Betteridge, Thomas. *Shakespearean Fantasy and Politics*. Hatfield: University of Hertfordshire Press, 2005.

Bisaha, Nancy. *Creating East and West: Renaissance Humanists and the Ottoman Turks*. Philadelphia: University of Pennsylvania Press, 2004.

Boas, Frederick S. *University Drama in the Tudor Age*. Oxford: The Clarendon Press, 1914.

Boling, Ronald J. 'Anglo-Welsh Relations in *Cymbeline*', *Shakespeare Quarterly* 51.1 (Spring 2000): 33–66.

Bowers, Rick. 'Tamburlaine in Ludlow', *Notes and Queries* 243 (1998): 361–3.

Bradbrook, M. C. *John Webster: Citizen and Dramatist*. London: Weidenfeld and Nicolson, 1980.

Brennan, Michael G. 'English Contact with Europe'. In *Shakespeare and Renaissance Europe*. Ed. Andrew Hadfield and Paul Hammond. London: Thomson Learning, 2005. 53–97.

Broude, Ronald. 'Roman and Goth in *Titus Andronicus*', *Shakespeare Studies* 6 (1970): 27–34.

Brower, Reuben. *Hero and Saint: Shakespeare and the Graeco-Roman Historical Tradition*. Oxford: The Clarendon Press, 1971.

Brown, John Russell, ed. *Antony and Cleopatra: A Selection of Critical Essays*. Basingstoke: Macmillan, 1968.

Brown, Stuart E., Jr., Lorraine F. Myers, and Eileen M. Chappell. *Pocahontas' Descendants*. New York: Genealogical Publishing Co., 1985.

Bullough, Geoffrey. 'Pre-Conquest Historical Themes in Elizabethan Drama'. In *Medieval Literature and Civilization: Studies in Memory of G. N. Garmonsway*. London: The Athlone Press, 1969. 289–321.

Burnett, Mark Thornton. '"The Heart of My Mystery": *Hamlet* and Secrets'. In *New Essays on Hamlet*. Ed. John Manning and Mark Thornton Burnett. New York: AMS Press, 1994. 21–46.

Butler, Martin. *Theatre and Crisis 1632–1642*. Cambridge: Cambridge University Press, 1984.

Camden, William. 'The Romans in Britaine'. In *Britannia*. Trans. Philemon Holland (1607). Online: http://e3.uci.edu/%7Epapyri/cambrit/romanseng.html.

Carey, Robert, Earl of Monmouth. *Memoirs*. In John Nichols, *Progresses of King James the First*. London, 1828.

Cavell, Stanley. *Disowning Knowledge in Six Plays of Shakespeare*. Cambridge: Cambridge University Press, 1987.

Cavendish, Margaret. *The Unnatural Tragedy*. London, 1662.

Cawley, Robert Ralston. 'Warner and the Voyagers', *Modern Philology* 20 (1922): 113–47.

Chandler, John. *John Leland's Itinerary: Travels in Tudor England*. Stroud: Sutton, 1993.

Chapman, George. *Caesar and Pompey*. London, 1631.

——. 'AN EPICED, OR Funerall Song: On the most disastrous Death, of the High-borne Prince of Men, HENRY Prince of Wales, &c'. In *An Epicede or Funerall Song*. London, 1612.

Charles, B. G. *George Owen of Henllys: A Welsh Elizabethan*. Aberystwyth: National Library of Wales Press, 1973.

Cheney, Patrick, 'Biographical Representations: Marlowe's Life of the Author'. In *Shakespeare, Marlowe, Jonson: New Directions in Biography*. Ed. Takashi Kozuka and J. R. Mulryne. Aldershot: Ashgate, 2006. 183–204.

Clapham, John. *The historie of Great Britannie*. London, 1606.

Coronato, Rocco. 'Inducting Pocahontas', *Symbiosis* 2.1 (1998): 24–38.

Crane, Nicholas. *Mercator: The Man Who Mapped the Planet* [2002]. London: Phoenix, 2003.

Crispin, Philip. 'Louis XII, Julius II and Pierre de Gringore's *Sottie du Jeu du Prince des Sots* (1512)'. In *Mighty Europe 1400–1700. The Writing of an Early Modern Continent*. Ed. Andrew Hiscock. Burlington: Ashgate, forthcoming.

Culhane, Peter. 'Livy and Titus Andronicus', *English* 55 (spring 2006): 1–13.

Curran, John E., Jr., *Roman Invasions: The British History, Protestant Anti-Romanism, and the Historical Imagination in England, 1530–1660*. Newark: University of Delaware Press, 2002.

——. 'Royalty Unlearned, Honor Untaught: British Savages and Historiographical Change in *Cymbeline*', *Comparative Drama* 31:2 (summer, 1997): 277–303.

Danby, John F. '*Antony and Cleopatra*': A Shakespearean Adjustment. In *Antony and Cleopatra*. Ed. John Drakakis. Basingstoke: Macmillan, 1994. 33–55.

Davies, H. Neville. 'Jacobean "Antony and Cleopatra"'. In *Antony and Cleopatra*. Ed. John Drakakis. Basingstoke: Macmillan, 1994. 126–65.

Dean, Paul. '"The Tragedy of Tiberius" [1607]: Debts to Shakespeare', *Notes and Queries* 31.2 (June, 1984): 213–14.

Dekker, Thomas. *The Whore of Babylon*. London: 1606.

De Luna, B. N. *Jonson's Romish Plot: A Study of* Catiline *in its Historical Context*. Oxford: Clarendon Press, 1967.

Desai, Rupin W. '*Hamlet* and Paternity', *The Upstart Crow* 3 (Fall, 1980): 97–106.

Dimmock, Matthew. *New Turkes: Dramatizing Islam and the Ottomans in Early Modern England*. Aldershot: Ashgate, 2005.

Donaldson, Beth. 'Pocahontas as Gift: Gender and Diplomacy on the Anglo-Powhatan Frontier', *Journal of the American Studies Association* 30 (1999): 1–17.

——. '"What means Sicilia? He something seems unsettled": Sicily, Russia, and Bohemia in *The Winter's Tale*', *Comparative Drama* 30.3 (Fall, 1996): 311–24.

Drayton, Michael, *Poly-Olbion*. In *The Complete Works of Michael Drayton*. Ed. J. W. Hebel, vol. 4, 5 vols. Oxford: Basil Blackwell, 1933.

Egan, Robert. 'A Muse of Fire: Henry V in the Light of Tamburlaine', *Modern Language Quarterly* 29 (1968): 15–28

Empson, William. *Faustus and the Censor: The English Faust-book and Marlowe's Doctor Faustus*. Ed. John Henry Jones. Oxford: Basil Blackwell, 1987.

——. *The Strengths of Shakespeare's Shrew*. Ed. John Haffenden. Sheffield: Sheffield Academic Publications, 1996.

Erne, Lukas. '"Popish Tricks" and "a Ruinous Monastery": *Titus Andronicus* and the Question of Shakespeare's Catholicism'. In *The Limits of Textuality*. Ed. Lukas Erne and Guillemette Bolens. Tübingen: Narr, 2000. 135–55.

Faery, Rebecca Blevins. *Cartographies of Desire: Captivity, Race, and Sex in the Shaping of an American Nation*. Norman: University of Oklahoma Press, 1999.

Findlay, Alison. *Illegitimate power: Bastards in Renaissance Drama*. Manchester: Manchester University Press, 1994.

Fisher, Jasper. *Fvimus Troes*. London, 1633.

Fletcher, John. *Bonduca*. In *Beaumont and Fletcher*, vol. II. Ed. J. St Loe Strachey. London: Ernest Benn, 1950.

——, Nathan Field and Philip Massinger. *The Knight of Malta*. London, 1647.

——. *Valentinian*. Ed. Martin Wiggins. Oxford: Oxford University Press, 1998.

Floyd-Wilson, Mary. 'Delving to the root: *Cymbeline*, Scotland, and the English race'. In *British Identities and English Renaissance Literature*. Ed. David J. Baker and Willy Maley. Cambridge: Cambridge University Press, 2002. 101–15.

Ford, P. Jeffrey. 'Bloody Spectacle in Shakespeare's Roman Plays: The Politics and Aesthetics of Violence', *Iowa State Journal of Research* 54.4 (May 1980): 481–9.

Fowler, Alastair. 'Two Notes on *Hamlet*'. In *New Essays on Hamlet*. Ed. John Manning and Mark Thornton Burnett. New York: AMS Press, 1994. 3–10.

Fraser, Antonia. *Mary, Queen of Scots*. London: Weidenfeld and Nicolson, 1969.

——. *The Gunpowder Plot: Terror and Faith in 1605*. London: Arrow, 1999.

Freedman, Sylvia. *Poor Penelope: Lady Penelope Rich, An Elizabethan Woman*. Bourne End: The Kensal Press, 1983.

Frye, Northrop. *A Natural Perspective: The Development of Shakespearean Comedy and Romance*. New York: Columbia University Press, 1965.

Frye, Roland Mushat. *The Renaissance Hamlet: Issues and Responses in 1600*. Princeton: Princeton University Press, 1984.

Frye, Susan. *Elizabeth I and the Competition for Representation*. New York: Oxford University Press, 1993.

Fudge, Erica. 'Pocahontas's Baptism: Reformed Theology and the Paradox of Desire', *Critical Survey* 11.1 (1999): 15–30.

Fumerton, Patricia. *Cultural Aesthetics: Renaissance Literature and the Practice of Social Ornament*. Chicago: University of Chicago Press, 1991.

Geoffrey of Monmouth. *The History of the Kings of Britain*. Trans. Lewis Thorpe. Harmondsworth: Penguin, 1966.

Gillies, John. 'Marlowe, the *Timur* Myth, and the Motives of Geography'. In *Playing the Globe: Genre and Geography in English Renaissance Drama*. Ed. John Gillies and Virginia Mason Vaughan. Cranbury, N.J.: Associated University Presses, 1998. 203–29.

Gleach, Frederic W. 'Pocahontas and Captain John Smith Revisited'. In *Actes du Vingt-Cinquième Congrès des Algonquinistes*. Ed. William Cowan. Ottawa: Carleton University, 1994. 167–86.

Goffman, Daniel. *The Ottoman Empire and Early Modern Europe*. Cambridge: Cambridge University Press, 2002.

Goldberg, Jonathan. *James I and the Politics of Literature: Jonson, Shakespeare, Donne, and Their Contemporaries*. Baltimore: The Johns Hopkins University Press, 1983.

Grant, Teresa. 'White Bears in *Mucedorus*, *The Winter's Tale*, and *Oberon, the Faery Prince*', *Notes and Queries* 48.3 (September 2001): 311–13.

Green, Rayna. 'The Pocahontas Perplex', *Massachusetts Review* 16.4 (1975): 698–714.

Green, Reina. 'Poisoned Ears and Parental Advice in *Hamlet*', *Early Modern Literary Studies* 11.3 (January, 2006). Online: http://extra.shu.ac.uk/emls/11-3/greeham2.htm.

Greene, Robert. *The comicall historie of Alphonsus, King of Aragon*. London: 1599.

——?. *A Pleasant Conceyted Comedie of* George a Greene, *the Pinner of Wakefield*. London, 1599.

Griffiths, Huw. 'The Geographies of Shakespeare's *Cymbeline*', *English Literary Renaissance* 34.3 (2004): 339–58.

Hadfield, Andrew. 'Shakespeare and republicanism: history and cultural materialism', *Textual Practice* 17.3 (2003): 461–83.

——. 'Tarquin's Everlasting Banishment: Republicanism and Constitutionalism in *The Rape of Lucrece* and *Titus Andronicus*', *Parergon* 19.1 (2002): 77–104.

——. 'Hamlet's Country Matters: The "Scottish Play" within the Play'. In *Shakespeare and Scotland*. Ed. Willy Maley and Andrew Murphy. Manchester: Manchester University Press, 2004.

——. '"The power and rights of the crown in *Hamlet* and *King Lear*: "The king – the king's to blame"', *Review of English Studies* 54 (2003): 566–86.

——. 'Tamburlaine as the "Scourge of God" and *The First English Life of King Henry the Fifth*', *Notes and Queries* 50.4 (December, 2003): 399–400.

——. '"The naked and the dead": Elizabethan perceptions of Ireland'. In *Travel and Drama in Shakespeare's Time*. Ed. Jean-Pierre Maquerlot and Michèle Willems. Cambridge: Cambridge University Press, 1996. 32–54.

Haig, Matt. *Dead Fathers Club*. London: Jonathan Cape, 2006.

Hamilton, Donna B. *Virgil and* The Tempest. Columbus: Ohio State University Press, 1990.

Hancock, Brecken Rose. 'Roman or Revenger: The Definition and Distortion of Masculine Identity in *Titus Andronicus*', *Early Modern Literary Studies* 10.1 (May 2004). Online: http://extra.shu.ac.uk/emls/10-1/hancroma.htm.

Hartog, François. *The Mirror of Herodotus: The Representation of the Other in the Writing of History*. Trans. Janet Lloyd. Berkeley: University of California Press, 1988.

Harvey, Richard. *Philadelphvs, or A Defence of Brutes, and the Brutans History*. London: John Wolfe, 1593.

Havely, Cicely Palser. 'Changing critical perspectives'. In *Shakespeare: Texts and Contexts*. Ed. Kiernan Ryan. Basingstoke: Macmillan, 2000. 145–53.

Hawkes, Terence. *Shakespeare in the Present*. London: Routledge, 2002.

Hayton, Alison G. '"The King my father?": Paternity in *Hamlet*', *Hamlet Studies* 9.1–2 (Summer and Winter 1987): 53–64.

Hentzner, Paul. *Travels in England during the reign of Queen Elizabeth*. Online: http://etext.library.adelaide.edu.au/h/hentzner-travels/.

Hodgkins, Christopher. 'The Nubile Savage: Pocahontas as Heathen Convert and Virgilian Bride', *Renaissance Papers* (1998): 81–90.

Hoff, Linda Kay. *Hamlet's Choice*. Lampeter: The Edwin Mellen Press, 1990.

Holderness, Graham. *Shakespeare Recycled*. Hemel Hempstead: Harvester Wheatsheaf, 1992.

Hopkins, Lisa. *Christopher Marlowe: A Literary Life*. Basingstoke: Palgrave, 2000.

——. 'The Dark Side of the Moon: Semiramis and Titania'. In *Goddesses and Queens: The Iconography of Elizabeth I*. Eds Annaliese Connolly and Lisa Hopkins. Manchester: Manchester University Press, 2007.

Hotson, Leslie. *Shakespeare's Sonnets Dated*. London: Rupert Hart-Davis, 1949.

Huffman, Clifford Chalmers. 'Bassianus and the British History in *Titus Andronicus*', *English Language Notes* 11 (March 1974): 175–81.

Hughes, Thomas. *The Misfortunes of Arthur*. London, 1587.

Huke, R. E., and E. H. Huke. *Rice: Then and Now*. Online: http://www.riceweb. org/History.htm.

Hulme, Peter. *Colonial Encounters: Europe and the Native Caribbean 1492–1797*. London: Methuen, 1986.

Hunt, Caroline. 'Hamlet, Tiberius, and the Elephants' Graveyard', *Shakespeare Bulletin* 23.3 (Fall 2005): 43–51.

Iversen, Erik. *The Myth of Egypt and its Hieroglyphics in European Tradition*. Copenhagen: GEC Gad, 1961.

James, Heather. *Shakespeare's Troy: Drama, politics, and the translation of empire*. Cambridge: Cambridge University Press, 1997.

——. 'Dido's Ear: Tragedy and the Politics of Response', *Shakespeare Quarterly* 52.3 (Fall, 2001): 360–82.

Jardine, Lisa. *Reading Shakespeare Historically*. London: Routledge, 1996.

——. *Worldly Goods: A New History of the Renaissance*. Basingstoke: Macmillan, 1996.

Jenkins, Elizabeth. *Elizabeth the Great*. London: Panther, 1972.

Jenkins, William Warren. 'The Princess Pocahontas and Three Englishmen Named John'. In *No Fairer Land: Studies in Southern Literature Before 1900*. Ed. J. Lasley Dameron and James W. Mathews. Troy, N.Y.: Whitston, 1986. 8–20.

Jones, Emrys. 'Stuart Cymbeline', *Essays in Criticism* 2 (1961): 84–99.

Jonson, Ben. *The Gypsies Metamorphosed*. In *Ben Jonson*, vol. vii . Eds C.H. Herford and Percy and Evelyn Simpson. Oxford: The Clarendon Press, 1941.

——. *Sejanus*. Ed. Philip Ayres. Manchester: Manchester University Press, 1990.

——. *The Vision of Delight*. In *Ben Jonson*, vol. vii . Eds C.H. Herford and Percy and Evelyn Simpson. Oxford: The Clarendon Press, 1941.

Kendall, Roy. *Christopher Marlowe and Richard Baines: Journeys through the Elizabethan Underground*. London: Associated University Presses, 2003.

Kenyon, J.P. *The Stuarts* [1958]. London: Fontana, 1966.

Kerrigan, John. 'The Romans in Britain, 1603–1614'. In *The Accession of James I: Historical and Cultural Consequences*. Ed. Glenn Burgess, Rowland Wymer and Jason Lawrence. Basingstoke: Palgrave, 2006. 113–39.

Kewes, Paulina. 'Contemporary Europe in Elizabethan and Early Stuart Drama'. In *Shakespeare and Renaissance Europe*. Ed. Andrew Hadfield and Paul Hammond. London: Thomson Learning, 2005. 150–92.

King, Ros. *Cymbeline: Constructions of Britain*. Aldershot: Ashgate, 2005.

Kirsch, Arthur. *Shakespeare and the Experience of Love*. Cambridge: Cambridge University Press, 1981.

Kistler, Suzanne F. 'The Significance of the Missing Hero in Chapman's *Caesar and Pompey*', *Modern Language Quarterly* 40 (1979): 339–57.

Klause, John. 'Politics, Heresy, and Martyrdom in Shakespeare's Sonnet 124 and *Titus Andronicus*'. In *Shakespeare's Sonnets: Critical Essays*. Ed. James Schiffer. London: Garland, 1999. 219–40.

Knowles, James. '"To Enlight the Darksome Night, Pale Cinthia Doth Arise": Anna of Denmark, Elizabeth I and the Images of Royalty'. In *Women and Culture at the Courts of the Stuart Queens*. Ed. Clare McManus. Basingstoke: Palgrave Macmillan, 2003. 21–48.

Koebner, Richard. '"The imperial crown of this realm": Henry VIII, Constantine the Great, and Polydore Vergil', *Bulletin of the Institute of Historical Research* 26 (1953): 29–52.

Lacey, Robert. *Sir Walter Ralegh*. London: Weidenfeld & Nicolson, 1973.

Lawry, J. S. '"Perishing Root and Increasing Vine" in *Cymbeline*', *Shakespeare Studies* 12 (1979): 179–93.

Lee, Nathaniel. *Lucius Junius Brutus*. Ed. John Loftis. London: Edward Arnold, 1967.

Leggatt, Alexander. 'The Island of Miracles: An Approach to *Cymbeline*', *Shakespeare Survey* 10 (1977): 191–209.

Levin, Harry. 'Shakespeare's Italians'. In *Shakespeare's Italy: Functions of Italian Locations in Renaissance* Drama. Ed. Michele Marrapodi, A. J. Hoenselaars, Marcello Capuzzo and L. Falzon Santucci. Manchester: Manchester University Press, 1993. 17–29.

Levy, F. J. 'Hayward, Daniel, and the Beginnings of Politic History in England', *Huntington Library Quarterly* (1987): 1–34.

Lindheim, Nancy R. '*King Lear* as Pastoral Tragedy'. In *Some Facets of King Lear: Essays in Prismatic Criticism*. Ed. Rosalie L. Colie and F.T. Flahiff. London: Heinemann, 1974. 169–84.

Little, Arthur L., Jr., *Shakespeare Jungle Fever: National-Imperial Re-Visions of Race, Rape, and Sacrifice*. Stanford: Stanford University Press, 2000.

Lloyd, Lodowick. *The Pilgrimage of Princes*. London, 1573.

Logan, Robert A. *Shakespeare's Marlowe: The Influence of Christopher Marlowe on Shakespeare's Artistry*. Burlington, VT: Ashgate, 2007.

McMullan, Gordon. *The Politics of Unease in the Plays of John Fletcher*. Amherst: University of Massachusetts Press, 1994.

McNulty, Robert, ed *Ludovico Ariosto's Orlando Furioso, translated into English Heroical Verse by Sir John Harington* [1591]. Oxford: The Clarendon Press, 1972.

MacLure, Millar, ed. *Marlowe: The Critical Heritage 1588–1896*. London: Routledge, 1979.

Macritchie, David. *Scottish Gypsies Under the Stewarts*. Edinburgh: David Douglas, 1894.

Maguire, Laurie. '"Household Kates": Chez Petruchio, Percy and Plantagenet'. In *Gloriana's Face*. Ed. S.P. Cerasano and Marion Wynne-Davies. Hemel Hempstead: Harvester Wheatsheaf, 1992. 129–65.

Magnus, Olaus. *Description of the Northern Peoples* [1555]. Trans. Peter Fisher and Humphrey Higgens. London: The Hakluyt Society, 1996.

Maley, Willy. 'Postcolonial Shakespeare: British Identity Formation and *Cymbeline*'. In *Shakespeare's Late Plays: New Readings*. Ed. Jennifer Richards and James Knowles. Edinburgh: Edinburgh University Press, 1999. 145–57.

Mallin, Eric S. *Inscribing the Time: Shakespeare and the End of Elizabethan England*. Berkeley: University of California Press, 1995.

Marcus, Leah. *Puzzling Shakespeare: Local Reading and its Discontents*. Berkeley: University of California Press, 1988.

Marlowe, Christopher. *Dido, Queen of Carthage*. In *Christopher Marlowe: The Complete Plays*. Ed. Mark Thornton Burnett. London: Everyman, 1999.

——. *The Jew of Malta*. In *Christopher Marlowe: The Complete Plays*. Ed. Mark Thornton Burnett. London: Everyman, 1999.

——. *The Massacre at Paris*. In *Christopher Marlowe: The Complete Plays*. Ed. Mark Thornton Burnett. London: Everyman, 1999.

——. *Tamburlaine the Great*. Ed. J. S. Cunningham. Manchester: Manchester University Press, 1981.

Marsh, D.C.R. *'The Recurring Miracle': A Study of Cymbeline and the Last Plays*. Lincoln: University of Nebraska Press, 1962.

Maslen, R. W. 'Sidneian Geographies', *Sidney Journal* 20.2 (2002): 45–55.

Mason, Roger A. 'Scotching the Brut: Politics, History and National Myth in Sixteenth-Century Britain'. In *Scotland and England 1286–1815*. Ed. Roger A. Mason. Edinburgh: John Donald, 1987. 60–84.

Massinger, Philip. *The Roman Actor*. In *Five Stuart Tragedies*. Ed. A.K. McIlwraith. London: Oxford University Press, 1953.

Matar, Nabil, and Rudolph Stoekel. 'Europe's Mediterranean Frontier: The Moor'. In *Shakespeare and Renaissance Europe*. Ed. Andrew Hadfield and Paul Hammond. London: Thomson Learning, 2005. 220–52.

Matthews, William. 'The Egyptians in Scotland: The Political History of a Myth', *Viator* 1 1970): 289–306.

Maxwell, Baldwin. *Studies in the Shakespearean Apocrypha*. New York: King's Crown Press, 1956.

Maxwell, Julie. 'Counter-Reformation Versions of Saxo: A New Source for *Hamlet*?', *Renaissance Quarterly* 57.2 (summer 2004): 518–60.

May, Thomas. *The Tragedy of Julia Agrippina*. Ed. Lyndsey Clarke. Online: http://extra.shu.ac.uk/emls/iemls/renplays/mayindex.html.

Mayall, David. *Gypsy Identities 1500–2000: From Egipcyans and Moon-men to the Ethnic Romany*. London: Routledge, 2004.

Mexia, Pedro. *The imperiall historie*. Trans. Edward Grimeston. London, 1623.

Michel, J. Y. 'Monuments in Late Elizabethan Literature: A Conservatory of Vanishing Traditions', *Early Modern Literary Studies* 9.2 (September, 2003). Online: http://extra.shu.ac.uk/emls/09-2/michmonu.html.

Mikalachki, Jodi. 'The masculine romance of Roman Britain: *Cymbeline* and early modern English nationalism', *Shakespeare Quarterly* 46.3 (Fall, 1995): 301–22.

Miles, Geoffrey. *Shakespeare and the Constant Romans*. Oxford: Clarendon Press, 1996.

Miller, Anthony. *Roman Triumphs and Early Modern English Culture*. Basingstoke: Palgrave, 2001.

Miola, Robert S. '*Cymbeline*: Shakespeare's Valediction to Rome'. In *Roman Images*. Ed. Annabel Patterson. Baltimore: The Johns Hopkins University Press, 1984. 51–62.

———. *Shakespeare's Rome*. Cambridge: Cambridge University Press, 1983.

Moffet, Robin. '*Cymbeline* and the Nativity', *Shakespeare Quarterly* 13 (1962): 207–18.

More, Henry (?). *Pathomachia: or, The battell of affections*. London, 1630.

Morris, Helen. 'Queen Elizabeth I "Shadowed" in Cleopatra', *Huntington Library Quarterly* 32 (1969): 271–8.

Muir, Kenneth. 'Elizabeth I, Jodelle, and Cleopatra', *Renaissance Drama* 2 (1969): 197–206.

Nashe, Thomas. *The Unfortunate Traveller and Other Works*. Ed. J. B. Steane. Harmondsworth: Penguin, 1972.

Neill, Michael. *Putting History to the Question: Power, Politics, and Society in English Renaissance Drama*. New York: Columbia University Press, 2000.

———. 'Monuments and ruins as symbols in *The Duchess of Malfi*'. In *Themes in Drama 4: Drama and Symbolism*. Ed. James Redmond. Cambridge: Cambridge University Press, 1982. 71–87.

———. 'Broken English and Broken Irish: Nation, Language, and the Optic of Power in Shakespeare's Histories', *Shakespeare Quarterly* 45 (1994): 10–28.

Nelson, Alan H. 'George Buc, William Shakespeare, and the Folger *George a Greene*', *Shakespeare Quarterly* 49.1 (Spring 1998): 74–83

Nicholl, Charles. *The Creature in the Map: Sir Walter Ralegh's Quest for El Dorado*. London: Vintage, 1996.

Oakley-Brown, Liz. '*Titus Andronicus* and the cultural politics of translation in early modern England', *Renaissance Studies* 19.3 (June 2005): 325–47.

Olsen, Thomas G. 'Iachimo's "Drug-Damn'd Italy" and the Problem of British National Character in *Cymbeline*'. In *Shakespeare Yearbook 10: Shakespeare and Italy*. Edited by Holger Klein and Michele Marrapodi. Lewiston: Edwin Mellen Press, 1999). 269–96.

Palmer, Daryl W. *Writing Russia in the Age of Shakespeare*. Aldershot: Ashgate, 2004.

———. 'Winter, tyranny and knowledge in *The Winter's Tale*', *Shakespeare Quarterly* 46.3 (Fall 1995): 323–39.

Parker, Patricia. 'Romance and Empire: Anachronistic *Cymbeline*'. In *Unfolded Tales: Essays on Renaissance Romance*. Ed. George M. Logan and Gordon Teskey. Ithaca: Cornell University Press, 1989. 189–207.

Parolin, Peter A. 'Anachronistic Italy: Cultural alliances and national identity in *Cymbeline*', *Shakespeare Studies* 30 (2002): 188–215.

Peacock, John. 'The Image of Charles I as a Roman emperor'. In *The 1630s: Interdisciplinary essays on culture and politics in the Caroline era*. Ed. Ian Atherton and Julie Sanders. Manchester: Manchester University Press, 2006. 50–73.

Peele, George. *The Battle of Alcazar*. In *The Stukeley Plays*. Ed. Charles Edelman. Manchester: Manchester University Press, 2005.

Pennel, Charles A. 'Robert Greene and "King or Kaisar"', *Notes and Queries* n.s. 3 (1965): 124–6.

Peterson, Douglas L. *Time, Tide and Tempest: A Study of Shakespeare's Romances.* San Marino: The Huntington Library, 1973.

Peyré, Yves. '"Excellent dumb discourse": le symbolisme des dumb shows de la tragédie élisabéthaine'. In *Tudor Theatre: «Let there be covenants »: Convention et théâtre.* Ed. André Lascombes. Tours: Peter Lang, 1998. 89–102.

Pincombe, Michael. 'Classical and Contemporary Sources of the "Gloomy Woods" of *Titus Andronicus*: Ovid, Seneca, Spenser'. In *Shakespearean Continuities: Essays in Honour of E. A. J. Honigmann.* Ed. John Batchelor, Tom Cain and Claire Lamont. Basingstoke: Macmillan, 1997. 40–55.

Poole, William. '*Julius Caesar* and *Caesars Revenge* Again', *Notes and Queries* 49.2 (June 2002): 226–8.

Preda, Roxana. 'The Angel in the Ecosystem Revisited: Disney's *Pocahontas* and Postmodern Ethics'. In *From Virgin Land to Disney World: Nature and Its Discontents in the USA of Yesterday and Today.* Ed. Bernd Herzogenrath. Amsterdam: Rodopi, 2001. 317–40.

Price, David A. *Love and Hate in Jamestown: John Smith, Pocahontas and the Heart of a New Nation.* London: Faber and Faber, 2004.

Pugliatti, Paola. *Beggary and Theatre in Early Modern England.* Aldershot: Ashgate, 2003.

Quiller-Couch, Arthur. 'Shakespeare's Workmanship: *The Winter's Tale*'. In *The Winter's Tale: Critical Essays.* Ed. Maurice Hunt. New York: Garland, 1995. 82–93.

Raman, Shankar. *Framing "India": The Colonial Imaginary in Early Modern Culture.* Stanford: Stanford University Press, 2002.

Randall, Dale B.J. *Jonson's Gypsies Unmasked: Background and Theme of* The Gypsies Metamorphos'd. Durham, N.C.: Duke University Press, 1975.

———. *Winter Fruit: English Drama 1642–1660.* Lexington: The University Press of Kentucky, 1995.

Ravelhofer, Barbara. '"Beasts of Recreacion": Henslowe's White Bears', *English Literary Renaissance* 32.2 (2002): 287–323.

Redmond, Michael J. '"My lord, I fear, has forgot Britain": Rome, Italy, and the (Re)construction of British National Identity'. In *Shakespeare Yearbook 10: Shakespeare and Italy.* Edited by Holger Klein and Michele Marrapodi. Lewiston: Edwin Mellen Press, 1999. 297–313.

Richards, Nathaniel. *Messalina.* Ed. Samantha Gibbs. Online: http://extra.shu.ac.uk/emls/iemls/resources.html.

Richmond, Hugh M. 'Shakespeare's Roman Trilogy: The Climax in *Cymbeline*', *Studies in the Literary Imagination* 5 (1972): 129–39.

Riggs, David. *The World of Christopher Marlowe.* London: Faber and Faber, 2004.

Robertson, Karen. 'Pocahontas at the Masque', *Signs: A Journal of Women, Culture and Society* 21 (1996): 551–83.

———. 'First Friday Talk'. Online: http://vassun.vassar.edu/~robertso/Poca/First_Friday_Talk1.html.

Robinson, W. R. B. 'Dr. Thomas Phaer's Report on the Harbours and Customs Adminstration of Wales under Edward VI', *Bullboard of Celtic Studies* (1972): 485–90.

Robson, Mark. 'Looking with ears, hearing with eyes: Shakespeare and the ear of the early modern', *Early Modern Literary Studies* 7.1 (May, 2001). Online: http://extra.shu.ac.uk/emls/07-1/robsears.htm.

Rogers, J. M. and R. M. Ward. *Süleyman the Magnificent*. London: British Museum, 1988.

Ronan, Clifford. *'Antike Roman': Power Symbology and the Roman Play in Early Modern England, 1585–1635*. Athens: University of Georgia Press, 1995.

Roper, Louis H. 'Unmasquing the connections between Jacobean politics and policy: the circle of Anna of Denmark and the beginning of the English empire, 1614–18'. In *"High and Mighty Queens" of Early Modern England: Realities and Representations*. Ed. Carole Levin, Jo Eldridge Carney, and Debra Barrett-Graves. New York: Palgrave Macmillan, 2003. 45–59.

Ross, Joan Warchol. *'Cymbeline's* Debt to Holinshed: The Richness of III.i'. In *Shakespeare's Romances Reconsidered*. Ed. Carol McGinnis Kay and Henry E. Jacobs. Lincoln: University of Nebraska Press, 1978. 104–12.

Sacerdoti, Gilberto. 'Three Kings, Herod of Jewry, and a Child: Apocalypse and Infinity of the World in *Antony and Cleopatra*'. In *Italian Studies in Shakespeare and His Contemporaries*. Ed. Michele Marrapodi and Giorgio Melchiori. Newark: University of Delaware Press, 1999. 165–84.

Salmon, J. H. M. 'Seneca and Tacitus in Jacobean England'. In *The Mental World of the Jacobean Court*. Ed. Linda Levy Peck. Cambridge: Cambridge University Press, 1991. 169–88.

Scalingi, Paula Louise. 'The Scepter or the Distaff: The Question of Female Sovereignty, 1516–1607', *The Historian* 41 (1978): 59–75.

Schanzer, Ernest. 'A Neglected Source of "Julius Caesar"', *Notes and Queries* 199 (May, 1954): 196–7.

Schwyzer, Philip A. 'A Map of Greater Cambria', *Early Modern Literary Studies* 4.2 (September, 1998). Online: http://extra.shu.ac.uk/emls/04-2/schwamap.htm.

——. 'The Jacobean Union Controversy and *King Lear*'. In *The Accession of James I: Historical and Cultural Consequences*. Ed. Glenn Burgess, Rowland Wymer and Jason Lawrence. Basingstoke: Palgrave, 2006. 34–47.

Scott-Warren, Jason. *Sir John Harington and the Book as Gift*. Oxford: Oxford University Press, 2001.

Sessions, W. A. *Henry Howard, The Poet Earl of Surrey: A Life*. Oxford: Oxford University Press, 1999.

Shakespeare, William. *All's Well That Ends Well*. Ed. Barbara Everett. Harmondsworth: Penguin, 1970.

——. *Antony and Cleopatra*. Ed. Emrys Jones. Harmondsworth: Penguin, 1977.

——. *Cymbeline*. Ed. Roger Warren. Oxford: Oxford University Press, 1998.

——. *Hamlet*. Ed. Harold Jenkins. London: Methuen, 1982.

——. *Henry V*. Ed. Gary Taylor. Oxford: Oxford University Press, 1994.

——. *Henry VI, Part One*. Ed. John Dover Wilson. Cambridge: Cambridge University Press, 1952.

——. *Henry VI, Part Two*. Ed. John Dover Wilson. Cambridge: Cambridge University Press, 1968.

——. *Henry VI, Part Three*. Ed. John Dover Wilson. Cambridge: Cambridge University Press, 1968.

——. *Julius Caesar*. Ed. Norman Sanders. Harmondsworth: Penguin, 1967.

——. *The Merry Wives of Windsor*. Ed. Giorgio Melchiori. London: Thomas Nelson & Sons, 2000.

——. *The Rape of Lucrece*. In *The Poems*. Ed. John Roe. Cambridge: Cambridge University Press, 1992.

——. *Richard III*. Ed. E.A.J. Honigmann. Harmondsworth: Penguin, 1968.

——. *The Tempest*. Ed. Virginia Mason Vaughan and Alden T. Vaughan. London: Thomas Nelson, 1999.

——. *Titus Andronicus*. Ed. Jonathan Bate. London: Routledge, 1995.

——. *The Winter's Tale*. Ed. J.H.P. Pafford. London: Routledge, 1988.

Shapiro, James. *Rival Playwrights: Marlowe, Jonson, Shakespeare*. New York: Columbia University Press, 1991.

——. *1599: A Year in the Life of William Shakespeare*. London: Faber and Faber, 2005.

Shepard, Alan. *Marlowe's Soldiers: Rhetorics of Masculinity in the Age of the Armada*. Aldershot: Ashgate, 2002.

Simonds, Peggy Muñoz. *Myth, Emblem, and Music in Shakespeare's* Cymbeline: *An Iconographic Reconstruction*. Newark: University of Delaware Press, 1992.

Soellner, Rolf. 'Chapman's *Caesar and Pompey* and the Fortunes of Prince Henry', *Medieval and Renaissance Drama in England* 2 (1985): 135–51.

Sohmer, Steve. 'Certain Speculations on *Hamlet*, the Calendar, and Martin Luther', *Early Modern Literary Studies* 2.1 (April, 1996). Online: http://extra.shu.ac.uk/emls/02-1/sohmshak.html.

——. *Shakespeare's Mystery Play: The Opening of the Globe theatre, 1599*. Manchester: Manchester University Press, 1999.

Speed, John. *The history of Great Britaine*. London, 1611.

Spenser, Edmund. *A View of the State of Ireland*. Ed. Andrew Hadfield and Willy Maley. Oxford: Blackwell, 1997.

Spurling, Hilary. *Elinor Fettiplace's Receipt Book* [1986]. Harmondsworth: Penguin, 1987.

Stanivukovic, Goran. '"The blushing shame of souldiers": the eroticism of heroic masculinity in John Fletcher's *Bonduca*'. In *The Image of Manhood in Early Modern Literature: Viewing the Male*. Ed. Andrew P. Williams. Westport: Greenwood Press, 1999. 41–54.

Stanton, Kay. 'Paying Tribute: Shakespeare's *Cymbeline*, the "Woman's Part", and Italy'. In *Il Mondo Italiano del Teatro Inglese del Rinascimento*. Ed. Michele Marrapodi. Palermo: University of Palermo, 1996. 65–79.

Strachey, William. *A Voyage to Virginia in 1609: Two Narratives: Strachey's "True Reportory", Jourdain's* Discovery of the Bermudas. Charlottesville: University Press of Virginia, 1964.

——. *The Historie of Travell into Virginia Britania* (1612). Ed. Louis B. Wright and Virginia Freund. London: The Hakluyt Society, 1953.

Streete, Adrian. 'Nashe, Shakespeare and the Bishops' Bible', *Notes and Queries* 47.1 (March 2000): 56–8.

Strong, Roy. *Henry, Prince of Wales and England's Lost Renaissance*. London: Thames and Hudson, 1986.

Stump, Donald. 'Marlowe's Travesty of Virgil: Dido and Elizabethan Dreams of Empire', *Comparative Drama* 34 (2000): 79–107.

Stymeist, David. '"Strange Wives": Pocahontas in Early Modern Colonial Advertisement', *Mosaic* 35 (2002): 109–25.

Suetonius. *The Twelve Caesars*. Trans. Robert Graves. Harmondsworth: Penguin, 1957.

Sullivan, Garrett A., Jr., 'Civilizing Wales: *Cymbeline*, Roads and the Landscapes of Early Modern Britain', *Early Modern Literary Studies* 4.2 (September, 1998). Online: http://extra.shu.ac.uk/emls/04-2/sullshak.htm.

Swärdh, Anna. *Rape and Religion in English Renaissance Literature: A Topical Study of Four Texts by Shakespeare, Drayton, and Middleton*. Uppsala: Acta Universitatis Upsaliensis, Studia Anglistica Upsaliensia 124, 2003.

Taylor, Anthony Brian. 'Lucius, the Severely Flawed Redeemer of *Titus Andronicus*', *Connotations* 6.2 (1996–7): 138–57.

Temple, Nicholas. 'Julius II as Second Caesar'. In *Julius Caesar in Western Culture*. Ed. Maria Wyke. Oxford: Blackwell, 2006. 110–27.

Tilton, Robert S. *Pocahontas: The Evolution of an American Narrative*. Cambridge: Cambridge University Press, 1994.

Vincent, Barbara C. 'Shakespeare's "Antony and Cleopatra" and the Rise of Comedy'. In *Antony and Cleopatra*. Ed. John Drakakis. Basingstoke: Macmillan, 1994. 212–47.

Virgil. *The Aeneid*. Trans. W.F. Jackson Knight. Harmondsworth: Middlesex, 1958.

Vitkus, Daniel. *Turning Turk: English Theater and the Multicultural Mediterranean. 1570–1630*. Basingstoke: Palgrave, 2003.

Warner, William. *Albions England* [1612]. Hildesheim: Georg Olms Verlag, 1971.

Weis, René. '*Caesar's Revenge*: A Neglected Elizabethan Source of *Antony and Cleopatra*', *Shakespeare Jahrbuch* (1983): 178–86.

Whitney, Charles. 'Charmian's Laughter: Women, Gypsies, and Festive Ambivalence in *Antony and Cleopatra*', *The Upstart Crow* 14 (1994): 67–88.

Williams, Deanne. 'Dido, Queen of England'. *English Literary History* 73 (2006): 31–59.

Wilmott, Tony. *Birdoswald Roman Fort: 1800 Years on Hadrian's Wall*. Stroud: Tempus, 2001.

Wilson, Richard. 'Visible Bullets: Tamburlaine and Ivan the Terrible', *English Literary History* 62.1 (1995): 47–68.

——. 'A World Elsewhere: Shakespeare's Sense of an Exit', *Proceedings of the British Academy* 117 (2002): 165–99.

Wood, Christopher S. 'Maximilian I as Archeologist', *Renaissance Quarterly* 58.4 (winter 2005): 1128–74.

Worsley, Lucy. 'The "artisan mannerist" style in British sculpture: a bawdy fountain at Bolsover Castle', *Renaissance Studies* 19.1 (2005): 83–109.

Yachnin, Paul. '"Courtiers of Beauteous Freedom": *Antony and Cleopatra* in its Time'. *Renaissance and Reformation* 15 (1991): 1–20.

Young, Anthony. '"Ripen Justice in this Commonweal": Political Decay and Regeneration in *Titus Andronicus*', *Renaissance Papers* (1998): 39–51.

Index

Printed in the USA
CPSIA information can be obtained
at www.ICGtesting.com
LVHW011754251123
764904LV00005B/79

9 780754 662631